THE HAPPINESS REBOOT

THE PATH TO RECLAIMING YOUR JOY

CRAIG M. ROBINSON

Published by River Grove Books
Austin, TX
www.rivergrovebooks.com

Distributed by River Grove Books

Design and composition by Greenleaf Book Group
Cover design by Janssen Robinson
Illustrations by Janssen Robinson

Publisher's Cataloging-in-Publication data is available.

Print ISBN: 979-8-90052-002-5

eBook ISBN: 979-8-90052-003-2

First Edition

Praise for *The Happiness Reboot*

"Robinson's ability to synthesize the familiar with the academic, in ways that allow the reader to relate to the material while constantly being surprised by its insights, make *The Happiness Reboot* both an entertaining and stimulating read. His rich life experience provides the perfect framework for his keen observational intellect to take us on a journey to discover where true fulfillment lies, after we shed the preconceived notions and beliefs that tend to obscure most people's paths."

—SALADIN K. PATTERSON, television producer and showrunner, *Frasier*, *The Bernie Mac Show*, *The Big Bang Theory*, *The Last O.G.*, *Dave*, *The Wonder Years*, *King of the Hill*

"In *The Happiness Reboot*, Craig takes the kinds of questions most of us avoid—about how we work, who we love, and what we believe—and treats them as the starting point for a more intentional life. It's thoughtful without being preachy, challenging without being judgmental, and deeply aligned with how I think about building a portfolio life."

—CHRISTINA WALLACE, author, *The Portfolio Life*; senior lecturer, Harvard Business School; speaker

"With *The Happiness Reboot*, Craig has produced an essential contribution to the literature on well being by offering a profound invitation to the reader to re-examine the structural foundations of their joy and fulfillment. He combines emotional depth with intellectual rigor and research to offer a crystallizing insight available to all: true and enduring happiness is out there for us, but only at our most deliberate and courageous."

—GREG SHELL, managing partner and Head of Inclusive Growth Strategy, Goldman Sachs

"After finishing Craig's book, my first thought was: If I could suddenly be a fresh naked baby again, what are all the inputs I would control to create a happy, satisfied, and fulfilled adult me? He questions many things we don't typically dig deep enough into, inspiring curiosity and exploration. For anyone ready for that journey, Craig's book is a wonderful guide."

—**MIGUEL MCKELVEY**, cofounder, WeWork;
cofounder, Unbound; partner, American Giant

"Craig's book weaves timeless insights from great thinkers on happiness and purpose—like Viktor Frankl—with his lived reality of navigating a demanding career and the many opportunities and complexities life places before us. He calls on us to define a through line not by traditional measures of success, but by a deeper understanding of who we are, what we're capable of, and what truly matters. It shows how committing to that path can become a powerful source of happiness."

—**DANIELLA BALLOU-AARES**, CEO and
cofounder, Leadership Now Project

*This is dedicated to those who left this world far too soon,
but not before leaving with me their wisdom and
best wishes for finding truth and happiness.*

I love you Mom, Aunt Brenda, and Uncle Dale.

CONTENTS

"Rarely do we find [people] who willingly engage in hard, solid thinking. There is an almost universal quest for easy answers and half-baked solutions. Nothing pains some people more than having to think."

—Dr. Martin Luther King, Jr.

PREFACE

"Two roads diverged in a wood, and I—I took the one less traveled by, And that has made all the difference."

—Robert Frost, "The Road Not Taken"

A little more than seven years ago, I was living the dream. I enjoyed leading large national and global businesses in my capacity as a c-suite executive; rubbing shoulders with the wealthy, famous, and powerful; and flying high according to the social standards of most—and certainly compared to my modest upbringing in Atlanta, Georgia. I had done everything "right" according to everything I had been taught, believed and, in turn, evangelized to others. I had graduated from the top schools and earned both the respect and admiration of my community. I should have felt there was nothing but bright skies ahead.

Yet if I was being honest with myself, I was not deeply happy or fulfilled in the ways I always imagined I would be. Success was not happiness. Money was not happiness. I had confused the optics of happiness with happiness itself. It seemed everything I had been taught was wrong—or at least not all the way true. I knew I had to make some life changes, but I was not sure how or where to start first.

As I set out to do the hard work of unpacking the component parts of my own unhappiness, I discovered a few things that would become the inspiration for this book. The reason why the answers had been so difficult and evasive is that I was asking the wrong questions. I was even afraid to ask certain questions of myself because the real answers might be painful, embarrassing, or usher in big changes I found scary. Replacing my conviction with curiosity was easier said than done. My steadfast commitments to my career, faith, and relationships—which took up a lot of precious real estate in my life and identity—left little remaining time, emotional capacity, and head space to scrape or cobble together anything meaningful to help change my trajectory. I was also loath to tinker with those three aspects of my life because my fragile ego and carefully constructed public-facing identity depended on them. I was unsure what alternative lifestyles and identities might replace them.

ASKING THE RIGHT QUESTIONS

Despite my uncertainty, I began searching for new truths like a snake slowly and awkwardly shedding its old skin. I made small adjustments here and there in the beginning, but eventually I made bigger life changes in an effort to fashion a lifestyle centered on my evolving expectations for my own happiness. From the outside, I might have looked lost. I left my church, left my job, relocated from New York City back to my hometown of Atlanta, and separated from my then-wife—all within a five-year period. At the same time, I started spending more of my free time reading, traveling, and reflecting more critically on my life. I also started seeing a therapist, working out, scuba diving more, and sitting around proverbial campfires with all types of curiously interesting folks.

These people were hippies, contrarians, and rebelliously critical thinkers whose lived experiences, philosophies, and lifestyles were wildly different from my own up until that point. In prior seasons of life, I might have judged or found little common ground with them, assuming our paths would have even crossed. Some of my new companions had little interest in traditional institutions of spirituality, relationships, and work, nor did they seem as preoccupied with creating wealth, living in America, or belonging to society in the way I was accustomed.

My openness and curiosity led me to meet and make more of these eclectic connections in almost every space I found myself—from art galleries and coffee lounges to Meetup gatherings for people of color interested in deepening their understanding of intimacy and sexuality. I surprisingly found myself enjoying the fellowship of the freethinkers more so than I did my old group of sometimes judgy, conservative, corporate types. It was kind of like being a freshman in college again, but at age forty-five. I was curious about their lived experiences, views, and values and what wisdom they possessed, and I was careful to leave my old biases at the door. I went off grid, so to speak, in an effort to turn down the societal noise that had been making it hard for me to reimagine what a new purpose and happiness-centered life might look like.

I might have looked to my friends like I was having a midlife crisis; but on the inside and to myself, it was just the opposite. I was starting to feel alive. As I began talking openly about my truth and quest for happiness, initially in small, safe spaces with close friends and later more casually and liberally with new acquaintances and in public forums, my vulnerability and transparency created opportunities for others to do the same. I had always been a regular guest speaker on panels, podcasts, and keynote forums, but mostly on professional topics. But during my season of transition and transformation, I used these speaking forums to begin articulating my emerging manifesto, which I now relate to you in the pages of this book.

My how-to podcasts and Zoom talks were always centered on themes of purpose and fulfillment, which soon led to listeners reaching out to me for advice, coaching, and follow-up support. I welcomed their communication and enjoyed helping. I also found comfort in knowing I wasn't the only one searching. Most of us were struggling to find deep and meaningful joy and happiness. Our circumstances, careers, and life stages may have been different, but our core needs and frustrations were the same: We had carefully and dutifully followed the playbook of what had been expected of us in our careers, relationships, and faith but had not seen the return on investment we'd expected.

I and the type of people I had gone to school, socialized, and worked with were good enough in most of the outward superficial ways, but not really great where it mattered most. It wasn't clear or obvious to most of us why this was the case. Perhaps because everyone seemed to be experiencing something similar, we had each normalized our attitudes of complacency and had begun to accept that this was life. A kind of cognitive dissonance crept in over the years, which made it easier to simply not think about what was missing or to completely numb ourselves from the pain with work, more vacations, and more extracurricular activities that served to distract us from what was missing in our lives.

REBOOT

I knew there was no alternative playbook. If I was going to feel happier and more fulfilled in my life, I would have to figure it out myself and be "okay" without knowing what it looked like—or how I would look. Yes, self-help and happiness books helped, a lot. Talking about my frustrations with friends helped. Therapy helped. However, ultimately, I had to embrace action and actually *make* some changes as opposed to talking about them. Many of those changes would be in my career, relationships, and faith, for starters. There was no better time than now to reboot my internal computer.

If I knew I had one hundred years left to live, I might make those changes more gradually than if I had one hundred days left to live. I might be inclined to tinker around the edges rather than undertake a complete reboot of the hard drive. As I was approaching my fiftieth birthday, I realized something that radically altered my perspective: I was, at most, halfway through my life expectancy. I decided that I would need to maximize every year of life I had left to compensate for those years already behind me. I felt an urgency to control-alt-delete my hard drive, wipe it clean, and load new happiness software and applications. So I did. And so can you.

There's no shortage of books on happiness or on topics such as finding your purpose or meaning and leaning in once you do. I have read many of these books and ingested and applied some of their key insights in my journey. Some of my favorites include those written by Arthur C. Brooks, Adam Grant, Gretchen Rubin, Mark Manson, and Dan Gilbert, who, through their research and storytelling, will urge you to be intentional with your happiness and not be afraid to start small (*The Happiness Project*[1]), challenge your convictions (*Think Again*[2]), embrace your purpose and true calling (*From Strength to Strength*[3]), or simply let go of what no longer serves you (*The Subtle Art of Not Giving a F*ck*[4]). I also found inspiration and practical wisdom for my professional journey in books like *Portfolio Life* by Christina Wallace[5] and *The Algebra of Happiness* by Scott Galloway.[6]

There are many authors that inspired me to write this book with the hope of building upon their work and addressing a growing interest in a more practical approach to happiness by professionals who, despite dutifully running the "happiness scripts" they were given for their careers and personal lives, are feeling short-changed. Rather than travel the fairly worn road of all the self-help books of the past decade whose insights, though timeless, don't directly speak to some of the emerging tensions and contradictions many of us became more conscious of in this post-COVID-era world, I am interested in exploring something a bit different: All the things you believe and do that knowingly reduce your happiness, or worse, lead to your misery. I am curious about the things you do to sabotage your own joy. I am committed to helping you interrogate the biggest assumptions, myths, and outright lies about what is right, proper, and necessary for you to be happy.

I'm also on a journey, wrestling with these very questions like everyone. And like everyone, I am biased by my unique experiences. I am a businessman and executive who spent most of my career working in the real estate and technology sectors. I am from Atlanta, but I am a global citizen, having lived in New York City, Washington, DC, Boston, and Europe. I have led global businesses with employees in every corner of the world. I am also African American and a Gen Xer. I am a brother, a son, and an uncle. Family is deeply important to me, even though I have no kids of my own. I am an adventure junkie and love scuba diving, traveling, and pushing my own boundaries. I am a Sagittarius (if that means something to you). I am a dreamer, critical thinker, and a contrarian but a powerful force when I come to embrace something with conviction. This is both a superpower and a massive liability I continue to keep in balance. However much we have in common (or don't), my hope is that those common threads are wide enough to bind us in a shared desire to be happy—or at a minimum, *happier*.

There is a famous quote that you must "be the change you wish to see in the world." This book was inspired by my personal journey—which continues—and my ultimate desire to live a life centered on my happiness and fulfillment. It's been a long, lonely, and sometimes painful journey. And I have often caused those I love and care about to experience pain as I've stumbled toward my truth. I have at times had to revisit the questions I have asked myself, to make sure the answers haven't changed. Each time I revisited the hypothesis, that we can experience true and lasting happiness if we are willing to challenge and potentially replace many of our "life scripts" for our careers, relationships, and faith, my answers were clearer, more confirming, and brought me greater peace and joy. This book is my manifesto, my therapy-out-loud. It is an invitation for you to join me in our shared quest to examine the tensions and dissatisfactions in your life with honesty and compassion, to help you design a new life for yourself—one centered on your happiness and fulfillment.

INTRODUCTION

Much of modern-day American culture, values, and ways of life was built upon early Puritan ways of thinking that insisted on working hard, being thrifty, and demonstrating discipline. In fact, it's hard to imagine the American caricature we know and sometimes love with pride—independent, entrepreneurial, and resilient—without considering the driving forces and influences of these early foundational beliefs and directives. While there was and continues to be a very dark side to America's origin story (e.g., slavery, genocide, theft, discrimination of all types), the inspirational images of Rockwellian Americans sacrificing much in service of ideals greater than themselves has offered a beacon of light unto the world. This inspiration is particularly true for the Western world and nations seeking democratic governments and open, capitalistic economies, both of which offer to create more individual liberties, economic mobility, and freedom. But most of all, they implicitly offer the promise of happiness.

Happiness, or the pursuit thereof, is in fact one of the foundational principles of our government, as written in the Declaration of Independence. The pursuit of happiness is one of three inalienable rights that every person has, alongside life and liberty. Having *a right to be happy*, or to at least try, is a powerful concept.

The promise of happiness has been a powerful call in this nation, beginning with the earliest attitudes of the settlers whose pursuit of happiness led them to defy English rule and enslave millions of Africans and fight a civil war to keep them enslaved. It can also clearly be seen in the hopes of millions of immigrants who came to America over the next two hundred years in search of a mythical place where one could work, own land, worship freely, prosper, and be happy. But has America delivered on its promise?

According to the Gallup Organization, most Americans are generally pretty satisfied.[1] This will seem fairly intuitive for most. The average American enjoys a fairly high standard of living, as evidenced by consistent infrastructure (even in rural areas), educational access, and a historically high employment rate (the average unemployment rate from 1948 to 2025 was 5.68 percent).[2] And according to the Pew Research Center, just over half of Americans are considered "middle class."[3] Though the percentage of those in the middle class has fallen by ten points since 1971 and roughly 8 percent of Americans still do not have health insurance (down from 15 percent in 2010 before President Obama's landmark Affordable Care Act), things are still pretty good for most.[4] In fact, the Gallup survey reported that "between 81 percent and 90 percent of US adults are either 'very' or 'somewhat' satisfied with their family life, current housing, education, job, community, and personal health."[5] Here are a few examples of what might be behind this overall feeling of satisfaction:

- The homeownership rate in the US has stayed between 63 percent and 69 percent over the past fifty-eight years and was 79.1 percent for those older than sixty-five.[6]

- The average household income in 2023 was just over $80,000, including family and non-family households.[7,8] This compares favorably to the Statista reported average global personal income of $9,733 per year in 2021.[9]

- US literacy rates are relatively high at 79 percent. This is in spite of some troublesome trends of increasing "low literacy" rates, with 54 percent of US adults having literacy skills below a sixth-grade level and 20 percent below a fifth-grade level, which may impact future US competitiveness.[10, 11]

- The US has been a largely stable democracy since 1776 with a 2024 Freedom Score (an independent measure of political and civil liberties) of 83/100.[12] That said, it is important to note that the US Constitution wasn't ratified until 1791, and the Civil Rights Act, which granted rights and protection to African Americans, was not enacted until 1964. As of this writing, US democratic institutions, norms, and stability are experiencing significant turbulence under the current Trump Administration.

A METRIC FOR HAPPINESS

Notwithstanding America's fairly high standard of living across most dimensions, the 2025 World Happiness Report[13] found that the US had fallen out of the top twenty happiest countries to number twenty-four. The US has never ranked in the top ten since the report was established in 2012. It peaked in 2012 at number eleven and has consistently trailed the Nordic countries who lead the world in happiness (e.g., Finland has ranked first for eight years in a row, and Denmark, Sweden, and Iceland are typically not far behind). Much of this recent decline is due to the outlook of younger Americans (below thirty), who brought the total weighted average score down with their age-cohort score of sixty-two. This downward trend in overall happiness was also evident in other Western, English-speaking countries like Canada and the UK.[14]

In another recent and relevant Gallup study, Americans were asked: In general, are you satisfied or dissatisfied with the way things are going in your *personal life* at this time? Less than half reported being "very satisfied" in 2025.[15] Similar to the divide in happiness along age cohorts reported in the World Happiness Report, the National Institute of Mental Health (NIMH) found depression rates to average just over 8 percent for all American adults. But this number more than doubles to 18.6 percent for young adults, aged eighteen to twenty-five years old.[16] And according to the Pew Research Center, most Americans are increasingly pessimistic about their future across a broad range of attributes, such as standard of living.[17]

How do we explain a population of people who are both generally satisfied about most things, but are seemingly less satisfied when it comes to their personal lives, pessimistic about the future, or, as is the case for our young people, increasingly depressed? Some of the editorial commentary from experts like Ilana Ron-Levey, managing director at Gallup, points to younger people "feeling less supported by friends and family, less free to make life choices and less optimistic about their living standards." Others, like John Helliwell, a founding editor of the World Happiness Report, point to cultural aspects of the Nordic countries that promote greater caring amongst their citizens as evidenced by their higher rates of returned lost wallets, as an example.[18]

Other, more clinical, answers are perhaps best provided by studying the foundational happiness research of Viktor Frankl, an Austrian neurologist, psychologist, and Holocaust survivor,[19] or his "positive psychology" disciples such as Martin Seligman, who have continued to refine our scientific understanding of happiness. I find more common sense wisdom in the stories of people like me. The universe of folks I know from school, work, and my community broadly who inspired me to write this book offer another perspective for us to examine.

I'm talking about your "high achievers." A person you might consider average to above average in their educational and professional attainments, who strives to embody happiness based on a number of superficial standards they have been conditioned to pursue. This person tries hard to do all the right things: going to the right school, studying the right major, getting the right job, marrying the right partner, living in the right neighborhood, having the right family formation, joining the right social clubs, and the list goes on. They are consumed by following the script with the expectation that happiness will follow. They are a "satisfied" but unhappy person, feeling the tension and cognitive dissonance between what they were told would make them happy and the emptiness they feel.

According to *Psychology Today*,[20] high achievers suffer from unhappiness in some unique ways. Roughly 25–30 percent suffer from chronic imposter syndrome and numerous other studies[21, 22] point to greater levels of low self-esteem, self-criticism, fear of failure, loneliness, work life imbalance, and burnout—despite looking amazing from the outside. Maybe this describes you. You may be happy on some basic level because of what you have achieved, but you are not as happy as you once imagined you would be—not as happy as you *aspire* to be. Why is that?

While many Americans have more of their basic needs fulfilled compared with many other countries, most Americans still want more and expect more. We want more money, faster cars, bigger houses, better bodies, more status—you name it. We've been living in the "super-size it" era, fueled in part by the perceived supremacy of American corporations, products, and culture. Additionally, the striver psychology of the American middle class (made possible by cheap debt) means everyone feels entitled to a shot at the next rung in the socioeconomic ladder. American folklore is full of legends about those who went from rags to riches, pulled themselves up, took the gamble, worked hard, and were rewarded with riches, fame, and happiness. This is the story we tell ourselves, and we believe it.

Our expectations are high, and happiness, though always seemingly in reach, is never easily attained. Our starting point is generally good, and hence the general satisfaction, but our happiness is generally fleeting. This is before we even get to notions of higher-level states of being like "fulfill-ment" (see the figure below).

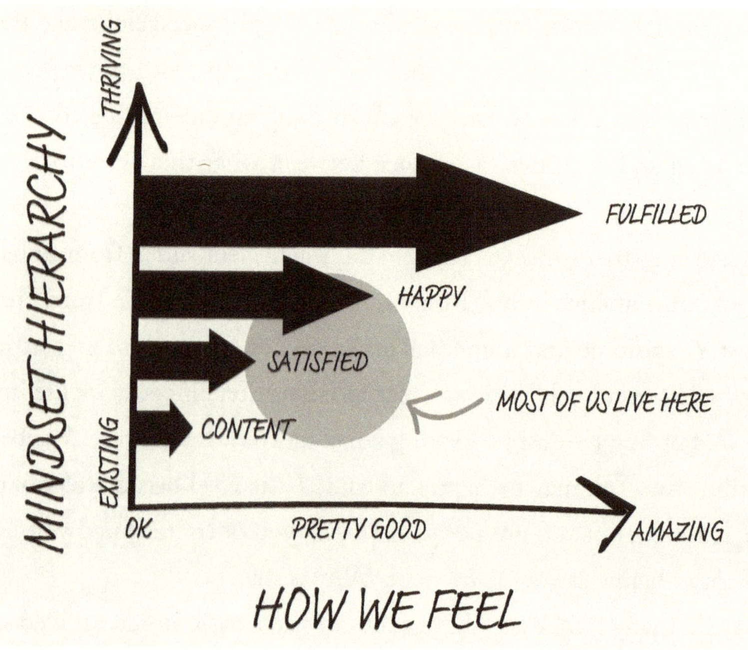

THE THEORY OF RELATIVITY

Abraham Maslow made famous the "hierarchy of needs," which one could surmise means our basic needs for food, shelter, and safety are necessary before we can really indulge the happiness of self-actualization. This makes sense. Many Americans might find their basic physiological and safety needs met but could be falling short in the higher levels of love and belonging, esteem, and ultimately, self-actualization.

Of course, we can't generalize, but we can draw some inferences from some of the cultural and societal trend lines that point to a canary in the coal mine. In the subsequent chapters, I address some of each, including the role of relationships (love and belonging), achievement and self-respect (esteem), and finding one's purpose (self-actualization). But first we have to acknowledge that some of these higher-level needs (and how, when, and if they are met) are subjective and relative to our expectations. How we experience love, belonging, or achievement is heavily biased by our expectations.

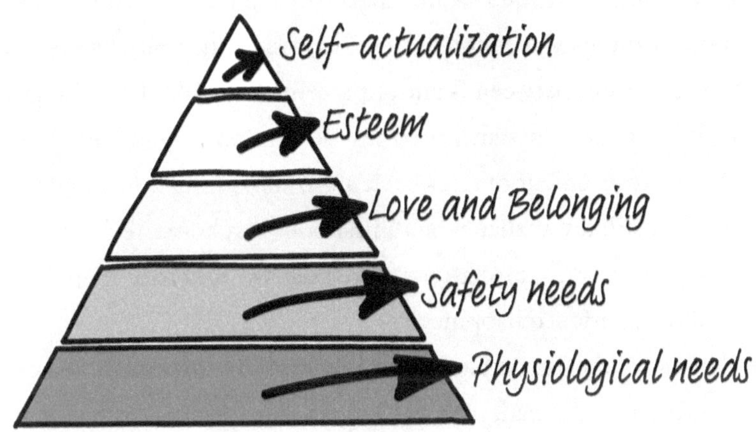

This leads me to wonder whether some important components of happiness are relative and largely based on expectations. Is one person's joy another's misery, or is it purely a mindset? To answer these questions, consider an economy improving from a recession. To some degree, economists will tell you, it does not matter how much the employment rate improves, it only matters how people *feel* about it. It only matters what people perceive to be the employment condition, which can be completely limited to their town, industry, or kitchen table. It's a big reason why the consumer confidence index is a powerful indicator of what we can expect from human behavior and future economic activity. It also matters what people believe to be normal.

When I bought my first home in 2002, the average mortgage interest rate was around 6.7 percent, lower by more than half of what it had been around the time my parents bought their first home. Years later, I refinanced to a record low (for me), and my perception of things was really optimistic. I felt fortunate and even more wealthy from just a rate drop of a little more than a point. Regardless of whether or not the new rate materially changed my life's wealth trajectory (spoiler alert, it did not), my perception of things was much better. Most recently, I purchased a home with rates hovering between 3 and 4 percent. I felt like I hit the jackpot once again. This new low anchored my perception of goodness in a way that made the movement of rates back up to something much higher than 3 percent, but still lower than when I first bought a home, feel cataclysmic. We quickly bake our expectations into how we feel and, therefore, our likelihood to experience happiness.

In the case of American happiness, I believe that we have baked certain things, both good and bad, into our happiness expectations. Social media has also played a powerful role. We see endless images of societies' definitions of beauty that include people "living their best lives." Endless photo dumps from a friend's vacation and snippets of lifestyles that inform new high-water marks for us to strive toward pepper the Internet. This phenomenon has proven to be damaging to teens, who don't have enough counter imagery, offsetting data, or even life experiences to push back on the daily bombardment of misleading social expectations.

It works the other way as well. We have baked a lot of low expectations into our happiness calculus. For example, many of us don't expect to find joy in our jobs. Most of us are not expecting to marry a soulmate who is perfect in all the ways we might have once dreamed of. Rather, we are content or satisfied with finding a partner with realistic and accessible attributes.

These are examples of how we have adjusted our expectations down to be reasonable given what we think is *possible*.

They say life is 10 percent what happens and 90 percent how you view it, meaning our mindset has a lot to do with how we perceive and experience what is happening. According to Sonja Lyubomirsky, happiness researcher and author of *The How of Happiness*, about 40 percent of our happiness is within our control, while 10 percent is impacted by circumstances and 50 percent our biology.[23] If true, this suggests that our structural unhappiness might not be structural at all—or at least 40 percent of it. Perhaps we can change some of our happiness outlook by simply being more aware and accountable for our expectations and what goes in our happiness quotient. But this is easier said than done. Much of this book is about how we can begin chipping away at the expectations we've amassed over the years that might be responsible for our unhappiness and replace them with our own unbiased and unmanipulated expectations for true happiness.

HOW TO READ THIS BOOK

This book unpacks and wrestles with the institutions, societal norms, and cultural forces that shape your expectations of happiness, the trade-offs you accept, and how you make major decisions. The best way to examine this is to start with the underlying assumptions and convictions that come long before your happiness—and stay with you long after your unhappiness. I have chosen to focus on three areas that act as the three legs of a table on which your best-laid setting has been prepared for the perfect, happiest dinner: work, relationships, and faith. But before we venture into a philosophical and practical discussion on happiness and ways to improve it, let's outline what I mean by "happiness" in terms of this book.

There is considerable research on happiness. Our understanding of happiness is evolving and spans a wide range of neuroscience, social science, philosophy, and theology. The categories of happiness range from pleasure (hedonic happiness) to higher levels of happiness that derive from purpose and growth (fulfillment). Within the range are hybrid forms that include both pleasure and fulfillment.

It would be happiness malpractice to talk about the theory of happiness without referencing some of the intellectual giants, such as Viktor Frankl, whose landmark research and psychotherapy called "Logotherapy" points to the power of finding meaning and purpose in life—with happiness being a natural byproduct.[24] While there are many contributors to the science of happiness, much of the work seems to build upon, refine, or apply Viktor's key ideas, which can be summarized as the following:

- Man's primary motivation in life is finding meaning, purpose, and significance. The absence of purpose, which Viktor termed an "existential vacuum," leads to unhappiness, specifically depression, aggression, and addiction.

- Happiness is the by-product of a purpose-centered live. In fact, happiness is the unintended consequence of finding meaning, rather than its objective.

- Suffering, as Viktor experienced in Nazi concentration camps, can be a path to understanding purpose and possessing meaning with the right mindset.

- Meaning can be discovered in three primary "values":
  - Creative values: Work, achievements, and contributions
  - Experiential values: Meaningful relationships and/or experiences with art, nature, and beauty
  - Attitudinal values: Mindset and attitudes toward suffering and circumstances

As a layperson, I find Viktor's research intuitive and aligned with the impulses I possessed long before reading about his work. Much of the research that has been done in the field since Viktor passed in 1997 seems to build upon and look for practical applications of purpose-centered living, meaningful relationships and belonging, mindset (in the face of hardship), and having impact. Even related theories on "flow,"[25] self-determination,[26] and post-traumatic growth[27] seem to reinforce Viktor's eudaimonic pathways to "well-being," "flourishing," and "happiness." In this book, I do not attempt to add any empirical science and academic work to that of these great academics, but rather editorialize, appropriate, and apply their theories to the real-life situations you experience. Moreover, I will occasionally simplify their concepts with a framework that makes the point easier to understand and apply.

My experiences and research have led me to unpack happiness even further, by examining its sources and the quality of the source. For example, happiness can be extrinsic (coming from outside sources—such as relationships and experiences) or intrinsic (coming from within—purpose, meaning, and growth). Sources can also be high-quality and long-lasting, or lower-quality and short-lived. There's then the idea of gross versus net happiness, which I describe as the difference between the maximum potential happiness from a said thing or person, and the actual happiness due to the loss, shrinkage, and friction that erodes our level of happiness along the way. I will spend more time on the latter than the former, as there is already a good body of work on gross happiness, but less on the leaks in the bucket that drain or leave us with far less than what we bargained for.

During the balance of the book, you will learn to interrogate your own convictions, particularly those that inform, shape, and govern the biggest assumptions we make from childhood to end of life. To start, I address those beliefs I think are the most powerful in shaping your identity, ideas, and instincts as an individual; those that are deeply rooted and have been reinforced over time by culture and institutions; those that, in the current age of social media, digital networks, and the pending amplifying effects of AI, will achieve an ever-greater grip on your psyche; and those that have significant and consequential influence, if not control, over your happiness—now and in the future.

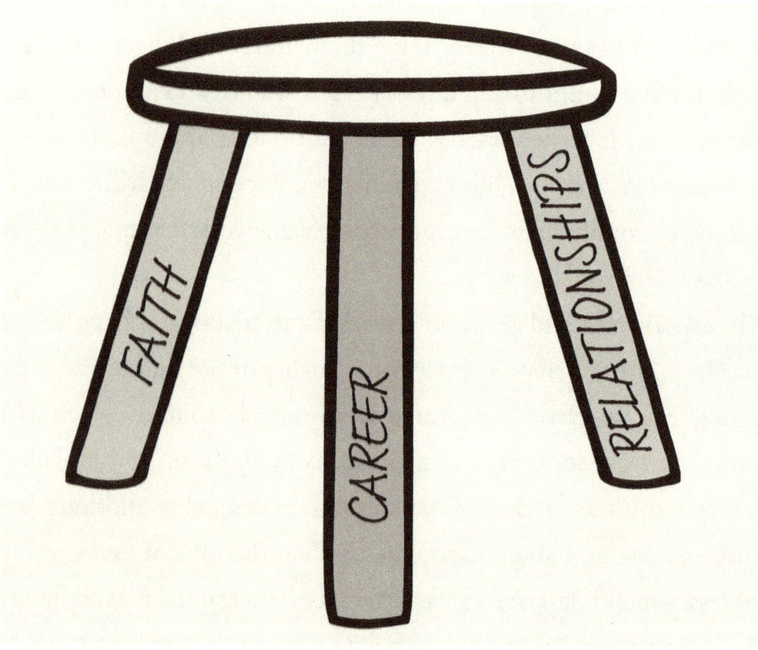

Each of the next three sections will examine the following areas of this happiness thesis:

Career: The costly and compounding choices about jobs and professions, spanning from college majors to retirement, that rob you of your happiness.

Relationships: The societal, cultural, and institutional forces that compel you to ignore your actual happiness, desires, and needs in romantic and familial relationships to serve principles and ideals that are not your own and may not serve you.

Faith: The things you believe that have little to no basis in fact or reason, holding you hostage with honor and virtue to systems of unhappiness that you yourself perpetuate.

Each section examines both the most common happiness assumptions informing the trade-off between sacrifice, purpose, and beliefs with the actual results, evidence, or potential scenarios that might suggest we revisit the hypothesis. I picked these topics in part because these are often the most powerful forces shaping and protecting our identities and are the most difficult ones to break free from as it relates to happiness. These are also the areas that have some of the longest-standing groove patterns that probably run on autopilot in your mind. They certainly were for me.

If by the end of this book you've pressure-tested your greatest convictions about your own happiness and are on your way to either recalibrating your life to make different decisions or sleeping more peacefully knowing that you're on the right track, then I can go on home to glory. My job will be done.

This book is the synthesis of ideas and musings that have been decades in the making. It is an invitation for you to join me in choosing curiosity over conviction, especially when it comes to your happiness, purpose, and life meaning.

SECTION ONE

A CALL TO ACTION

They say life is short. For some, it really is, but for most, death is generally unexpected and feels too soon, regardless of how long one actually lives. I was inspired to write this book after years of reflecting on this (obvious) truth and what its implicit and explicit implications are for happiness. The average life expectancy in the US, according to the Centers for

Disease Control, is age seventy-seven; for women it's age eighty and for men it's age seventy-five. And although it's been averaging down somewhat since COVID-19, this is a significant improvement over what was an average forty-seven-year life expectancy for Americans in 1900, sixty-eight years in 1950, and seventy-nine years in 2019, before the pandemic.[28] These gains have generally trailed behind for African Americans and African American men, in particular.

While the average life expectancy has more recently been trending down, the retirement age has not. The average retirement age, based on when you can draw down on your Social Security benefits, is now sixty-seven (or sixty-six if you were born before 1954). So if we're living in the fictitious world of averages (which we do not), the average person would have ten years of unencumbered life between work and death to enjoy . . . well, life. Unfortunately, most Americans are unable to live purely off of their Social Security. Many must continue to work beyond retirement age to supplement their income, thereby eroding whatever amount of life they might have once imagined they would have to enjoy before death.

One final thought on the depressing retirement–death gap (or lack thereof for most) is the reminder that we do not live in the world of averages. An average is not a real thing. It's a mathematical concept. Our death will be an absolute number of years from birth. It might be around the average age of seventy-seven (or sixty-nine for me, a Black male), but it could also be a number far sooner than the average. Or perhaps it could be much later, like it is for the average Asian American. That's the problem with averages. Averages are for spreadsheets, not for living. Your life isn't a calculation to be deferred until some hypothetical point in the future. It's a gift to be opened now, and every day you postpone your happiness is a day you might not get back.

CHAPTER 1

LIFE IS SHORT, YOU JUST DON'T KNOW IT YET

"A man who lives fully is prepared to die at any time."

—Attributed to Mark Twain

I remember when I first started thinking about my mortality in earnest. It was during my first bout of COVID-19. It was bad. I was living in New York City and lying in bed, unable to move without significant effort. Even a trip to the toilet was a calculus of energy, timing, and urgency. Although my condition eventually got better, I spent a week or two spiraling into reflections of my life and mortality. I had no choice. I was bedridden in the bedroom of my Harlem brownstone, listening to the ambulances whisk down nearby streets daily, only to be punctuated with intermittent pot-banging from neighbors who gleefully expressed solidarity with nurses and healthcare workers. A glutton for punishment, I left the news running 24/7, which was focused almost exclusively on reporting the US and global death count—by the hour. I was thinking about death *a lot*.

This was not my first time reflecting on death, but in the past, I thought about death retrospectively. Meaning, "I could have died had XYZ or ABC happened." In most cases, those events did not change how I thought about life or lived my life. For example, nearly ten years before my first brush with COVID-19, I was rushed to Mount Sinai Hospital in New York City in the middle of the night with debilitating pain. The back pain and loss of feeling in my leg led ER doctors to order an MRI. The results showed a blood clot on my spine. In what seemed like minutes, medical staff prepared me for emergency spinal surgery.

There was only one known surgeon in their network who had seen what I now know to be a rare condition that causes clots from spontaneous bleeding, and he was the best qualified to operate on me. This surgeon (who I will never forget) was on his way to join his family for vacation but got a frantic call from hospital staff—as he was literally heading out the door—summoning him to perform my surgery. Had their call come a little later, after he had already boarded his flight, it might have missed him. I also might have missed the saving grace of having the only doctor with experience with my condition conduct my operation. The only thing I remember before he put me under was him saying, "I can't promise you anything. You might be paralyzed after this, but we will do our best." That he did. A few months later, I ran a half marathon with my then-girlfriend. It's been fifteen years since, and I have lived a full and healthy life, but it could've gone a different way.

I also reflected on near-death encounters before my surgery. I spent my thirtieth birthday in December 2004 in Phuket, Thailand. I am a classic Sagittarius: outgoing, a dream chaser, charismatic, a lover, and loyal to a fault, but I can also be unfiltered, get bored easily, and turn hot or cold on a dime. By spending the first two weeks of my thirtieth birthday in Asia, and specifically Thailand, I nearly dodged the great Tsunami bullet of 2004 that took the lives of more than 5,000 unexpecting souls in Thailand (more than 227,000 deaths across the broader region). I am sure I met many of those unsuspecting Thai coastal inhabitants while I vacationed that week, had tailored suits made in their shops, jogged the Phuket beaches and waved to the local tourist peddlers in the mornings, watched Thai kickboxers, and ate the best Thai food ever. The irony of this near-death experience is that my buddy and travel companion who was celebrating his fortieth birthday had in the final days of our trip suggested we extend our stay by a week or so because we were having so much fun. Although I seriously considered it, I ultimately decided to stick to our original itinerary given the holiday plans I had in place with my family. The tsunami landed December 26th, a few weeks after we left. As I watched the news clips of the waves rushing over the coasts at speeds of 500 mph and heights of one hundred feet, I knew we would have certainly died had we stayed.

While in Thailand, we also bungee jumped from what was the tallest bungee in the region. We had met two beautiful, friendly, and ultra-adventurous Bangladeshi British sisters who were backpacking the area earlier in the day. They and my buddy really hit it off. Before long, they had devised a plan to bungee jump and insisted I join them. I am somewhat afraid of heights, but all the way afraid of falling from heights. So it took some serious peer pressure before I found myself at the top of the lift, staring into what looked like a pond in the middle of the jungle. After a few false starts, I finally jumped and, for an extra fee, the bungee operators took a pic of my resulting heroic swan dive. It was worth it. I looked like an Olympic diver, even if I yelped the entire way down. That's neither here nor there. A few years later, my buddy came across an article about the bungee jump facility where we had made our heroic "Olympic" jumps. It had collapsed (or the cord broke) in a sudden and catastrophic incident where someone had died. *Oh shit, that could have been us,* I thought once again.

A few years earlier during the summer of 2001, I had just finished my first year of business school at Havard and was working on Wall Street as a summer intern at Goldman Sachs in its mergers and acquisitions group. The work was grueling. I remember twenty-plus-hour days and nights being common. I don't think I took a single weekend off that entire summer outside of moving out of my temporary dormitory housing at New York University in August 2001. I worked on a few noteworthy transactions, including an IPO carve-out of a business unit from a larger company and a sell-side investment banking deal.

I was horrible at all of it, and I knew it a few weeks into the summer. I was not called to be an investment banker. While I did not enjoy the work, I appreciated the exposure (brief as it was) to an elite world of intense banking culture. It is demanding, draining, and nonnegotiable, but it wasn't entirely bad. I remember there being a "nap room" at 85 Broad Street where you could check out a bed for a few minutes or hours if you absolutely needed some quick shut-eye before heading back to your duty station. This would all change a few weeks later on September 11, 2001.

LIFE IS TOO SHORT

I had only been back in business school a few weeks after a summer in and around the World Trade Center (WTC). Although I never worked in the buildings, I walked by the WTC, had drinks and meals in them, and occasionally had meetings there until my summer internship ended in August 2001. So it was close enough to home to strike a nerve when I watched—over and over and over again—the news clips of the two planes crashing into the towers. Something about the images of people who were early enough to work (or never left from the night before) to be caught in the horrific attacks on our country haunted me.

I was horrified by the scenes of people faced with the unbearable heat from the flames inside the building, choosing to jump dozens of stories to their death from windows versus bear the intense fire at their backs. I was particularly captivated by the image of the wave-like motion of office papers, falling down from those windows like snow onto the ground below. It meant something more to me. I reflected on the many proposals, decks, and papers I had toiled over the weeks prior and imagined myself in the WTC, cranking hard the night of September 10 on some deadline that a senior exec might have demanded we stay to complete. I imagined taking a black car limousine, the standard transportation for all bankers, to the office super early to get ready for a big client meeting, as was often the case. At that moment, as I stared at the papers on the TV, I thought to myself, *Life is short . . . we just don't know it yet.*

And was it worth it? Is it worth it?

I was forty-nine years old at the time I wrote this manuscript and had already brushed shoulders with death more times than I would have liked. I take nothing for granted. My mother was forty-nine years old when she finally agreed to see a doctor about a lump in her breast. She had thought, for however long she did, that the lump was the hardened tissue from when a kid had accidentally thrown a softball that hit her chest. Perhaps it is not entirely crazy to imagine as a layman that one might have a lasting bruise or scar tissue from that type of impact, but it is more likely the case that my mother was in denial.

It was also the case, as I learned later, that she did not have health insurance. We never talked about things like insurance in my house. I also didn't know if my mother had a will, medical directives, or anything important that someone thinking about death might consider. Although I was two years out of college, living in Belgium on a year-long client assignment with a prestigious accounting firm, to her, I was still a kid. She insisted on maintaining the parent–child authority, even after adulthood. However, after her visit to the doctor and upon my return to the States in the winter of 1999, my mother shared she had breast cancer and spoke to me as equals.

I froze in disbelief. I had not known anyone personally that had died from cancer. I would later understand that both my paternal grandparents had died from cancer, along with their daughters and my two aunts. All of whom I had met maybe once or twice before they died. My mother, on the other hand, I had known and experienced all my life as a fierce and strong woman who never showed any signs of weakness. She was a Taurus, born May 1, 1950, and known by all for her sharp tongue if she disapproved. She was tough and not always the warm and friendly type, but she was steadfast about some things that reflected her love language.

She insisted that her boys (me and my brother, Janssen) got a better education than she had, and she sacrificed much for it. We benefited immensely. The other thing my mother was, if nothing else, was a woman of faith. She was Christian in the tradition of Southern African Americans, including our family, which came from a lineage of African Methodist Episcopal (AME) preachers and pastors going back to the post–Civil War Reconstruction era. My great, great, great-grandfather, George Washington Gholston, who was born enslaved to his father in 1860, would go on to be a successful business-man (farming), an AME preacher and founder of a church that still stands today, as well as a trustee of Morris Brown College, a historically Black college in Atlanta.

My mother came from this tradition. So it was no surprise that she met the news of stage 4 cancer with what most believers turn to in these moments: faith. "God will heal me," she said. "He can do it, and if we pray, touch, and agree, it will be done." I took comfort in her faith—if not my own.

In the subsequent months, she and I grew closer than we had ever been. Unfortunately that was not saying much given how troublesome and conten-tious our relationship was during much of my teen years—but that's another story. At this moment, she opened the door, just a crack. I took her to some of her radiation and chemo appointments, weighed in on wig choices, and ultimately dropped by the house more often to check in. However, in April 2000, a few months after her diagnosis and what we thought were successful lump and mastectomy surgeries, she suffered a seizure. We rushed her to the emergency room only to learn that the cancer had spread to her brain, liver, and stomach. They gave her six months to live, but she died a few weeks later, just eight days after her fiftieth birthday. It has been twenty-five years since that day, and I still mourn and question its meaning.

My maternal grandfather, who I never met, died from a heart attack at age forty-two. My maternal grandmother died at age sixty-five from diabetes complications. At the time of this writing, my mother, who was the eldest of eight, is only survived by two living siblings. She, her deceased siblings, and her parents died before the average life expectancy of seventy-seven years old. Life was shorter than they could have ever imagined. There was no way they could have known it.

I lost six close relatives during COVID-19 and in the years immediately following its wrath. The deaths were mostly caused by what I call the "Big C's": COVID-19, cancer, and cardiovascular disease.

I have seen death more than I care to reflect or discuss—and I sometimes intentionally suppress those memories. However it's the realization that most if not all of those I lost did not expect that they would see death a year prior to their passing. All had been following their daily routines until perhaps months, if not days or hours, before their passing. For most, death came suddenly.

Whether we have a hundred years to live, a hundred days, or something in between, our time (as best we know) is probably finite. But our pathways to happiness and joy are not. They are infinite. While we may not have a lot of control over how long we live, we have lots of control over *how* we live and what we do with the life we're given. The first and most important step in reclaiming our happiness is acknowledging and embracing the power to choose our paths. Our paths are not necessarily defined by our careers, faiths, and relationships, but these are important and easy places to start our lifelong journey of reclamation.

REFLECTION QUESTIONS

1. Can you recall a time in your life when you were forced to confront your own mortality or the fragility of life (e.g., personal illness, a close call, the death of someone you knew)? Describe that moment and its immediate impact on your thoughts and feelings.

2. Did that experience lead to any significant shifts in how you perceived your life or career at the time? If so, were those changes lasting, or did the urgency fade?

3. How does the idea of "finite time" currently influence your daily choices, particularly concerning your happiness and fulfillment? Are you living as if your time is limited, or with an implicit assumption of indefinite time?

4. Considering your time is finite, what is one concrete action related to your happiness or fulfillment that you have been putting off? What would be the true cost of not taking that action now?

5. What is the smallest, most immediate first step you could take this week to begin reclaiming your happiness in a way that is not defined by external expectations, but by your own internal compass?

CHAPTER 2

WHAT IS HAPPINESS?

*"When I was five years old, my mother always told me
that happiness was the key to life. When I went to school,
they asked me what I wanted to be when I grew up.
I wrote down 'happy'. They told me I didn't understand the
assignment, and I told them they didn't understand life."*

—Unknown

"I care less what you think, but I do care *how* you think." Those words stuck with me for weeks and months after I heard them spoken by the dean of the Harvard Business School during one of our alumni board meetings. We were discussing his goals for how the school could encourage constructive discourse on campus following the then-recent Gaza conflict between Israel and Hamas. Although it was a culturally and politically charged topic that had resulted in violence, firings, resignations, and endless examples of cancel-culture, the dean was propelling the conversation someplace higher. It was a better and more constructive place. By suggesting that we reflect on why and how we think, he was encouraging us to reflect on (not evangelize) our own assumptions, biases, and understanding of the facts. If we could just slow the conviction cycle down long enough for curiosity to have a shot, we might actually make progress.

The dean's reframing of the conversation was powerfully simple and seemed appropriate for what I wanted my readers to do as well. If this book is successful, it will not be because it tells you what to think. No, that's not success. Instead, I encourage you to reflect on *how* and *why* you believe what you do. What evidence do you have to support your *why*? Is it your why or someone else's why? Have you revisited your convictions, updated and informed them with new data, new facts, new science, or even your own lived experiences? Have you ever had (or given yourself) safe space to revisit those convictions, particularly those asking the most from you? Can you take stock of those spaces that are both slowly and quickly eating away at your happiness?

Before you can use this book to explore all the things that are blocking, eroding, and undermining your happiness, I present some of my base-level thoughts on the concept of happiness. I have already referenced some of the more technical and scientific definitions of happiness in the introduction and will continue to reference the work of Frankl, Seligman, and others throughout the book, when helpful. However, I want to add some of my own (non-scientific) dimensions to the concept of happiness that might be helpful to you and also get you warmed up for the steeper climb in the chapters ahead.

QUADRANTS VERSUS COORDINATES

They say that happiness is not the destination but the journey. Some say it's a state of mind. Some say that the pursuit of happiness is a "hedonic treadmill." We're either always in search of it—or it dissipates just as soon as we have it, leaving us never satisfied or ever in possession of it. Buddhists believe that nirvana is the highest state of being, free from passion, greed, hatred, and ignorance. Is it even possible for humans to achieve such a state—and to not want for or desire more happiness? And if so, can it be sustained over time?

To be honest, I am not entirely sure, nor am I convinced it matters for my thesis. What and how we experience happiness spiritually, psychologically, and emotionally is a slightly different question than what *causes* happiness and unhappiness. A scientist can point to the parts of the brain that light up when humans experience what they perceive to be "well-being," but you don't need to understand the technical nature of neurotransmitters to understand when something is enhancing or depleting your joy. There are obvious chemical realities to creating, stimulating the production of, or even injecting dopamine, endorphins, and serotonin into the body. But for more practical reasons, I prefer to think about the big and small sources of our happiness. I have tried to make this a bit easier to understand and apply by creating what I call the "Happiness Quadrants."

"What are happiness quadrants, Craig?" Well, I am glad you asked.

If happiness (or any of the other emotional states aforementioned) was a discrete destination, we could mathematically describe it as a geometric coordinate, a finite place in time, in this dimension. It's something that could be discovered, plotted, and mapped for future travelers to find again. There are many books, evangelists, and podcasters who offer formulaic approaches to finding happiness as though it were a discrete and fixed place capable of being found. Moreover, so many clinics and retreats have built up tents and roped fences like lines to a Disney ride where happiness can be made accessible for all . . . for a fee. They typically sound something like, "If you do these three things, I promise you will be happy in ninety days or your money back."

While there might be a measure of underlying credibility or science worth entertaining in some of these happiness manifestos, I'm going to go out on a limb and say I doubt it. Or rather, your commitment to finding happiness and curiosity for different paths and philosophies—as evidenced by your attending the said workshop, buying the book, or listening to the podcast—is a big part of the value you achieve, and it is therefore worth something.

But the issue with these "coordinate" approaches is that most conceive that happiness can be any number of things for any number of people. Plus, it can change over time, due to hedonic leveling or the inability to plot "feelings" and states of mind. Additionally, how do you account for the varying levels of happiness—from satisfaction as measured by the Gallup organization to nirvana as measured by a Buddhist? Perhaps a more sustainable framework for thinking about the range of things over time, across people and generations, that account for happiness is a quadrant. Let me raise a white flag in retreat before I start offering my thoughts. These are just ways to think about happiness, not in fact a definition of happiness.

How to Plot Your Happiness

In my quadrant framework, on an x- and y-intersecting axis, you have an endless number of potential x- and y-coordinates, but the definition of the boundaries and metrics of the x- and y-axis are what I find more concrete.

Imagine that your happiness could be defined as follows: Happiness can be high or low, in terms of quality, impact, and sustainability (among other attributes). This is our y-axis that runs vertically. Happiness can also be intrinsic or extrinsic, in terms of whether the happiness is generated by internal or external sources. This is our x-axis that runs horizontally. The intersection of these two lines creates four quadrants.

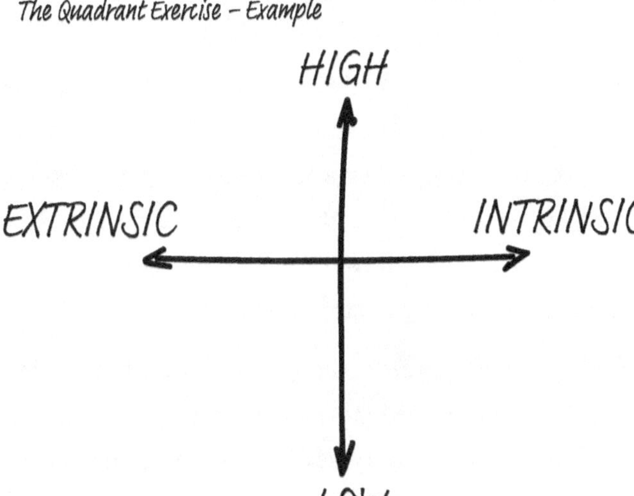

- *The Upper Right Quadrant* (happiness sources that are high and intrinsic): These sources of happiness are the most fulfilling because they originate from within, induced by meaningful, intentional, and enduring values (e.g., living a life centered on purpose). I liken this quadrant to the essence of Frankl's research and our need for a "self-transcendent" meaning and purpose. The proverbial light bulb is like your LED option, because it shines super bright and for a long while, using less electricity.

- *The Lower Right Quadrant* (happiness sources that are low and intrinsic): These happiness sources are good and important but perhaps are less impactful or enduring (e.g., donating to your favorite charity). The light bulb shines bright enough, but only for a brief while and then eventually flickers out. These are like your traditional 60-watt light bulbs that you're constantly having to change out in your old bathroom fixtures.

- *The Upper Left Quadrant* (happiness sources that are high and extrinsic): These are really powerful sources of happiness that originate from things outside of us, such as quality experiences or special moments with friends. These require effort, time, and maybe money to make it possible. They also require people and things outside of our own being. These are like the really bright light bulbs that shine on movie sets and industrial settings. Powerful, but requiring a good deal more energy than our LED bulbs.

- *The Lower Left Quadrant* (happiness sources that are low and extrinsic): These are immediate sources of gratification, satisfaction, and pleasure, but they are typically short-lived and not as meaningful (e.g., buying new sneakers, eating your mom's apple pie, or getting wasted). These sources can also have negative consequences when overindulged and are generally the least efficient source of lighting, like an old Polaroid camera flash.

I do not believe that any quadrant is inherently good or bad. They are available for us to draw from for the optimal composite mix of sources. While it is possible for all of your happiness to come from one quadrant, it is probably not ideal or sustainable. For example, there is great joy that can come from taking a magical vacation to the Maldives (upper left), but it is costly, takes time, and is difficult to do every time you need to experience happiness. The same is true for the joy that comes from the "quick fix" sources (bottom left), like buying new sneakers or drinking your favorite bourbon. These can be great but can also be problematic if the only time you are happy is when you buy new sneakers or drink alcohol. In fact, Frankl and Seligman would argue that a life purely focused on hedonic pleasures (bottom left) eventually leads to unhappiness. While high intrinsic sources can be deeply meaningful, a life without the other quadrant sources could be dull and less colorful than it need be.

When I was growing up, nutritionists and medical experts popularized the idea of a balanced meal. The science behind the theory that promoted a fixed percentage of protein, grains, vegetables, and carbs in each meal has since evolved a bit, but the image of the plate divided up like a pie chart is very useful here. Our four quadrants should be balanced in the way that optimizes your happiness, taking into consideration cost, effort, impact, and time, as an example. If each quadrant were a food group (similar to a nutritionally balanced diet), it might look something like this if I filled it out:

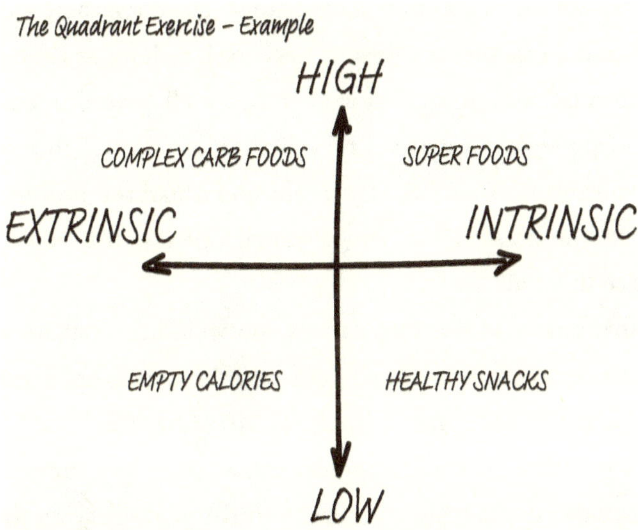

- *Upper Right:* Writing this book with the goal of helping others to find greater happiness.

- *Lower Right:* Helping friends rewrite their resume so that they can pursue their dream job.

- *Upper Left:* Traveling to the Maldives to scuba dive.

- *Lower Left:* Drinking a few of my favorite spicy margaritas at the local taqueria after work.

If the aforementioned makes sense, despite my warning, many of you will feel the urge to prioritize the quadrants, rank them, and maybe strive to eat nothing but superfoods or feel shame if all of your happiness currently comes from binge watching *The Real Housewives* and eating Krispy Kreme donuts. Though neither would likely lead to optimal happiness, the goal is not to feel pressed to try to be superhuman or to feel shame for actually being human. The idea is to simply be intentional with how you balance and allocate your investments (in time, talent, and treasure) to generate the happiness lifestyle that you desire.

There are not really good or bad decisions (although there are certainly trade-offs and consequences for any decision), as long as they are intentional, informed, and *yours*. Unfortunately, we all have limited time and capacity, so trade-offs are a real thing in this version of the universe. If you find yourself unbalanced, you might undertake the process of rebalancing. Like the tires on your car, if you change one tire, you often need to rebalance them all.

One final note and warning. Just as you wouldn't rebalance your tires every day, week, or month, obsessing over your happiness quadrants is probably a bad idea too. In his book, *The Subtle Art of Not Giving A F*ck*,[1] Mark Manson warns that chasing happiness can actually be counterproductive and lead to misery.[2] Plotting your day with the goal of trying to optimize your sources of happiness is not the goal. But being intentional and aware of how you spend your day is the point of the exercise.

It is perfectly rational and reasonable to have your focus be to find your joy in the right happiness quadrant or quadrants without being overly obsessed with the exact coordinate. But all of these forms of happiness are what I refer to as "gross happiness," meaning they are the maximum form of happiness that you experience before the detractors erode them. This is why I developed what I refer to as "net happiness," a concept I explore in the next chapter.

The Quadrant Exercise – Example

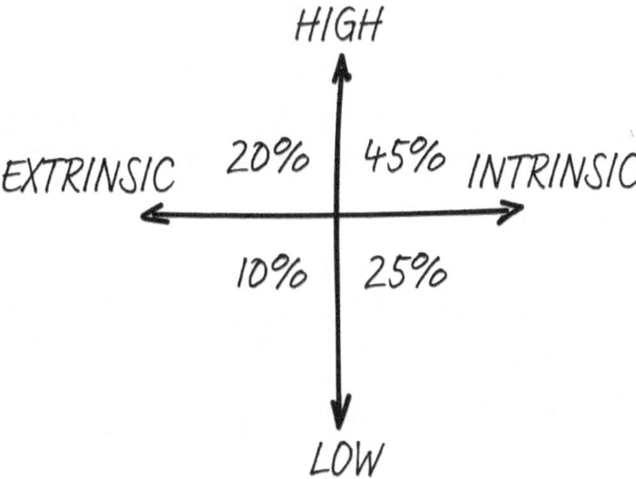

An example of how one might plot their ideal allocation of time.

The Quadrant (versus coordinate) Exercise

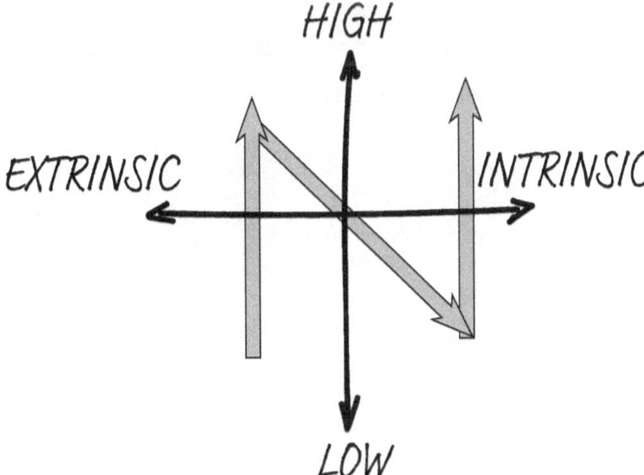

An example of how one might reallocate some of their time to better balance.

REFLECTION QUESTIONS

1. Take two to three minutes to quickly jot down a list of moments you felt happy over the past month. Try to generate a list of at least ten moments, or as many as you can.

2. For each moment in your list, place next to it an "H" for those moments that felt like high and enduring levels of happiness or an "L" next to those that felt like low and temporary levels of happiness.

3. Now, go back through your list and place an "E" for those that came from extrinsic or outside sources and an "I" for those that came from intrinsic or internal sources.

4. Lastly, add up the number that you listed as "H & I," "L & I," and so on. Place the number for each in the appropriate quadrant.

5. What if anything did you find surprising about your allocation? Are there any quadrants that are significantly more concentrated than others? How do you feel about that? What, if anything, would you change to your quadrant weightings?

CHAPTER 3

GROSS VERSUS NET HAPPINESS

*"When one door of happiness closes, another opens, but
often we look so long at the closed door that we do not see
the one that has been opened for us."*

—**Helen Keller,** *We Bereaved*

What if your gross level of happiness was a perfect 100 out of 100, meaning the happiness that came from the steak dinner, Caribbean vacation with your bestie, dream job, or fifty-year wedding anniversary was absolutely perfect? Chances are you are living inside of a computer program, like the one in *The Matrix*, or something even better. However, it's highly unlikely that perfect is achievable or at least sustainable over time. Why?

Like every other facet of life on Earth, we experience friction. Friction and drag will eventually slow an object in motion, like the way wind balloons an open parachute, breaking the fall of the jumper. Gravity, drag, friction, resistance—whatever you want to call it—is life's way of reminding us that for every action, there is an opposite but equal reaction. I imagine the laws governing our happiness to be similar. For every source of joy, there are counterforces that can work to undermine and offset your joy.

When I was younger, I would experience a meaningful sense of dread following some great news. I would anticipate an opposite but equally bad thing waiting to happen, just around the corner, as a cosmic response to my good fortune. Before you dismiss this fear I once had as ridiculous, think about how many times you or someone you've known has said, "This is too good to be true." It's the same mindset and fear.

We are sometimes unwilling to embrace our gross happiness because we are already anticipating that it will be reduced to a more realistic net happiness. My mother would take this fear a step further but using religious ideology. If we received what she viewed as a blessing from God, she would immediately warn us that the "devil will be jealous and look for ways to steal your blessing" or to "be careful, the Devil is going to be busy after this." So it was more than just physics, it was the laws of good and evil that required us to settle for something less than pure happiness.

Our gross happiness is what we seek to experience, which is possible in theory, but the reality that remains after life happens (be it perceived or real) is our net happiness. Here are a few simple examples to help illustrate the idea.

- During that dream trip with your bestie (maximum potential gross happiness), your happiness is slightly less because the flight was delayed and your luggage was lost, but you eventually get to the resort and reclaim your luggage a day later and have a great time for the balance (actual net happiness).

- At your dream job, you may love what you do, who you do it with, and the impact it makes (maximum potential gross happiness), but you have to commute an hour, and that sucks (actual net happiness).

- During your fifty-year anniversary with your partner (maximum potential gross happiness), you are celebrating love and community while also secretly worrying about your partner's recent cancer diagnosis (actual net happiness).

I no longer believe that these "net events" are cosmic or spiritual in their origin, but rather they are realities of living in a world where things can and often happen. Net events don't have to be "good" or "bad." Those are judgment terms and attributions that are purely of our creation. I also subscribe to the Viktor Frankl school of thought suggesting that suffering in itself is not always bad, but rather how we view it and the opportunity it offers us to lean into our purpose. Further, those intrinsic and extrinsic sources of joy are all still very happy moments. Just a little less happy than ideal because of some normal and sometimes unavoidable drags that come with living on Earth. As the saying goes, "life be life-ing." This is our net happiness.

That said, we are not completely helpless. We can manage our net happiness by mostly managing, mitigating, or minimizing the drag. We can mitigate with insurance or extra precautions, minimize with our mindset (i.e., stoicism), or even manage by compartmentalizing. But our "net" has a few levers that we can pull to reduce the drag, should we decide. For example, my net happiness at the perfect job described above might increase with a hybrid work schedule that allows me to work from home a few days a week. Or rather than wait a day for the rescheduled flight following the canceled flight to Jamaica, I can opt to shell out a few extra dollars to rebook and take an earlier flight. Or in the case of stoic thinking, I can channel my inner strength and discipline by focusing on the positives and less so on the things that are out of my control. So in the case of the delayed flight, I could resist the temptation to be angry and instead, view the opportunity as the extra time I now have to spend with a friend in the Delta Sky Lounge pouring back free drinks.

Our net add-backs don't have to be responsive. We can anticipate detractors to optimize and design for our happiness in advance. For example, I love scuba diving. It is an upper left quadrant event for me (high happiness and extrinsic), but I hate carrying my scuba gear (i.e., the tanks, BCD, fins) from the dive shop to the boat and cleaning off the salt water from my gear after my dives. So I am willing to pay a bit more for dive shops that have extra staff to help with these small detractors to my gross happiness.

We can also amplify the gross. I imagine that there are moments of happiness that are literally perfect 100s, but those that could go from a solid 80 to a 90 also offer ways to increase our net. For example, if your dream trip with your bestie is truly an 80/100, it might be possible to make it even better (a 90/100) if you and your friend embarked on a meaningful excursion (versus drinking mojitos at the resort), where you hiked a challenging mountain and experienced the reward of looking over the countryside from a rarely seen vantage point. That memory and joy would last longer and be more meaningful—even if your flight was delayed. Again, our net and gross happiness can be influenced by our mindset, our behaviors, and the quality of the underlying intrinsic and extrinsic happiness source.

THE LAW OF HAPPINESS EXPECTATIONS

Our gross happiness is informed by our expectations. If we have high expectations, there is a greater chance we will be disappointed when happiness falls short. If we have low expectations, there is a greater chance we will be delighted when we exceed them. Being in spaces that inform and shape our expectations, such as social media, can have a massive impact on our happiness.

This may explain why some people in America are seemingly unhappy, even when they appear to have so much more than people in other parts of the world, where having very little is to be expected. It's likely also a close cousin to the comparison thief that robs our joy when we compare what we have with someone else who has slightly more or less. The comparison informs our sense of what is possible and what we feel we deserve. Research from Harvard Health shows that our happiness diminishes with more choices.[1] Said differently, we are happier when we have fewer options, spend less time comparing, and can more quickly settle on what is the expectation watermark. I refer to this theory as the law of happiness expectations.

I recently had an opportunity to think about my theory on happiness expectations when I saw a CNN article about the happiest countries, which I introduced in the Preface. The article was reporting on an annual study (since 2012) called the World Happiness Report (WHR)[2] that is commissioned and conducted by the UN, University of Oxford, and Gallup. I was obviously intrigued and excited to read the article given my passion for the topic, and the announcement coincided with me writing this book. After skimming the first few lines and seeing Denmark referenced, I was reminded that a friend years ago recommended that I read a book about why Scandinavia was home to the happiest people on earth. *Ah yes,* I thought to myself. *I really need to go back and dig into this claim.* Prior to reading the CNN article and starting the book (that I never completed), it had never occurred to me that:

1.   There was such a thing as the "happiest people on Earth."

2.   Happiness could be measured to provide for a ranking system between countries and regions (the way we measure life expectancy rates).

3.   There was something we might learn from these people that was applicable to people anywhere.

I want to set the record straight before I dive into what I ultimately learned and concluded from my research and reflection. The happiest place on Earth is actually Finland, which has held this title for the past eight years (as of 2025). However, Denmark is a close second, followed by Iceland and Sweden. Of more than 140 countries that are surveyed year over year (147 were surveyed in 2025), the Nordics are as consistent as top contenders of happiness as the East Africans are in winning virtually every marathon.[3] While I could more easily imagine and explain the advantages that an Ethiopian or Kenyan runner might have against other runners from training in higher altitudes, it was not obvious why Nordic and Scandinavian people have a leg up on the rest of us. It was also less clear what the next sixteen countries in the top twenty happiest countries had in common.

I have lived in and/or visited seven of the top twenty. I lived and worked in Belgium (14th) for a year and spent considerable time managing teams and business operations across Europe, which is home to fourteen countries on the top twenty list and seven in the top ten. I have also worked extensively in Canada (18th) and traveled to or vacationed in many other contenders on the list, including Costa Rica (6th), Mexico (10th), and Israel (8th). I have a good sense for these places—yet did not find their rankings intuitive, especially after noting that the USA didn't even make the top twenty in 2025.

In fact, I generally found Belgium, where it rains an average of two hundred days each year, to have a fairly cold vibe. Not surprisingly, research points to a positive correlation between nice weather and happiness—but that's beside the point. While I found most of the Belgians I met to be nice externally, I didn't find them to be particularly warm, inviting, or happy (except when pouring back one of the hundreds of their legendary beers). Furthermore, as a brown-skinned man, I experienced a good bit of hostility and racism at worst and often felt invisible at best. After I learned the history and methodology of the ranking, it all made sense why Belgium was on the list.

In 2011, the United Nations General Assembly started inviting their member countries to measure their citizens' happiness and enact public policies to maximize their happiness based on the findings. The methodology is straightforward. The attitudes of each country's citizens are captured for a range of metrics, such as:

- Real GDP per capita

- Social support

- Healthy life expectancy

- Freedom to make life choices

- Generosity

- Perceptions of corruption

After seeing the component parts of the methodology, it all made sense to me—mostly. Many of these metrics are generally proxies for a person's basic needs being met, à la Maslow's hierarchy. One could even argue that they are the basis for a person's satisfaction more so than true happiness. These are a person's basic and fundamental life needs, attributes that need to be met. But happiness is not only about having access to adequate healthcare, good education, a safe neighborhood, and economic stability—or is it?

When I compare these attributes with the research I've seen on fulfillment, which places more weight on purpose, belonging, and growth, it's hard to see how these WHR happiness index metrics tie directly to what I'm advocating. When I think about the intrinsic and extrinsic sources of happiness, these satisfaction metrics at best point to the foundations and supporting systems for higher-level, self-actualization type happiness to be achieved in greater levels.

The countries ranked in the top ten happiness index are countries that generally have very strong social safety nets. They are places where people have the social and political freedoms to spend their time and effort doing as they please. However, I believe that whether or not any person is actually happy has more to do with what they do with their time than the environments that surround them.

For example, how do we explain why countries like the United States are not even in the top ten—or even twenty as of this past year? This is true despite Americans having most of their basic needs met in what is arguably one of the best working democracies that boasts providing its citizens with unmatched independence and freedom. It's true that our American safety nets are not as robust as those in countries such as Canada or Belgium, where, in exchange for fairly high tax rates, you get many things for free. Generally speaking, most Americans have a fairly high standard of living relative to other countries in the developing and developed world.

The answer may be found in one word: expectations. In places like America, we have no shortage of ambition and expectations that we will create wealth and fame and be happy. We believe that our expectations are just within reach, assuming we work hard enough, hustle hard enough, or are talented enough. These notions are planted and reinforced from day one, culturally, politically, and socially (because we grow up consuming hip-hop videos, social media, or for us Gen Xers and older, watching *Lifestyles of the Rich and Famous*).

Even if or when our basic needs are met, we find ourselves disappointed when we ultimately don't end up living up to the hype because of these unrealistic expectations and hopes. Our expectations need not be lofty, like being rich and famous. They could be something more reasonable, like having a middle- to upper-middle-class standard of living with a reasonably good-looking and healthy spouse and kids. The point is that our happiness (or lack thereof) may begin with our expectations. And expectations are all about our mindset and less our conditions.

Let's try another example. If I am earning $100,000 a year, which would be a very comfortable household income in most parts of the US (and the world for that matter), I am generally unhappy if my expectation was that I would be making $150,000 or more. Or if I make $150,000, but my neighbor boasts of making $200,000 (what a jerk, right?), the comparison with my neighbor and expectations that I should have the same might rob me of my potential joy. This is particularly sad when we consider that the actual living standards between a $150,000 and $200,000 household income are probably not wildly different. It's just the perception of the $50,000 difference that causes unhappiness.

Now let's shift our attention to the countries that rank lowest on the list. Many of them are in the Middle East and Africa, where I have visited many times. In fact, my ex-wife's family is West African, and my earliest international travels as a high school student were to Senegal as student exchange ambassador. I have traveled to Ghana, Egypt, Kenya, Morocco, and Tanzania (twice). I also have tons of African friends that I came to know from my time in school and work. Although I have not lived there and cannot speak to what life is like on a day-to-day basis, I have a reasonably good appreciation for what the index might be missing.

Zimbabwe was one of the countries in the rankings (143rd) that caught my eye in particular. Although I have not been there and cannot speak to the moods and attitudes of the common person, I do have a wonderful Zimbabwean friend with whom I shared the happiness index report for her reaction. Let's call her Anj. She is a former African fashion model and stylist who was born in Zimbabwe but has also lived in Europe and the US. That is to say, Anj is someone who can compare and contrast the lifestyles of those in her home country with the lifestyles of those ranked as one of the happiest places.

Zimbabwe, once nicknamed "the breadbasket of Africa," was a place admired for many of the socioeconomic attributes that are today viewed as reasons for why someone might be fairly unhappy living there. It is a country that has been ravaged by a cruel dictator, high inflation, inconsistent electricity, and lack of basic infrastructure. In the decades following its independence, it has declined in most of those traditional social economic indicators for progress. So it is not difficult to see why a country like this would, on the surface, be viewed as an unhappy place. But Anj shared some of her reflections on why the people themselves are happier than the index suggests.

Anj shared a story about her grandparents, who lived on a small farm that provided most of their food. They did not have much, but were a proud, close-knit family that took time to enjoy the simple pleasures of life. Life was not only simple, but her people were also happy. Her grandparents were typical of many Zimbabweans she saw growing up, which she describes as warm, humble, and resilient.

Anj, who now lives in Manhattan, shared a comical story of her cousin in Zimbabwe, who would be so happy if she woke up in the morning and found the electricity was running. Her cousin would rush around the house frantically and joyfully, alerting everyone living in the compound to "give me your phones!" Her cousin would gather everyone's phones to take advantage of the intermittent window for which they might have enough power to not only charge their phones but maybe watch a favorite show on YouTube. Something that we take for granted here in the US provided a moment of happiness for her cousin.

Her family embraced and enjoyed the readily accessible sources of joy, such as going to church together or drinking at the community pub where they might watch cricket, rugby, or football (American soccer). The local kids, although running in the streets barefoot, would play soccer all day outside, laughing, smiling, and perhaps experiencing greater happiness levels than many of the wealthier kids in the US suburbs who would not only play with name-brand shoes in coiffure soccer fields, but have all the other high-end soccer gear and trappings.

As a bit of an exercise, I asked Anj to rattle off the attributes that come to mind when she thinks about the joy she associates with Zimbabwe and here's what she shared:

- Pride

- Contentment

- Curiosity

- Humility and humanity

- Resilience

- Simplicity

- Values grounded on respect, spirituality, and faith

- Warmth

- More commonality than division

- Community

- Unaffected by outside noise

- Authenticity

- Natural storytellers

As Anj shared with me the attributes on her list, her voice and energy actually lit up not only with pride and her fondest memories but with happiness. Her list, without me nudging or editorializing, spoke plainly to some of the fundamentals of fulfillment, like belonging, community, and purpose, even if they were noticeably void of what the WHR looks for in defining happiness.

So how do we square this against the happiness index, or the attitudes and outlook about happiness in the United States, Belgium, or Denmark?

I suspect the Law of Happiness Expectations might help explain one other dimension at work.

THOSE MOST SATISFIED HAVE LOW OR REALISTIC EXPECTATIONS

When Anj's cousin woke up in the morning, surprised to find electricity working, she was happy. But her expectation was just the opposite—that there would not be electricity, and therefore her low expectations were exceeded when she could charge her cellphone. Exceeding her expectations, as low as they might be for Western standards, brought her happiness. But if someone has fairly high expectations, and their actual experiences fall below their expectations, there might be a feeling of unhappiness. If my expectations are that I will see my friends at the local pub and enjoy a good soccer match, I have a greater chance of being happy if that condition can not only be met but met consistently—and heightened when my favorite soccer team wins.

I believe that happiness, which has intrinsic and extrinsic sources, is both correlated with one's expectations (which can be high or low) and also one's actual ability to consistently meet, exceed, or fail to reach those expectations. However, the relationship between happiness and satisfaction can be complementary versus interdependent. Satisfaction, happiness, and fulfillment are like the three layers of a cake, with satisfaction being on the bottom, happiness in the middle, and fulfillment on the top. Note, one could argue that so-called contentment is the actual base level of a four-level cake. If satisfaction happens when our basic needs are met or upon some minimum level of achievement, one can theoretically be content in situations where their basic needs go unmet. As in Frankl's description of meaning in suffering, contentment in less than satisfactory situations can be achieved with a certain mindset. But for simplicity's sake, let's stick with the three experience levels for now.

Unlike the perfect three-layer cake that your mom might've made as a kid or you've seen in the bakery, not every layer of the cake must be the same width and thickness. The base layer of the cake (satisfaction) might be thin, as it is in the bottom 10 percent of those countries indexed by WHR. The next layer (happiness), which can come from other sources, could be thicker.

An individual with a strong sense of purpose, belonging, and growth (like some of Anj's friends and family in Zimbabwe), independent of where they live and how much of their basic needs are met (like layer one in Denmark), can experience meaningful fulfillment. They all share a relationship with each other, primarily as a consequence of the person's mindset and outlook, but they are not necessarily dependent upon each other.

To be clear, I imagine anyone living in Afghanistan, Congo, or Zimbabwe—or any country that currently ranks low on the world happiness index—wants economic stability and growth, healthcare, education, and everything else in that satisfaction bundle of goods. Of course they want those things and deserve them. I also imagine that the folks in Belgium, Denmark, and the Netherlands want to experience as much community, joy, and cheer (and sunny weather), in addition to all the luxuries that come with a government and society that provides for most of their basic socioeconomic needs and civil liberties.

Finally, as a personal testament to the hopes and desires of someone living in America that has both his base level of needs in place and a fair amount of happiness, I also want to feel fulfilled. I want to have my cake and eat it too. We all do.

MAXIMIZING THE AREA UNDER THE CURVE

By now, you can see that I love to use math and science to make philosophical and sometimes emotionally charged points. Here is another one. If we can agree that happiness is not necessarily one single defining thing (a coordinate) nor are the points all equal (the quadrant), it is reasonable to believe that happiness can be both big and small, and powerful in its cumulative effect. Benjamin Franklin is believed to have said, "Happiness consists more in small conveniences or pleasures that occur every day, than in great pieces of good fortune that happen but seldom to a man in the course of his life."

If I have one great day out of seven, that's likely less desirable than having five amazing days out of seven . . . for ten consecutive weeks! Would you rather have fifty-two consecutive weeks of small but consistent pleasures each day, or two weeks of maximum joy (you win the lottery), followed by fifty weeks of misery (treating a painful and potentially terminal illness)? I'm going to guess we would rather the surface area of our joy be maximized to cover as much time and space as possible.

I would rather have happiness in many facets of my day (work, family, personal, volunteer) over as many days as possible. This is another reason for having happiness sources in all four quadrants versus just one. I think of the mathematical illustration of this concept as the area under the curve. In the following diagram, imagine that the x-axis is time and the y-axis represents potential happiness. I would rather have the area be as large and expansive as possible, rather than see it spike for a moment and then flatline. If possible, we want to make decisions in life that maximize our gross and net happiness in as many areas of our life as often as possible (i.e., it's your normal day-to-day life versus a one-off life event). In her book, *The Happiness Project*,[4] Gretchen Rubin offers very practical suggestions for how you can do this. She encourages making small, consistent changes in your daily habits that bring you joy. She describes the powerful cumulative effect these small steps, versus big life transformations, can play in leading to lasting and meaningful happiness in your life.

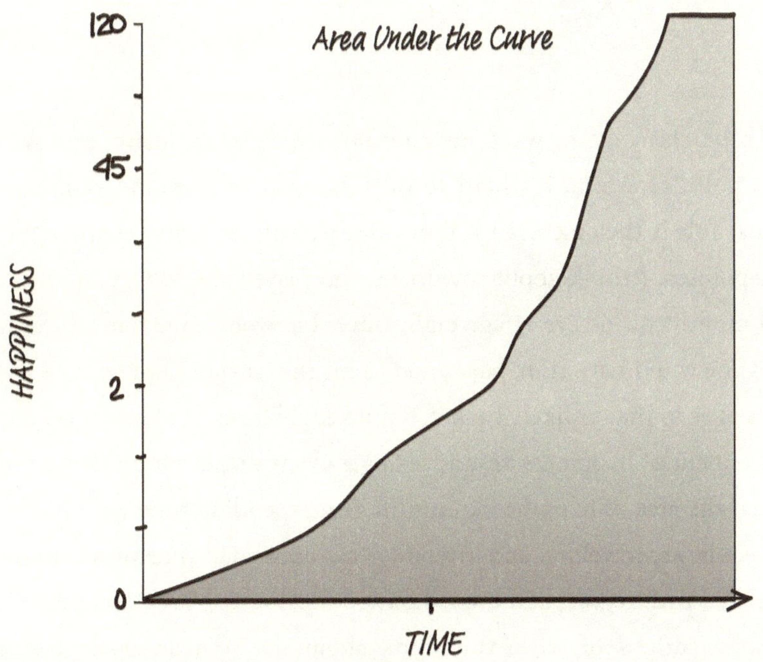

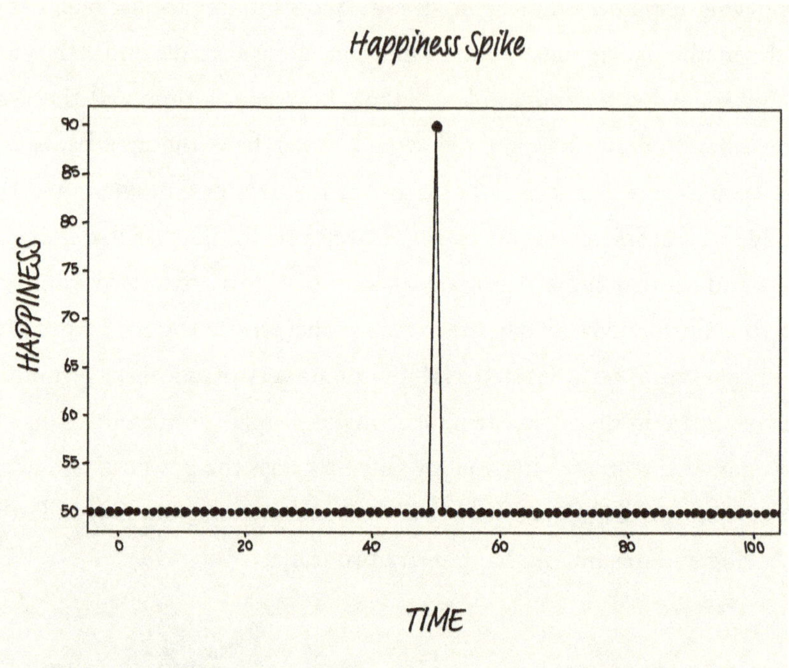

To be clear, these two things are not mutually exclusive, and we can want both. However, it's hard to organize your life around rare, one-off events. This is the case even if they offer potentially game-changing levels of happiness. I think about my uncle who played the lottery up until the final months of his life at age eighty-five. He would imagine all the happiness he could have if he happened to hit the jackpot. Not that he put all of his eggs in that unlikely basket, but he could have. Had he organized his life's pursuit of happiness around a single event versus a lifestyle that maximized the area of happiness in his life (e.g., spending time with his nieces and nephews, traveling, and attending his book club meetings), he might have died with regrets and missed out on maximizing joy during his life.

So regardless of what you think about the sources, quality, magnitude, and even sustainability of your potential happiness, the best way to maximize the area of happiness is to find ways to ensure it happens regularly and in as many aspects of your life as possible. There are things we knowingly and unknowingly do (or don't do) that can reduce that happiness, thereby shrinking the net happiness to something less than desirable. In some cases, these detractors are of our own doing.

In the next section, we will examine the detractors, low expectations, and deferred (if not forfeited) happiness that stem from our careers and professional choices.

REFLECTION QUESTIONS

1. For the list of happy moments listed in the earlier exercises, how many were recurring versus one-off?

2. Are there any one-offs that have the potential to be recurring? What potential changes would you have to make for these moments to be recurring or last longer?

3. How could you expand the happiness area under the curve, considering both the time and amplitude associated with your happy moments?

4. When reflecting on some of your greatest sources of potential happiness, are there drags that you remember or anticipate (resulting in a lower net happiness) that you could take steps to alleviate?

SECTION TWO

DO WHAT YOU LOVE

Career is the first of my three-part thesis (and table leg). Why? We typically start making big structural decisions about our careers early in life—high school and college—when adults encourage us to focus on certain subjects over others or to pick a major based on "what pays well." These early decisions can be hard to reverse later in life and are often commitments we make long before the average person picks a spouse and starts a family. Career also represents a significantly larger amount of our time (each day, week, month, and so on) than the time we typically spend worshiping in a temple, mosque, or church. So it's a big deal.

Whether your work is a nine-to-five or a nine-to-grind, it is likely a very important part of your life, livelihood, and identity. Most Americans will spend about one-third or more of their typical weekday working, one-third sleeping, and one-third tending to everything else. This is not necessarily ideal, but a reasonable assumption for the average eight-hour working-day professional. If you've had jobs like the ones I have had, you probably spend way more than eight hours a day working and often take work home, commute to and from work, check emails throughout the night or weekend, and, if nothing else, stress about work when you should be spending time being present with loved ones and doing activities that bring you joy.

MAKE A LIFE, NOT A LIVING

"My fundamental feeling…has been from the very beginning the same as it is today: that it's our responsibility to make spaces that people feel happy in."

—Miguel McKelvey, WeWork Blog

Long before the rise and fall of WeWork and its cofounder and CEO, Adam Neumann, the company had a massive impact on me and millions of others who were inspired by WeWork's mission, ambitions, and achievements. WeWork, in its heyday, was an organization that encouraged everyone to make a *life*, not just a living. Our iconic black tees with "WeWork" spelled out in white letters encouraged everyone who saw them to do what he or she loved. Our company mission was bold, provocative, and perhaps presumptuous. WeWork intended to elevate the world's consciousness—one workspace at a time.

It was both an *inspirational* and an *aspirational* brand. The company, which had more than fifteen thousand employees at its height, inspired us by what they achieved against the odds, in record time, and all while defying financial gravity. We aspired to live up to its creed and spread the gospel of work hustle and happiness. Why? Because we believed that the future would be amazing. We were inspired to make the workplace not just a place where people worked, but one that fostered community, stoked innovations, maximized productivity, and was fun. We were determined to burden "work" with the yoke of our most basic human needs for belonging, purpose, and growth. WeWork wasn't just a coworking company, it was a *movement*, and I was one of its disciples.

THE MISSION

In 2009, it was easy to embrace the hustle counterculture. The world was in the middle of a massive recession that saw unemployment levels reach 10 percent,[1] fueled by the contagion of the residential mortgage collapse. Our institutions had failed us. Large corporations had laid us off. Banks had cheated us. Our investments in home ownership, historically the most expedient path to wealth creation for most working Americans, was underwater . . . or worse . . . and the government had let it all happen. The wealthy got bailed out while the rest of Americans watched their dreams vanish as fast as you could say credit default swaps.

Talented knowledge workers, both employed and unemployed, were open to a new vision, a new promise, and a new religion. This vision centered on self-determination, entrepreneurship, and hustle. But more than that, people wanted to find joy, connections, and meaning in their work. They wanted to be happy. We were also already seeing numerous examples of the self-made tech-bro "unicorn" CEOs (the gods that author Scott Galloway describes so well) that made something from nothing, largely by *not* playing by the old rules.

As a side note, they quickly created new rules fashioned in their favor that created a host of other problems that we can explore later. Their signature look of skinny jeans, spunky tee shirts, and custom Air Jordans signaled it was cool to be your authentic self, make millions, and have fun in the process. The prop-tech, fin-tech, health-tech, and every other type of tech company created out of thin air would go on to become more valuable than many of their analog counterparts that had been decades, if not more, in the making. Everyone wanted to be a part of where the hockey puck was going—way, way up! We also wanted our lives to matter. We wanted to believe in the values of our employers. We wanted to win, but most of all, we wanted to be happy.

During the course of your career, you may not have considered your work as a potential source of joy or happiness. And most likely, that's no fault of your own. Work, especially for Gen Xers and older, generally was never viewed as a source of joy or happiness. It was purely a place to earn a living, build a career, and develop relevant skills that would secure a place in the great and flat global economy. Work was perhaps your brand, your identity, or maybe a source of status, if you were so lucky to have that type of gig. But one thing it was not was a source of deep and meaningful happiness.

Instead, you were sold a bill of goods that dictated happiness must come on your own time: nights and weekends, holidays, vacations, family time, or better yet, retirement. Many of the executive superstars who regularly grace us with their "how I made it" wisdom on podcasts, in books, and on countless panels also warn us that the idea of "work-life balance" is *not* a real thing. It sounds nice, they say, but if you really want to be successful, you need to measure balance on the fulcrum of a life weighted at one end with hard labor and at the other end with life *after* hard labor. In other words, the balance you seek will be deferred until later in life, after retirement— maybe. Or you pick a season, perhaps to raise children, take a mental health sabbatical, or pivot between jobs, during which time you intentionally set your ambitions aside for a season to recalibrate. But to be clear, you were still in the game and committed to winning. As Oprah Winfrey once said, "You can have it all, just not all at once."

We were not offended by the expectations that happiness was best left at home. In fact, we encouraged this way of thinking with our own behaviors and social nudges. As an example, we might entertain a colleague's reflections on happiness during a brief interaction at the water cooler or with some basic small talk at the beginning of a conference call or Zoom meeting (e.g., "How was your weekend, Jim? Did you guys get away for the holiday?"). All of that was performative. Most were not really interested in their coworkers' sources of joy, unless it helped break the awkward silence while waiting for the rest of the meeting attendees to show up.

MAKING WORK *WORK*

Work and society have masterfully created strict boundaries between our work and our personal lives. In the rare case that someone actually does what they love, we often assume it comes at the price of earning a less competitive wage, slower career growth, or less outward status and success. When I was young, I can remember adults cautioning my peers and me against picking jobs that we loved but couldn't make a lot of money, like the idea of the "starving artist." As a side note, my brother was bold enough to ignore them all and choose a life and career as an artist. He's not only successful, he's also happy.

If a successful person and particularly a wealthy person, however you define that, ever said they did what they loved, we sucked our teeth and thought, *Yep, easy for you to say. You're rich.* We assumed for so long that successful, wealthy, accomplished people earned the right to be happy after heaping spoils into their retirement funds, 401Ks, and personal balance sheets. They did not really enjoy the ride—just the spoils.

Work hard, play harder (implicitly later) is an idea that was deeply rooted in the American Puritan psyche with the image of the hardworking farmer who must sow and labor their fields if they are to reap a harvest in the spring season. As the Bible warned, you will reap what you sow—or, as we often fear, you *won't* reap if you *don't* sow.

We brought these binary attitudes to work. While some younger work cohorts, namely Millennials and Gen Z, were asking a bit more of their employers—namely to reflect and hold true to their values—they, too, wanted some of the same trappings that we older cohorts wanted. They desired money, impact, growth, and the chance to work for a cool company. It is true that in this post-pandemic era workers have been loath to return to the conundrum of working nine-to-fives (or nine-to-grinds, as I often say), commuting hours to get to and from work, and sacrificing personal life to make work *work*. There has been real push for individual happiness and freedom as exemplified in the demand for hybrid work, but it remains to be seen if these trends will be secular or seasonal.

Until this point in my career, I had been a successful real estate executive. I had run large national and global businesses with thousands of employees and been responsible for billions of dollars in revenue or resources. I thought I was happy at the time, but in hindsight, I was not. I was successful, making decent money and feeling pretty good about "winning" in a game that few African Americans have traditionally been invited to even participate in. I came from a culture and family that understood the burdens of being the "only" in the room or the first. And I was accustomed to being "othered" in school and work—which made success, when it finally came, feel sweet and akin to happiness.

I was also of the school that believed joy would come from opening the door a bit wider for others like me to follow behind. So I took joy in proving that those like me—other "othered" people—belonged in these executive roles and from also generating resources that I could pour back into my community. Yes, I had earned millions, more than I ever thought possible, but I was not fulfilled and definitely not really happy.

I wanted and needed more in life. I just didn't know how to go about it or where to look. I had a wonderful partner, we took amazing vacations, and we felt community in our church and Harlem neighborhood, but I still felt empty in some major ways. I worked way too much—an average of six days a week, ten- or twelve-hour days (or more)—and was on email and text at all hours of the night. I was fatigued with office politics, code-switching, and wrestling with intermittent bouts of imposter syndrome. The emotional stress had also taken a physical toil on my body. I had become overweight, prediabetic, and a regular consumer of Zoloft for anxiety and what was likely in reality mild depression. On the outside I was crushing it, but on the inside, I was feeling crushed.

It was around this time that I began second-guessing the assumptions I had made about work/life balance and started pushing back or questioning the scripts I had been running for decades. For the first time in my career, I was feeling the urge to seek out happiness in what I did professionally. I had mostly found what I now know to be satisfaction, not joy, in my success. I was ambitious, hardworking, and moving up professionally, but the things I was *not* really gnawed at me.

I was not showing up as my full and authentic self. I mistook success for fulfillment. I thought that if I could accomplish and accumulate enough, I could one day enjoy the spoils such as getting in shape, spending more time with family, nurturing my marriage, scuba diving more, and doing something in public service to give back. I had assumed that those would be the defining attributes of life in my sixties. My forties were for cranking, climbing, and conquering. But I was slowly but surely coming to grips with the plain fact: I was wrong. Around this time, I was also beginning to notice tech and startup culture permeate my world. The idea that you could work hard, make a difference, make money, *and* be happy was just too tempting and radical of an idea to ignore. WeWork was my on-ramp. Perhaps this book will be yours.

THE INTERVIEW

To this day, I can vividly remember my final interview with WeWork's CEO, Adam Newmann, when I was being considered to lead his newly created business unit, Powered By We (PxWe). Adam and his chief commercial officer and loyal lieutenant, Dave Fano, desired to create a global division that would complement WeWork's core coworking business with a paid service offering that provided design, construction, and management services for real estate occupiers and owners of space. There were countless businesses, large and small, that wanted the benefit of WeWork's deep insights into the nature of work, design aesthetic, and community, but preferred to lease or own their space instead of placing their employees in WeWork buildings.

PxWe also had the not-so-subtle goal of expanding WeWork's reach beyond its own coworking spaces into the other, more traditional spaces of companies, accessing tens of millions of employees around the globe. It was a clever way to add members to WeWork's platform without using WeWork's capital to build spaces. We would design, build, and manage spaces for companies for a fee and recurring fees if they also bought our technology. PxWe would also balance out the unit economics of the capital intensive and cyclical coworking business with a business that could generate immediate and less-cyclical cash without spending massive capital up front. I was a perfect candidate for the job, having run large real estate service businesses for some of the most respected public and private service companies.

My interview experience foreshadowed what the next few years would bring. Adam's executive assistant had warned me to not wear a suit, but instead a T-shirt and jeans. "Don't come off too corporate," she cautioned. "Adam will not see you as a culture fit and be suspicious." So I did my best to dial it down, leaving my cufflinks and tailored suits at home. I had never worn jeans and a T-shirt to work. I did not have sneakers that were meant for anything other than running in Central Park, and I was a little bit too heavy at the time for skinny jeans. Translation: I was no tech bro and did not look the part. So you might understand why I was a bit intimidated when Adam asked me to meet him at his home for my final interview.

I drove three hours in New York City traffic to meet Adam at his home in the Hamptons. In classic Adam style, he was not there when I arrived. Dave Fano and I stood in his driveway, waiting for Adam to eventually get home for the meeting *he* had requested. I remember sweating in the summer sun, awkwardly making small talk with David, who would later go on to be a friend, confidant, and one of the smartest folks I encountered at the company. Dave was apologetic for Adam's delay but also used the opportunity to prepare me for what was to come. These were the normal shenanigans for being on the exec team at WeWork.

Adam eventually arrived in an SUV packed with his many kids and wife, Rebekah, and also a few servants who seemed to attend to and anticipate everything Adam and his family might want. Adam, perhaps preoccupied with the logistics of getting his family out of the car and into their beach-front home, walked right past me and David, barely even acknowledging our presence, much less apologizing for being late.

We followed Adam and his caravan into the house, sat quietly in his man cave, and watched him balance multiple calls (on multiple phones) with a host of real estate titans, like Starwood's Barry Sternlich, all while his servants brought him food, drink, or whatever he desired. There was so much commotion, and he had not yet even welcomed us to his home.

Eventually, after things settled a bit and Adam had wrapped up a few of his calls, he locked eyes on me. I could tell he had no idea who I was or why I was there. David prompted him, "This is Craig, who is going to run PxWe for us."

"Oh yes, that's right," Adam said as he leaned in.

He drilled me about my background, my track record, my views on the market and the like. At times, I felt Adam was more interested in finding some weakness in my candidacy than in really understanding anything I had to say. I was not his typical profile for an executive. I was Black, in my forties (old for WeWork, in my estimation), corporate, and from the real estate world he sought to disrupt. I am also 5'8" (on a good day) so not even a big physical presence alongside Adam's towering height.

Adam looked like the Jesus that I remember seeing in the stained-glass windows in so many of the Black churches I knew from back home. He was tall, slender, and Jewish, with long, flowing hair that made him the perfect look for a Messiah role in any cult movie. The only deviation from the European-fashioned images of Jesus, which looked more Nordic than Palestinian, was Adam's dark hair and dark eyes. So there, he was not totally the version of Jesus I remember, who was typically blonde and blue-eyed. But he did ultimately rise to the occasion as the real estate community's messiah—for a few years at least, until he was not.

After WeWork's failed IPO attempt, Adam would eventually be cru-cified so to speak, in the press, trade journals, and real estate community alike. But I had no idea at the time that some three years later, Adam would be stripped of his crown and his glory and left naked for commoners and speculators to inspect for any remaining signs of divinity.

But not in the summer of 2018. He was building a space-bound, half-rocket ship, half-ark that was about to take off and take as many believers as possible along for the epic voyage. I was determined to be on the rocket ship. After a grueling interview, I could sense that Adam was pleased and wanted me on the team. His curiosity shifted to personal matters, perhaps to gauge culture fit.

"Craig, do you have kids?" he asked.

"No," I replied quickly.

"Why not?" he responded with serious concern.

I explained awkwardly how my wife and I had not been able to conceive. We had endured five miscarriages and two rounds of IVF. It was not the conversation I wanted to have, or one I thought appropriate in typical work culture, but accepted this new opportunity to be vulnerable and connect with my future boss.

Adam pressed on and insisted my wife and I try again, but this time with "his guy," who was a spiritual guru who he assured me could get us pregnant. He then invited his wife, Rebekah, to ask me questions. "Craig, are you a good husband?"

Oh sheesh, I thought to myself. *This interview is officially going off the rails.* "I do the best I can, but marriage is tough," I said politely and looked to pivot back to the conversation of the business. She seemed satisfied with my answer. Little did I know at the time, but my wife and I would file for divorce a few years later.

After navigating the most awkward interview ever, Adam got really serious. He asked me with a solemn stare, "Do you smoke?" I didn't know much about Adam's love for pot and tequila, so I had not assumed that he was asking about smoking weed during an interview. I thought, *Maybe he wants to celebrate my new employment with a cigar.*

No cigar. This was Adam's way of kicking the interview into third gear and making sure I was going to fit in with his leadership team. I politely declined the weed, assuming that this was likely a hidden-camera moment and that even thinking about puffing with Adam would make me a laughingstock if the tape ever leaked. Plus, I was a Black man trying to climb a professional ladder when so many Black men were in prison for weed possession, and here my future boss was offering me a blunt. *No thanks,* I thought.

But I did feel my cool factor with Adam wearing off. He was obviously disappointed. Adam tried to redeem me and the interview by offering me shots of tequila. *Ugh,* I thought. The last time I had taken shots of tequila it did not end well. I had been in Bali at a cool "beautiful people" lounge with an infinity pool and a made-for-TV scene straight out of an episode of *Grown and Sexy.* But it was not sexy for me. I threw up everywhere, in the elevator and on myself. I am not quite sure what happened after that. I passed out. So taking shots was not a good idea for me in my final round. I declined and watched my standing with Adam plunge. So I tried to salvage things. "How about vodka?" I replied. Adam lit back up like the inflatables in front of the used car lots. I was back in his graces as I took vodka shots, and he smoked his weed. I was in, and on my way to making the world a better, happier place.

THE GOSPEL OF MEANING, PURPOSE, AND HAPPINESS

The coworking business never achieved profitability at any consistent or meaningful enterprise level while I was there—or perhaps not enough to service the debt and capital commitments that had fueled their meteoric growth to more than eight hundred locations around the world. For those less familiar with how these coworking companies make money, let me break it down for you, quick and simple.

WeWork would lease a lot of space for the long term from a building owner. In exchange for the long-term lease and some guarantees from WeWork, the building owner would fund a good bit of the capital that WeWork needed to build out a really cool and attractive space. WeWork's lease with the landlord for the space would be at market rental rates (or in some cases, greater than market). WeWork could, in turn, subdivide the space into smaller offices, suites, or desks and rent them to individuals and smaller teams for days, weeks, or months at a time. In exchange for these shorter and more flexible terms for a turnkey, amenity-filled space, WeWork would charge its tenants ("members") a monthly rate somewhere around 1.5-2x WeWork's underlying rent. This profit spread made sense as long as a few things held true:

1. The space had to ramp up and remain filled at some minimum occupancy level at this rental premium to break even and eventually make money.

2. The unit economics had to survive the ups and downs of real estate market cycles, vacancies, and changes in market rent. For example, if market rents fell below what WeWork had leased the space for years prior, then the 1.5x rental premium charged to a member could be much higher than space they could easily find elsewhere.

3. You couldn't keep plowing money into the same space to re-lease (with aggressive incentives, commissions, and so on), repair it, and/or modify the space to accommodate a prospective member. If so, you would risk plowing more money into the space than your original analysis likely assumed.

4. Finally, a competitor couldn't open a space down the street and discount their prices for a product that was just "good enough" to steal your demand. Otherwise, you would likely have to do the same and ultimately find none of your original profit assumptions panning out.

So while coworking could make money and did for periods of time, the fixed rent/arbitrage model would eventually fail at some point in the real estate cycle. Later, competing coworking companies, like Industrious (where I worked later as chief growth officer), would usher in new structures that did a better job of mitigating the risk of downside with variable lease structures and management agreements. But these less risky, more complex structures necessitated a slower growth rate than WeWork and its funders desired back then.

In the years that followed, we believed and preached a gospel of meaning, purpose, and happiness in our work—made possible in part by the spaces that we designed, built, and managed. We built beautiful spaces that made people proud to associate with their place of work and encouraged community building through the thoughtful layout that made chance encounters less chanced. The placement and comfort of furniture encouraged impromptu gatherings to problem solve or innovate, and a host of social events embracing everyone's authentic self was invited and welcome. My team delivered millions of square feet of spaces for organizations around the globe. Both large and small companies wanted the same thing, we thought. Large companies wanted to be nimble, entrepreneurial, and attractive to great talent—in a capital-efficient manner. Smaller companies, which were inherently nimbler and more entrepreneurial, wanted to scale into larger companies in a capital-efficient manner. But employees of all company sizes wanted to feel valued, engaged, and happy. This resonated with me personally, which made me a compelling evangelist.

My team designed, built, and delivered spaces for organizations around the globe, ranging from the large tech behemoths like Amazon, Facebook, and Salesforce to small offices for celebrities such as Will Smith and Arianna Huffington. It was all great, until it wasn't.

In my final months with WeWork, the company was in turmoil. While we had been preaching the gospel to a growing congregation, the debts and company burn rate (the amount of money we were spending each month to cover our expenses) had been piling up massively. The company was only as financially successful as its last fundraise, and the spigot had turned off suddenly and unexpectedly. WeWork's primary financial backer, SoftBank, a large multinational Japanese investment company under the leadership of Masayoshi Son ("Masa"), had abruptly decided to back out of earlier pledges to plow billions more into the company, and there weren't a lot of other sugar daddies in the wings.

So WeWork's executive team, but principally Adam, felt compelled to push forward with an IPO in a Hail Mary throw for more money. The company was not ready and had none of the prerequisites you'd want to see in an IPO candidate. It was nowhere close to being profitable, there were questionable and excessive uses of cash by Adam, and a lack of governance had allowed a number of major conflicts of interest to emerge, like Adam leasing buildings that he owned back to the company or Adam selling the rights to "We" (one of WeWork's brand identities) to the company for millions. According to the *Wall Street Journal*, Adam had taken $700 million out of WeWork before the IPO, which would go on to fail remarkably and make the company into the laughingstock of the industry.

I often describe WeWork as a rocket ship that was designed to travel to Pluto—or farther—if you listened to Adam. The rocket burned the most expensive fuel available, funded by SoftBank and other venture capitalists, and was never designed to glide or fly in Earth's orbit. It had no wings, just massive jets capable of taking us from the world of office into the worlds of housing, schools, retail, investment funds, technology, and other attractive total addressable markets (TAMs). The ship was never thought to fly like other aircrafts . . . hence not having any of the prerequisite FAA-mandated parachutes, landing gear, or wings.

Subsequent CEOs that came after Adam's removal tried desperately to shed excess weight (with rounds of layoffs, restructuring, and unit closings), build landing gears, and prepare its investors for the rough landing ahead. And that it was. The company finally fell into bankruptcy in 2024, and with it any dreams of intergalactic space travel. However, what survived was a dream of making work a place for something more than work.

Today, professional talent want their work to be a source of meaning, connection, and joy in part because of the WeWork-era gospel. Though companies such as Google had already been using culture and workspaces to attract and retain talent for years, WeWork productized and popularized the ideas for the masses. Talent would not only expect of their employers great spaces, flexible work schedules, and company values that reflected their own but also an acknowledgment that their humanity and well-being were important. Work would no longer be able to ignore our need for happiness and nor would we.

Although I left the company prior to its final demise and subsequent restructuring, feeling dispirited and angry with Adam (who negotiated a platinum parachute from SoftBank while the rest of us got nothing), I held firm to the dream of finding happiness in my professional life and continued to refine and revisit it in my own way. I was intent on never going back to the version of me that needed Zoloft to go to work. I was committed to preaching the gospel, even if the church and pastor stood no more. My brief time at WeWork, and the treasured friendships that I made—and maintain—with Miguel McKelvey, Dave Fano, and countless others, inspired me in deep and lasting ways that ultimately gave rise to this book you're reading today.

FULFILLMENT BEYOND SATISFACTION AND HAPPINESS

One of my chance encounters while running PxWe at WeWork was meeting Aaron Hurst. Aaron is the author of *The Purpose Economy* and a leading expert on the science of purpose and fulfillment at work. Aaron's research and work brought a scientific and research-based legitimacy to what we at WeWork already felt and knew at our core. Much of WeWork's research had been intended for marketing and sought to prove the productivity, talent engagement, and business agility that businesses experienced in our spaces. While it was self-serving (to help drive more sales), we also believed it. I got to know Aaron, and his views on the future of work and fulfillment resonated with me. His message was clear. The future of work is not about happiness, but fulfillment.

We invited Aaron to be a guest speaker at a number of our client events. In his talks, he often reminded us of the history of work for mankind. The original purpose of work, as he explained, was purely survival. Early humans worked (by farming, hunting, etc.) to survive. There were no elaborate expectations for joy, engagement, or purpose in catching prey or, for agrarian communities, to reap a harvest. If work didn't happen, the consequences were far more drastic than happiness. You likely died. Later, with the industrialization of work, he argued, the purpose of work shifted to an output-based system that valued homogeneity. Lines of workers did the same thing, day after day, in unison. Managers did not tolerate individuality or independent thinking, nor did they desire for their workers to do anything other than show up—and not strike. Avoiding a strike was as close as work needed to get to happiness.

Later, mostly in the era that I came into the workforce, we shifted to a service and information-based economy. More of our economy was generated by knowledge work and knowledge workers. Work that was once done in the fields of Mesopotamia or the factories of Detroit, Michigan, was now increasingly done in banks, consulting firms, technology companies, and consumer goods conglomerates that depended on people capable of marketing, finance, strategy, operations, innovating—thinking. As Thomas Friedman helps readers understand in his book *The World Is Flat*, this work could also be distributed to far-flung parts of the earth where talent was capable, hungry, and willing to do work, for less.

Most managers of the thinking class viewed employee engagement as the ultimate score for the health of the workers' marriage to their jobs. Employee engagement is basically a measurement for how committed, dedicated, or even excited an employee is to their work. An annual survey typically captured the employee sentiment of engagement, and managers in turn would study the results, looking for signs of levers they needed to pull to squeeze out *more* engagement. Engagement was thought to directly drive productivity, and I am sure there are studies that either support the claim or make enough of the case.

But in practice, I imagined it to be a better measure of an employee's willingness to come in early, crank out emails over the weekend, miss their kid's baseball game, cancel a date, or whatever thing in life might compete for their engagement. Aaron would joke it was a way for employers to measure how much more you would work without more pay. As of today, employee engagement is still viewed as a reasonable score card.

But engagement does not speak to our fundamental need to feel alive, feel joy, or feel connected. Engagement is a transactional metric that says "I am motivated to do this thing" without regard to why. Maybe I can't afford to lose this job, so I will work hard to be viewed as irreplaceable. Maybe I believe this job will get me the skills or access I need so that I can compete for the job I really desire. Maybe it's about the money, status, or optionality that I think the work will give me. And while there are big differences between a job and a career, most people would do neither for free, and most of us don't expect either to bring us joy.

But why not? Aaron offered a new take on what work needs to do in order to unlock these mysteries of the human condition. Although I use "happiness" as a catchall word throughout the book, I really like Aaron's philosophy that work should be a source for more than happiness. It should be a source for deep, meaningful, and lasting fulfillment.

Aaron, who was influenced by the Gallup organization's research on the topic, believed that fulfillment comes when we have three things:

1. Impact. We need to feel a sense of purpose and meaning in our lives. What we do needs to matter and be impactful.

2. Engagement. Humans are social animals and need belonging (community) and meaningful relationships.

3. Growth. People need to feel like they are growing, learning, and being stretched. We need to be getting better in some way.

Without these three ingredients, we struggle to be fulfilled. But that was hardly the kicker for me. The real breakthrough came from Aaron's biggest conclusion relative to work and why it is critical to our happiness. We have a less than 1 percent chance of being fulfilled in life if we are *not* also fulfilled in our work.[2]

Newsflash! This means that you couldn't detach work from your need for fulfillment, even if you wanted to. This intuitively makes sense, especially if we consider how much of our lives we spend working. The most common estimates suggest people spend ninety thousand hours working during a lifetime (or 13 percent to 16 percent of your life depending on how long you live, and perhaps a little over 20 percent of your waking hours). This equates to a forty-hour work week, fifty weeks per year, and forty-five years of work (age twenty to sixty-five years) and an eighty-year life span.[3]

But imagine you don't live an average lifespan (and die before the average age), and also imagine that you work longer than forty hours a week—if we factor in commute time, emails and calls at home, or even the time you spend thinking about work outside of normal work hours, the actual percentage of your life spent working could be significantly higher. My grandfather Hubert Simpson, who died at age forty-two and at times worked two or more jobs to support his family, is a sad reminder of how averages can be misleading if you are planning your life around them. According to Pew Research, 19 to 22 percent of people work past sixty-five years of age as of 2023, up from 11 percent in 1987.[4] The amount of time we spend working (and doing things related to work) is likely much higher for most people.

So imagine you spend another third sleeping, ideally, and a few hours each day doing chores, admin, and other essentials. That would leave the balance for joy and meaningful activities—family, friends, hobbies, worship, vacation, or whatever you see fit. And that's assuming you're not parenting or taking care of an aging parent. See the following table for a quick illustration.

Weekly Time Breakdown	
Without Kids	**With Young Kids**
Total Hours in a Week: 168 hours *Sleep:* 56 hours (8 hours/day × 7 days) *Work:* 40 hours (8 hours/day × 5 days) *Work-Related Activities:* 10 hours (2 hours/day × 5 days) *Daily Essentials and Chores:* 35 hours (5 hours/day × 7 days)	Total Hours in a Week: 168 hours *Sleep:* 56 hours (8 hours/day × 7 days) *Work:* 40 hours (8 hours/day × 5 days) *Work-Related Activities:* 10 hours (2 hours/day × 5 days) *Daily Essentials and Chores:* 35 hours (5 hours/day × 7 days) *Childcare:* 17.5 hours (2.5 hours/day × 7 days)
Leaves 27 hours per week	**Leaves 9.5 hours per week**

Assumptions:
- Sleep: The average adult is advised to get seven to nine hours of sleep per night. We'll use the mid-range average of eight hours.

- Work: The standard full-time work week is forty hours, which averages out to eight hours per day (in the US).

- Work-Related Activities:
  - *Commuting:* The average one-way commute in many developed countries is around twenty-five to thirty minutes, or about one hour a day for a round-trip.
  - *Getting ready:* Personal grooming, showering, and dressing for work can take an average of thirty minutes.
  - *Working from home/thinking about work:* This is the most difficult to quantify. Many studies show that people who work from home often struggle to "unplug." Let's estimate this mental burden as an additional thirty minutes of cognitive load or minor work tasks.
  - *Total work-related activities:* Approximately two hours.

- Daily Essentials and Chores: This includes a wide range of non-optional activities.
  - *Eating:* Preparing and eating meals takes time. This can be estimated at about two hours per day.
  - *Household chores:* Cooking, cleaning, laundry, grocery shopping, and other household management can take an average of one to two hours a day, with women and parents typically spending more time on these tasks. Let's use an average of one and a half hours.
  - *Personal care:* Time for hygiene, taking care of children, or running personal errands can add up to another one and a half hours.
  - *Total essentials:* Approximately five hours.

Based on our illustrative example of how time can get consumed by work and life's necessities, the remaining hours of free time per week to otherwise pursue joy, happiness, and fulfillment translates to an average of just over 3.8 hours per day (1.3 hours per day with kids). However, this time isn't evenly distributed. The majority of this time is likely available during the two non-working days, with very little left on the five working days. This weekly perspective illustrates how the quest for joy and meaning often becomes a weekend-centric endeavor for many people—at best. Is this enough time to fulfill your happiness needs? Maybe, but I doubt it, and Aaron's research also suggests it.

So why not make your career, jobs, and work in part responsible for your happiness—or better yet, your purpose, belonging, and growth? Why would you even consider jobs that did not speak to these basic needs? Why do we encourage kids to study subjects and pick majors in college or skills in trade schools based purely on what will "make them money"? Why would you stay in a job, even if it pays well and you're good at it, if it drains your soul? You shouldn't.

In the following chapter, I offer frameworks that will help you reflect, evaluate, and potentially pivot in your career, if by chance you are not in a fulfilling career or job already. While no one can tell you what work will ladder up to your happiness quotient, you can answer a few questions that might move you in the right direction.

REFLECTION QUESTIONS

1. What does a typical twenty-four-hour day look like for you? Quickly jot down: How much time do you spend working? Sleeping? Doing things that bring you joy? See the following table. What, if anything, surprises you? What, if anything, would you like to change?

Typical Day		
Activity	**Hours Per Day** **(Avg. over a seven-day week)**	**Percent of Total**
Sleeping		
Getting Ready for the Day		
Commuting		
Eating		
Working		
Chores and Necessities		
Exercising		
Doing Activities That Bring You Joy (e.g., worshiping, volunteering, time with friends, hobbies, etc.)		
Other: Describe____________		
TOTAL	24 Hours	100 percent

2. Do you agree with the premise that it's difficult to be fulfilled in life if you're not fulfilled in your work? Why or why not? What are your counterarguments or alternative perspectives?

3. What societal or personal beliefs have you held about the role of work in your life that might have prevented you from seeking deeper fulfillment in your career until now?

4. How do you personally define "employee engagement" in the context of your own work experiences? Can you think of a time when you were "highly engaged" at work but perhaps not truly fulfilled? What was the difference in your experience between the two?

5. What underlying motivations (e.g., money, fear of job loss, skill acquisition, status) might have driven your engagement in past roles, and how did these motivations align or conflict with your deeper needs?

CHAPTER 5

FINDING YOUR G.E.L.

*"The happiest people are not the ones
who achieve the most. They are the ones who
spend more time than others in a state of flow."*

**—Ikigai: The Japanese Secret to a Long and Happy Life
by Francesc Miralles and Héctor García**

I recently connected with a mentee of mine for one of our regular check-ins. Let's call him Mike (not his real name). Mike had just completed his first year at a top 25 business school and was getting ready for his summer internship, an important professional experience MBA students use to help pivot between careers, test their target job assumptions, or to help improve their chances of securing a full-time offer from their summer employer. For Mike, he was angling for a combination of the three. But in my forty-five-minute call with Mike, I heard a few things that gave me pause.

I had met Mike a few years prior to him starting business school, when he was working in the accounting department of a company where I was an executive. Mike came from a modest working-class home, went to a large state school for undergraduate college, and hustled hard to land a professional job after finishing college. He was smart, scrappy, and ambitious. But most of all, Mike was singularly focused on being successful based on some loosely defined concepts he's probably held for years, but mostly the vague and crowdsourced standards of his business school peers.

When we chatted, I asked about the rationale for selecting the summer internship he had accepted with a small private equity firm. He rattled off a few rehearsed soundbites that sounded very familiar to those I probably used some twenty-five years ago. He offered reasons, like "path to wealth creation," "this will make me more attractive to recruiters," and "the firm is crushing it." Though I am sure he felt his rationale was original and projected confidence, he was running one of the standard scripts that many of us download and run when selecting careers. They are not bad, just not necessarily likely to lead to our authentic happiness—and maybe not even success.

I went on to ask him how he enjoyed his first year of classes, which are typically foundational in nature and the prerequisites before diving into the second-year electives that typically align with your professional interests. He said he did "okay" but admitted that he did not like Finance nor did he do well in the class—one that was the most important skill needed for his summer job. He did however enjoy strategy, marketing, and operations, and thought he would really enjoy running a business in the long run. So why, I asked, was he not pursuing what he was truly interested in doing versus primarily pursuing jobs that were "paths to wealth creation" and sexy, if I could paraphrase his motivation.

THE PATHS WE CHOOSE

There are few things I have enjoyed more over the course of my career than mentoring. I especially love mentoring mid-career professionals who are, perhaps for the first time in their lives, dealing with the consequences of their biggest life and career decisions—discovering the trade-offs and determining how they line up with their authentic truths. It's typically around this time that the world they once imagined for themselves and their career is now facing off with the realities of life. They've tasted success but likely also disappointment. They've earned big promotions but perhaps also know the sting, embarrassment, or blow to pride that comes from being passed over for a promotion or getting laid off. They also now probably have a better sense for how hard or easy, or to what degree, their professional dreams may necessitate happiness trade-offs.

While some will use these moments (setbacks, dissatisfaction, and so on) to reflect on the merits of their early assumptions about their career calling and purpose, others relish in their determination and plow right ahead. The latter may blow right past important signs and signals that say in bright red letters: "This is not your lane. This is not your calling. You're not fulfilled."

In the book *Now Discover Your Strengths*, which a mentor had me read right out of business school, the authors encourage us to discover and embrace our strengths early on. This may seem like the obvious thing to do, but it's not often what we do instinctively. In the West, and America in particular, we are encouraged to do just the opposite—focus on improving our weaknesses. If you were average in math in school but got an A in art class, chances are your parents would put you in summer math camp versus send you to art school for the gifted. I was guilty of this for years. In business school, I tended to take more of the classes where I felt vulnerable—finance and accounting—versus the ones I enjoyed and was curious about, such as organizational behavior and marketing. I did this not because I enjoyed finance or was particularly good at it, but because I was building a bulletproof version of me that would be able to compete and land any job I wanted. The things that I enjoyed and did well in were classes I opted not to take more of. I was probably more like my mentee, Mike.

I continued to do this in my professional career as well. For example, I typically got year-end performance feedback and, as a manager, I also gave performance feedback to my teams. No matter how much positive feedback I got or gave, my instinct was to spend as much time and energy as I could focusing on the areas where I fell short, not exploring how to further develop or exploit my strengths.

We also gravitate towards jobs, roles, and careers that we know may not bring us joy or play to our strengths but will bring us future optionality, money, or status. For example, I worked in investment banking one summer during business school as an intern. I had no deep interests in capital markets, sales and trading, or corporate finance, and what I knew of the lifestyle for bankers was anything but attractive to me. I had heard that bankers could expect to work twenty-plus-hour days for weeks at a time and would be expected to drop anything on a dime to be available at work. I had heard horror stories of bankers leaving funerals early (or not going at all) because a major deliverable was due. But for some reason, I took one of the highly coveted banking jobs knowing all of this, in spite of this. Why? Well, I reasoned, this job will help me get into real estate private equity, development, or something on the investment side of commercial real estate. I would put in my time, pay my dues, and earn a right to enjoy my work—later.

It turned out that every assumption I made about the summer internship gamble was way off. First, I was awful at the type of work we did. It did not play to my strengths. I am good at sales, marketing, strategy, and building relationships. I am horrible at creating and maintaining complex Excel sheet models, making detailed pitch decks that are purposefully void of creativity, and, most of all, working effectively with less than five hours of sleep. I also found myself growing resentful of the fact that I had no control over my schedule. I could never promise a friend that I could meet for drinks or dinner. It all depended on when we finished in the office. On a Friday or Saturday, we could easily work until 9 p.m., 10 p.m., or midnight. I hated not having autonomy. The only thing I enjoyed was the sound of me saying, "I work at Goldman in their M&A group." It was sexy and I honestly thought it would advance my career.

It did not. The things that I ultimately did well in my career, like building and scaling real estate service businesses, had nothing to do with banking or the image of myself I wanted to promote during that brief summer internship. Although I didn't have any philosophy or sense for the role of happiness in work, I instinctively knew that this was a bad career choice for me.

G.E.L.

As my career progressed, I became more self-aware, prouder of my strengths, and more honest about my weaknesses. I also paid more attention to moments when I felt alive and joyful, and others when I felt dread. With outward success came mentees and folks who wanted to know my formula for success.

Almost on a whim, I came up with the acronym G.E.L., which has proven to withstand the test of time and continues to resonate with most. I have since read of other frameworks that offer similar guidance, like *Ikigai*, which graphically captures in a Venn Diagram the Japanese concept for "reason for being."[1] However, G.E.L. is not only an acronym but also a geometric framework for triangulating your optimal career, function, or raison d'être.

Each time I meet with a prospective mentee or even offer career advice to colleagues and friends, I ask them to complete my G.E.L. questionnaire. Here is how it works.

G.E.L. QUESTIONNAIRE

1. *[G] What is it that you are naturally GOOD at?*

What is your superpower? What are your strengths? What comes easy for you but perhaps harder for someone else? Don't just limit your answer to terms that describe work functions. Zoom out and think about your strengths more broadly. Reflect back to your school days, volunteerism, work . . . any time or point when you realized you had a gift or a knack for something unique. Perhaps it was public speaking, solving complex puzzles, bringing people together, or something creative. It really doesn't matter. The key is not to be so narrow in defining the strength that you miss out on the underlying broader strength that could have many applications.

So why is finding your G so hard and evasive for some? There are three very common reasons. The first reason is ego. We want to be good at the cool and sexy things. If our G is not cool per se, we might not embrace it. Two, we are determined to get good at something we think is within reach with just a bit more practice and a bit more effort. And while that may be true, it will never be the same G as it is for someone for whom it is their natural gift. If you have to work hard to be good at your G, it's not your G. Third, finding G might be hard for some because they have not been introspective or had enough experiences to really zero in on something actionable.

One last risk with finding your G. If you anchor on something too specific, you miss the bigger strength. For example, you might be good at solving crossword puzzles. But it might also be, more broadly, that you are gifted at pattern recognition, solving complex problems, or seeing signals in the noise. Each of these could have applications in an endless number of settings.

For me, I learned early on that I was really good at synthesizing and making complicated things simple (typically through storytelling and writing). I could also be a compelling communicator, which I first experienced in sixth grade when I won an oratory contest and, thereafter, each time I was called to speak in front of large crowds. In group settings, I found that building trust and followership came naturally, which served me well in leadership roles, which I seemed to have often in high school, college, and work. I also had a knack for spotting trends and pattern recognition and seeing the big picture (or the key issue), which I discovered early in my consulting and sales roles. How about you? What are some of your superpowers?

2. *[E] What is it that EXCITES you?*

What gives you energy? What is it that fuels the last or extra mile (which is always the least crowded)? What would you consider doing for free or without prompting? When you talk about a certain thing, do you notice your energy level, voice, and animation elevating a bit? If so, you've probably found your E. It's your rocket fuel. My E was easy for me to find.

I love big ideas, challenger brands, David and Goliath type stories. I gravitate towards big political, policy ideas, and campaigns as well as new tech and innovation and contrarian ideas and business models. But I also get energized by more nuanced things, such as sources of inspiration, the human spirit to press forward, the power of nature, and authentic connections with others. I began to really understand this about myself when I had leadership roles in challenger brand companies with teams that shared my passion for wanting to change the status quo, make a difference and win, not just by doing something better, but by doing it differently. I also noticed that I was always reading certain books, like ones written by Malcom Gladwell or Adam Grant, that challenged the way I thought about big and small things. I could consume those books like candy, always wanting more. And finally, I often found myself deeply inspired by leaders who had big and positive visions for a world that did not yet exist, like Barack Obama and Steve Jobs.

Wow, just writing that paragraph lit my fire. I know this is my E. What's yours? It's probably worth noting that not everyone shares this view. In his book *Algebra of Happiness*, Scott Galloway warns against

continued →

following your passion as a primary motivation but rather allowing your passion to be the byproduct of first finding something you're good at and then mastering it. And while I agree with many of the tenets of the book and understand the rationale behind Scott's warning, I believe that your E is a critical component part—alongside mastery of your G.

3.   *[L] What gives you the LIFESTYLE you want?*

How do you balance risk and reward or stability and control versus freedom and spontaneity? Do you need an abundance of work-life balance, or do you thrive in intense environments? What role does compensation play in your calculus?

My brother decided long ago that he'd never want to work in corporate America. The thought of office cubes and corporate politics made him sick, so the life of an artist was fitting for him. On the other hand I didn't mind corporate environments so much (at the time). For some of my friends, my million-miler status would be grounds for therapy. But for me, I enjoyed it and my Delta Airlines diamond medallion status. I am risk-averse and struggled to get comfortable with 100 percent commission roles where I could have made more money or being an early employee in a startup that could go under. Too much risk drives me nuts. I am comfortable not being a billionaire if it means I have more work-life balance, less risk, and more time to be—happy.

In *The Algebra of Happiness*, Scott also encourages us to work harder in our twenties and thirties, earlier in our careers, to achieve a certain escape velocity that will serve us well later. Once again, I see it slightly different. If you're in your G.E.L., you don't have to run harder in one season at the expense of your happiness. Being in your G.E.L. means you are excelling professionally in a way that's sustainable (imagine running a marathon versus sprinting) and happier for it!

Once you've identified your G.E.L. components, put them together in a fully balanced way that makes the triangle equilateral. If you distort the triangle from an equilateral to an isosceles triangle, you will run into problems. For example, if you find yourself in a role that plays to your strengths (G) and your passion (E) but does not deliver on the lifestyle (L), you will be angry and resentful. You might say to yourself, "I'm creating so much value and doing what I love, but I am not making any money, or I never see my kids." Or you may say to yourself, "I have no idea if this opportunity is going to pay off and be worth it."

If you find a role that plays to your lifestyle (L) and passion (E), but not your strengths (G), that means you are not going to be a top performer in your organization. You love what you do, and it gives you a great life, but since you are not the best at it (or even as good as the person sitting at the desk next to you), chances are you won't move up, or worse, you may get weeded out as a mid- and lower-tier performer.

Finally, if you find a role that plays to your strengths (G) and lifestyle (L), but not your passion (E), you're doing it for the wrong reasons and will burn out. Motivation without passion is an expensive and inefficient fuel source. In their book *Ikigai: The Japanese Secret to a Long and Happy Life*, authors Francesc Miralles and Héctor García describe this feeling as being in your "flow." Like my G.E.L., the Japanese concept of flow means (in work, for example) you are doing what you love, are good at, and creates value for people who are willing to pay you. That's the path to happiness and fulfillment.

Example G.E.L.

In my example, G.E.L. looks something like this: I am in my G.E.L. when I can scale and lead growth businesses, companies, or initiatives that are challenging the status quo, making a big impact, and likely to matter. I will be at my best in organizations that are well-resourced (funded), collegial, and not overly (if at all) political. When I reflect on the roles where I was most successful *and* happy, I was in my G.E.L.

They also aligned with Aaron's framework too. I felt most fulfilled when I was in roles that gave me purpose, growth, and belonging—and played to my strengths and desired lifestyle.

How about you? Take a few minutes to reflect on your past roles. How well do they line up with your G.E.L.? Did you feel fulfilled? If you have not had enough experiences to know what your G.E.L. might be or you are still unsure, you might need to test a hypothesis. You might also need more data points. In this scenario, I suggest adding an O to your G.E.L. to create G.E.L.O.

The O in G.E.L.O. is for "optionality." Recent grads with little work or lived experiences might not yet know what they want and what they're good at or appreciate the nuances and trade-offs of corporate culture, risk, and reward. For them, they need to have experiences. But not *mindless* experiences. They need to take note of their experiences. They should reflect on when things feel good, and when they feel draining. They need to pay attention to their energy levels, effort levels, and anxiety levels. Having roles that offer a nice O are perfect.

Think about roles, situations, and companies where you get exposure to lots of functions, situations, cultures, and so on. It might not always be in work situations, either. I enjoyed summer internships, consulting roles out of college, and general management rotations because they gave me "optionality" to test different assumptions. Working in banking during my MBA summer was a great option. I could test my assumptions and conditions for success before making a big commitment. This series of testing can take years, if not longer. The key is to be self-aware at all times and to be honest with yourself. Chances are, you will know sooner than others if you are not in your G.E.L. But if you're not honest with yourself (i.e., in denial about your G), your teammates and managers will see it soon enough.

Finding your G.E.L. is one important step to finding work that brings you purpose, meaning, and growth. It's one step in ensuring that what you do for a living ladders up to the life you want. Happiness and fulfillment will be key to sustaining anything you want or need to do over time. You can cram and crank through a tough role or poor organizational fit, but chances are you can't stay there long—and you certainly can't win.

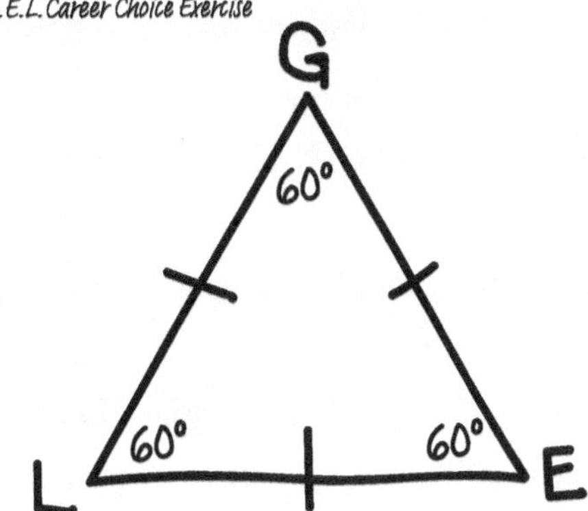

G.E.L. Career Choice Exercise

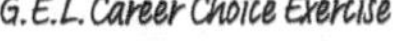

G.E.L. Career Choice Exercise

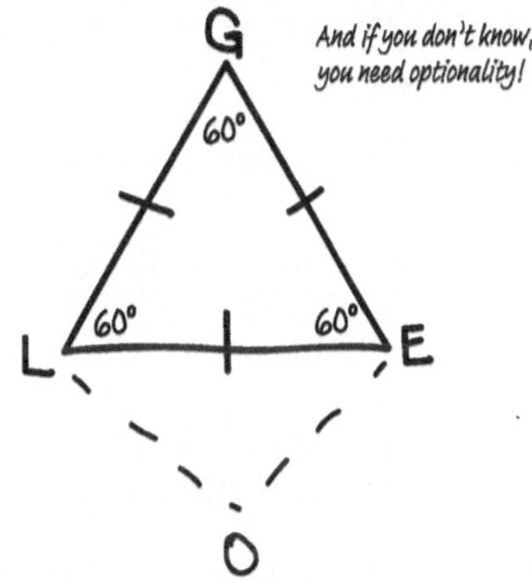

While we are often encouraged by our parents or friends to select college majors, summer internships, and ultimately careers that offer the promise of money and success, they may not lead to happiness. Our best chance of finding happiness in our work is to find work that aligns with our G.E.L. When you're in your G.E.L., chances are you are also experiencing "flow." This does not mean that work will come easy or that you won't have tough days, but by and large you are playing to your strengths and passions, on your terms. And if you're "flowing" in an environment that reflects your values and purpose, challenges you, and offers community, you have a much greater chance of being fulfilled in life.

One final note on finding your G.E.L.: It's likely not a single job, function, or activity that unlocks your rocket fuel. It may very well be many things that you are good at doing, passionate about, and are capable of providing the lifestyle you want. You may even discover different G.E.L.s in different seasons of life. In her book *Portfolio Life*, Christina Wallace suggest that we diversify our sources of work, income, and opportunities for impact, growth, and belonging, as a more prudent and sustainable path to happiness.[2] I agree and have followed this approach in my own life. I have an active portfolio of things that I do that align with my G.E.L. For example, I enjoy and earn money from consulting, coaching, advising, public speaking, writing, and occasionally from taking on longer-term executive roles in organizations. There is no need for any *one* thing to be *my* thing. The same can be true for you.

REFLECTION QUESTIONS

1. Reflect on a significant career decision you've made
    (e.g., choosing a major, accepting a job, pursuing a promotion).
    What were your primary reasons for that decision?

2. What external pressures (e.g., parental expectations, peer success, societal definitions of prestige) might have influenced your rationale, and how might these have differed from your intrinsic desires?

3. Can you identify a specific instance in your academic or professional life where you intentionally pursued something you struggled with, rather than something you excelled at or genuinely enjoyed? What was your motivation for doing so?

4. Take out a sheet of paper and jot down the key attributes of your G.E.L.

5. What trade-offs have you consciously or unconsciously made between G, E, and L in your past roles, and what has been the personal cost of those trade-offs?

6. How might your career path have differed if, at key junctures, you had prioritized deepening your existing strengths and passions over shoring up weaknesses?

CHAPTER 6

THE SCATTER PLOT EFFECT

"The ultimate measure of a man is not where he stands in moments of convenience and comfort, but where he stands at times of challenge and controversy."

—Dr. Martin Luther King, Jr., *Strength to Love*

Being in your G.E.L. does not mean that things come easy, and it does not mean that you will always be winning. In fact, just the opposite. Nowhere in Aaron's ingredients for fulfillment (purpose, belonging, and growth) or my G.E.L. (good, excited, and lifestyle) did we use the words "winning," "rich," "status," or any of those much-sought-after goals. The absence of happiness in any given moment is not necessarily unhappiness. Nor is it necessary for purpose and growth to come without effort, resistance, and searching.

Early in my career, I would devour the monthly editions of *Black Enterprise* magazine, which spotlighted successful Black business leaders and their achievements. I can remember feeling awestruck by the images of powerful, accomplished, and beautiful professionals, entrepreneurs, and rising talent—all who looked like me. I had also grown up in Atlanta, a city known for its large and growing Black middle and professional class. Atlanta is one of the few cities that has consistently boasted three things for African Americans since the Reconstruction era and early 1900s: 1) economic capital, from a thriving and diverse middle class, 2) political capital, from its large voting population that elected Black leaders in every branch of local government, and 3) social capital that originated from its Civil Rights institutions, HBCUs, churches, entertainment, arts, and other social organizations. These three forces reinforce each other and continue to perpetuate what I and my friends refer to as "our Wakanda." Author and political commentator Charles Blow in his book *The Devil You Know*[1] writes with greater precision how some of these forces can be found in other parts of the South and offer a compelling opportunity for economic, political, and social progress for Black people.

For me, growing up in Atlanta during the 1970s, 1980s, and 1990s, I knew no other world. I grew up seeing Black teachers, politicians, businesspeople, activists, doctors, and the like. Although I did not live in a particularly nice neighborhood, I was exposed to what was possible by osmosis. I had role models, even if they were not "mine" per se and only seen from a distance.

Notwithstanding the plume of Atlanta's Black mystique, my household and immediate surroundings were a bit more troublesome and challenging. My father had left me, my brother, and my mom when I was ten years old. My mother struggled with substance abuse and depression for most of my teens. Even though my mother remarried and held our family together, it always seemed like we struggled financially, emotionally, and otherwise. We lived in an area of Atlanta known for drugs and prostitution. My mother insisted that our schooling take place elsewhere—in a Black private school in the historic Old Fourth Ward neighborhood, next door to MLK's birth home, and later to a public school in a more upwardly mobile middle-class neighborhood.

A few decades earlier, my neighborhood and street had been a White working-class community. But as families like mine arrived, White flight took hold, leaving our southwest neighborhood to become increasingly Black and working class, and over time, less diverse, less resilient, and less safe. You could drive the streets of my neighborhood and see signs of once-nice tree-lined streets with neat bungalows, respectable post-war brick homes, and occasionally a stately home belonging to someone important. Over time, many of these homes fell into disrepair, some became drug fronts, and others were occupied by families like mine.

We were not poor by any stretch, but we looked more middle class than we actually were. This was true for Black people in general, I thought. No matter our pain or suffering, we were going to look better than we were. We were too proud of a people to "look a mess." We showed up in church every Sunday morning looking our best, even if we were down to our last dollar, fighting a terminal illness, or strung out on drugs. We looked a million bucks even if all we had was a single dollar to our name.

I struggled with this contradiction. I saw examples of what was possible in and around Atlanta's middle and elite classes, even while my day-to-day experiences were far humbler. I decided early on that school would be my safe passage between these worlds. I commuted from my neighborhood in the "SWATS," as we affectionately referred to parts of southwest Atlanta, to a public school that boasted one of the best math and science magnet programs in the city and had alumni who had made it to Ivy League schools, military academies, and the like. My high school, Benjamin Elijah Mays (named after the great African American educator and president of Morehouse College), even today celebrates a proud alumni roster of Atlanta mayors, famous musicians, scientists, athletes, and businesspeople. In 1993, I graduated salutatorian of my class. I was student government president and had been admitted to MIT. I set out to build a life for myself that was informed by what I knew was possible, based on what I had seen, even if I had no clue how.

WHEN RANDOM IS NOT RANDOM AT ALL

Fast-forward a few years, I began my career like so many, looking for examples in books, my workspace, and even magazines such as *Black Enterprise* for how to fashion myself. I would absorb the biography of a keynote speaker at motivational conferences like the text held secret meanings and clues to success. I would reverse engineer a successful person's career path in hopes of making sense of my own decisions. Even after I decided I wanted to return to graduate school for my MBA, pivot into commercial real estate, and ultimately public service, I still found myself captivated by the biographical stories of famous CEOs, innovators, and political leaders. The case method of learning business management principles resonated with me during my time at Harvard Business School. It was an opportunity to do more of what I had been doing all my life: studying what "successful" people, the protagonists as we called them, did in major life-defining decisions, potentially perilous business predicaments, or even in moral dilemmas as leaders.

Like my fellow B-school classmates, we imagined ourselves as the protagonist. We would imagine sitting in the commanding chair of the USS *Enterprise*, like Captain Kirk, calmly making decisions about whether to launch a product or not, buy a company or not, close a division or not, apply a certain accounting treatment or not, idle the plant or not, or even pull the Tylenol off the shelves of thousands of stores if you thought the pill bottles might have been tampered with, as was the dilemma in our James Burke Tylenol case study.

So it was not a surprise, as I started to experience some success in my career, that I told my own story using the same formula. If I was invited to speak to high school students, college kids looking for jobs out of college, or even teens in Harlem, where I mentored for years, I would tell my story the way I read the stories of my mentors. From the bottom left, to the top right. That's the way the story *always* goes. We would align a series of key decisions, key successes, and other life-defining moments in a way that made for a clean and easy-to-understand narrative. It also made it deceptively easy to reverse engineer.

You might recall in your high school math classes that the equation for a line is $y=mx+b$, where m is the slope of the line. All you need to do, if given the slope and a constant (b), is plug in your own x and y values. That's how we often interpreted and made sense of the formula for success. Plug in your own assumptions for x and y and let the formula do the rest.

I now believe this to be misleading at best.

If someone neatly plucks out a few data points in their life journey, lines them up in a neat orderly fashion that generally points up and to the right, this is probably the work of fiction. Our lives are not neat, predictable lines that follow "if, then" statements. In reality, our lived experiences are messy, unpredictable, random, and highly interdependent with a host of other variables that never make it into our biographies.

We never talk as much in our biographies about the role of luck, chance, or even the saving graces of a mentor, sponsor, or manager who saw our potential before we did. We certainly never talk about our failures, blunders, or major losses when trying to describe the reasons for our success. When talking about our happiness, we rarely talk about our unhappiness.

Perhaps we really believe our hype and intentionally dial down the noise that we feel is not relevant. We might be fixated on mirroring the same stories of our role models who we believe we are exemplifying. Or just maybe, we don't really know why we've been successful—and that thought is far too scary. Why? Because it means we don't know for sure if or how our success might continue.

I have come to describe this phenomenon as the scatter plot effect. In statistics, we learn of a mathematical concept called regression. In lay terms, we can look at scatter plots and determine if there is enough correlation and relationship in what looks like random dots on a graph to draw a line that reveals that the scatter plot is actually not random at all. We do this in our lives as well.

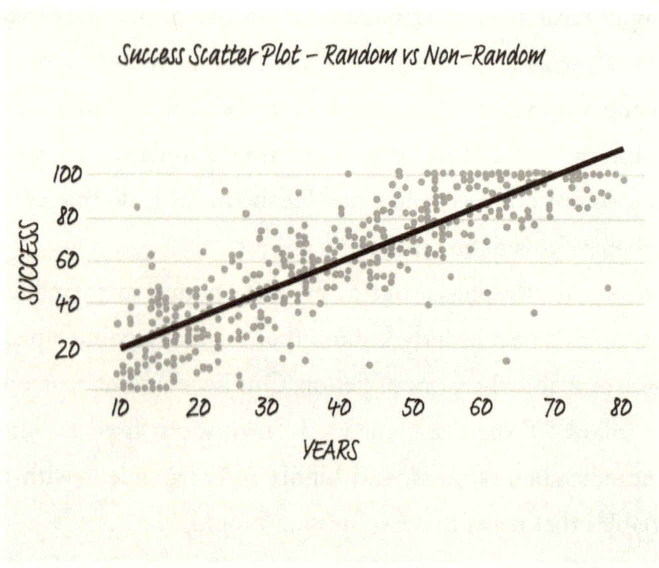

Life can look random. If you were to plot your life on a graph from left to right, with the x-axis being time and the y-axis being progress, you might see a bunch of dots (think key events in your career so far) that look random.

I got a job; I got laid off; I met someone at a conference. That person became a mentor; I applied for a job; my mentor had a friend who worked at the company. That person put in a good word for me; I got the job; my offer package came with a small equity option. The company has an IPO five years later; I created wealth; I find out I have cancer; I take time off to heal. The hospital in my city has a new oncology ward with an academic who is studying my specific cancer; I get unique access to the latest therapy and live happily ever after; I write a book about how I made it.

Ta-da! This is a series of fictitious random events (scatter plot) that I will insist is actually a straight line. If I am really feeling myself, the line is not straight and linear but exponential because of some inflection point when things really took off in your career.

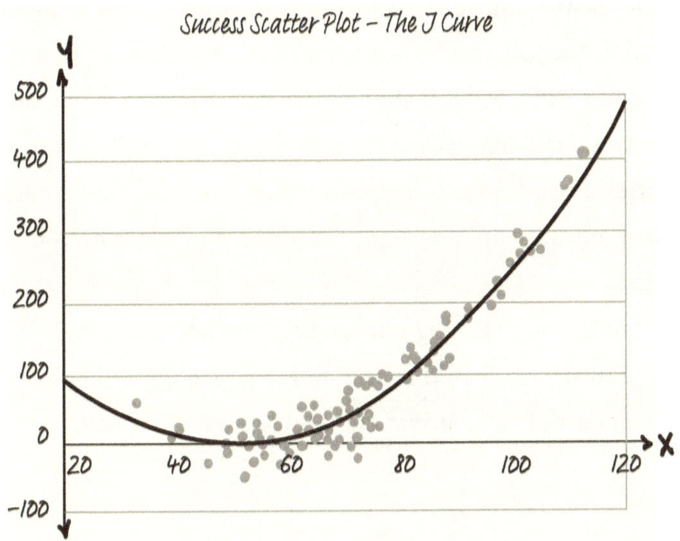

This is a dangerous and misleading way to reflect on our stories and to interpret them for others. Not so much because it's mathematically inaccurate, or heavily biased to favor a certain narrative (a confirmation and selection bias of sorts), but because it also misses out on the most powerful parts of the story to actually learn from.

You are more likely to encounter hardships, trials, and tribulations than chance encounters with people who will be mentors who hook you up with jobs at pre-IPO unicorns. You are also to both benefit and suffer from the role of chance, timing, and environment. This is a point Scott Galloway argues that I agree with: Being in the right "super cities," spaces, or even companies at the right time can have a big impact on the opportunities available to you in your career journey.[2] So why not say that?

Perhaps there is more to be learned from the fictitious example just mentioned of how that person handled their layoff, the vulnerability and humility of asking a mentor for help, or the decision to rebalance their life when faced with a health scare. Or maybe we can talk about the luck and fortune of working for a company that, without you knowing at the time you took the job, might successfully IPO and create wealth—when so many others did not have that experience. Maybe we can learn more from how you dealt with adversity than we can from how you celebrate your victories. Specifically as it relates to happiness, I find it more powerful to talk about unhappiness as a motivation and something that we can *all* relate to.

As we think about plotting our career paths, and particularly those that give us fulfillment, we should expect and embrace the setbacks, hardships, and failure as part of the journey, and perhaps the best parts.

REFLECTION QUESTIONS

1. How have you typically narrated your own career journey when asked to describe your success? Does it often follow a neat, upward-sloping line?

2. Can you recall an instance where an unexpected event or interaction (a "random dot") fundamentally shifted your trajectory in a way you couldn't have predicted or planned? What was that event, and what was its long-term impact?

3. If you were to honestly plot your career path as a scatter plot, what would some of the most surprising or seemingly unrelated dots be? What did you learn from those specific moments, even if they didn't fit a clear narrative?

4. Reflect on a time in your career when you experienced a
    significant setback, failure, or period of deep dissatisfaction
    (e.g., layoff, missed promotion, burnout, job you hated).
    What did you actively learn about yourself, your values,
    or your true priorities during that challenging period
    that you might not have learned from a "victory"?

5. If you were to define career success based solely on the insights
    from this chapter, how would your definition differ from the one
    you might have held at the beginning of your professional life?

CHAPTER 7

PIVOTING WITH P.P.P.

"Every day is a chance to begin again."

—Attributed to Catherine Pulsifer

Just because you've been doing a thing for a long time does not make it right. Just because you've invested time and talent in a job or career that's not a fit does not mean you need to see it through. In finance, we call these wasted investments "sunk costs" or "throwing good money after bad." Forget about the past and get excited about the future. It doesn't really matter when you come to the realization that you are not in your G.E.L. and unhappy; you can do something about it. But first you need to envision a different future. A professional life that is simpatico with the life you want to live. I credit the writings of Arthur C. Brooks in his books *Strength to Strength* and *Build the Life You Want,* which he coauthored with Oprah Winfrey, for encouraging me to embrace my next season. As he predicted for those who pushed through blockages of ego and fear of the unknown, we would find happiness and gold in those hills. I have.

While Brooks's book has deeply resonated with mid- and late-career folks such as myself, I believe it's never too early (or late) to start aligning your career with your happiness. I even wish there were more classes taught in college or grad school to encourage self-discovery and reflection on those things that will ultimately lead to true meaning in our jobs and careers *before we* pick majors and first jobs. But should you find yourself past that season and well into your career, and upon reflecting on the frameworks from the prior chapters for fulfillment and G.E.L., you suspect you need to make some changes, I can offer some practical steps to consider. This chapter is about how to pivot either slowly or quickly, but intentionally.

THE THREE P'S (P.P.P.)

I once had a mentor share a few words of advice that were once shared with him, that I will share with you. In the marketplace of talent, our value is defined by three P's: People, Process, Product.

Regardless of what you've been doing professionally for the past few years or decades, you have a market value that is loosely defined by:

1. *(P) People:* You have a professional and social network that is valuable. Think about who you know (key talent, customers, suppliers, and so on) and who knows you (can vouch for your brand). The value you bring to a job or company is your access to people and social networks.

2. *(P) Process:* After some point in your career, you are perceived to have some level of mastery of a function, skill, or key process in an organization. You might be known for being a guru of sales, marketing, finance, operations, general management, HR, or something else. It could be a few things. But ultimately, there are key processes in an organization that you are qualified to run, manage, conduct, and so on. These skills are valuable.

3. *(P) Product:* Over time, we also develop expertise in not only functions but industries, sectors, and/or products. You might have undisputed credibility and tenure in certain domains, such as technology, entertainment, real estate, banking, investments, and so on. You know a product and industry well, and that is valuable in the marketplace.

Together, your social networks, functional skills, and domain expertise make up a big part of what someone is willing to pay you. If your current P.P.P. is not aligned with your G.E.L., then it's time to pivot.

A pivot can be slow and methodical, or immediate and drastic. A gradual and strategic pivot might mean giving up one P in exchange for another. Said differently, two P's can stay constant while the third P changes. For example, maybe I love what I do (sales), and I love the industry that I do it in (real estate), but I want to do it in a different country to better align with the life I want. Perhaps moving to another country will mean I need to build a new network of People who will eventually know and vouch for me. A company in another country will value my sales and real estate expertise enough (Process and Product) to give me time to build and establish new networks and relationships with prospective customers. I will be bringing enough to the table that my value is validated in my compensation and title.

Or perhaps I want to stay in the same market (New York City) and industry (real estate) but change functions from sales to general management. I am leveraging my network (People) of real estate owners and brokers in Manhattan and my deep knowledge of office buildings, which is valuable, while I learn a new skill—how to manage teams and businesses as a general manager. These are examples of pivots.

These are also examples of pivots that do not typically require you to take a step back or reduce your expectations for compensation or title. You might even make the case for a promotion. But should you need to change two or three of your P's, you are planning for a bigger makeover that might cost you a bit more. For example, if I want to leave NYC, real estate, and sales and pivot more drastically into operations in the technology sector and relocate to Tokyo, I am preparing for a major makeover that will probably require me to take a few steps back in order to eventually move forward. That is, of course, unless you make the three pivots over time.

That said, changing out more than one P and absorbing the costs of that might not be a bad thing. Your calculus might be that it's worth taking the step back in order to get in the right lane faster and maximize the time you plan to spend in your G.E.L. or a role, company, or environment that fulfills you.

The key is to remember why you are pivoting to begin with. You are making changes to bring your work and happiness into greater alignment. The sooner you can make these changes, the sooner you will experience true fulfillment.

REFLECTION QUESTIONS

1. Can you identify a specific area in your professional life where you might be experiencing the "sunk cost fallacy"—continuing something primarily because of the time, effort, or money you've already invested? What is it, and what are the reasons you continue?

2. If you were advising a friend who was in your exact situation, what specific advice would you give them about moving past their "sunk costs" and pivoting? Why is it often easier to advise others than to follow our own advice?

3. If you are considering a career pivot, which of your "Three P's" (People, Process, Product) are you most willing to change, and which are you most eager to keep constant? Why?

4. Describe a potential gradual pivot for yourself by holding two P's constant and changing just one. What might that look like, and what new opportunities or challenges would it present?

5. Now, imagine a drastic makeover where you change two or three of your P's. What would be the biggest cost of such a pivot (e.g., reduced compensation, temporary step back in title, loss of familiar networks)? What would be the biggest gain in terms of aligning with your G.E.L. and overall happiness?

CHAPTER 8

FOR THE LOVE OF MONEY

*"If it takes money to be happy, your search
for happiness will never end."*

—Attributed to Bob Marley

One of the most common arguments I have heard for linking one's work to their happiness is the assumption that work's financial rewards can be used to buy happiness, but research shows this idea is actually more nuanced.[1] Before I dive into the nuances and limitations of money-bought happiness, let me spend a few minutes on what I believe is a fair claim for those in the camp of wanting more money to advance their happiness goals.

Some of the leading researchers in this area conclude that there is a positive correlation between money and happiness (or emotional well-being). For example, money allows one to "buy" freedom, experiences, and the ability to be charitable. It is also true that money can insulate us from potential drains on our happiness, like the ability to fix a leaky roof when the alternative might have otherwise been to have water drip onto your head in bed or get on the roof and fix it yourself. Money also affords a certain minimum standard of living, security, and access to health that is necessary for a base level of satisfaction.

That amount of annual household compensation needed before happiness plateaued was thought to be about $75,000[2] based on research published in 2010 by Daniel Kahneman and Angus Deaton. So one's happiness would increase with incremental household income, from $0 to $75,000 per year, after which an individual would see no additional happiness with added income. More recently published research by Matthew A. Killingsworth, Daniel Kahneman, and Barbara Mellers[3] suggests that happiness does increase with more money for most people, but only up to about $500,000 per year (versus $75,000).[4]

Note: According to ADP, 0.79 percent of jobs in the country paid more than $500,000 per year in 2024,[5] so not exactly a large sample size to study. But the research went further, breaking the group of happier people into two buckets. One group experienced increased happiness in a consistent and steady fashion as their incomes increased gradually over time up to $500,000, while the other group, about 30 percent, reported being "happiest" when their income increased just over $100,000. But they also found an even smaller minority of individuals in the study for whom happiness did not increase beyond $100,000.

While the current research makes the case that money plays a role in our happiness by affording us the opportunity to travel, contribute to charities, and enjoy hobbies (like scuba diving), it is less clear about when and where we experience diminishing returns beyond certain thresholds, be it $75,000, $100,000, $500,000, or more. It's also not clear what these findings might mean for the happiness of most US households which earn less than $100,000 (the average is a little over $80,000 per household and a little under $45,000 per person according to the Census Bureau's 2024 findings).[6] Let's also not forget that the "happiest country on earth," Finland, boasts an average annual salary in 2025 of $50,000 and a median of $46,000 (which means that half the country makes less).[7]

Are those with less money just as capable of finding happiness in other non-monetary means, like those we explored in early chapters? There is also growing research that speaks to the power of our mindset, which can supersede the role of money. As an example, a person with a negative mindset versus a person with a positive mindset might experience the role of money and its impact differently. Regardless of your views on money and its potential, our work, which offers an opportunity for purpose, community, and growth, can generate powerful feelings of well-being and fulfillment, even if it does not pay a massive six-figure salary. Equally, as this book argues, your happiness can be depleted by doing meaningless work, even if it pays $500,000 or more.

NET HAPPINESS

Academics and scientists have spent decades interrogating the aforementioned and will probably continue doing so for years to come. This is not my lane, fight, or ministry, and I will be as curious as you are as to what they conclude when the dust settles.

Instead, I want to refer back to the concept that I discussed earlier called net happiness. Gross happiness applies to all of the research that speaks to intrinsic and extrinsic sources of joy, well-being, and happiness feelings. Your career can be a source of gross happiness. The "net happiness" is the happiness that is left after all of these detractors are applied. Some detractors that result in a lower net happiness are things we can potentially address with money. Money does play a role in removing detractors (such as the leaking roof) and thereby increasing your net happiness. But I want to caution anyone who believes that money itself or the pursuit of money can be an enduring source of happiness. In fact, it may be just the opposite.

In my profession, I have known and worked for a number of wealthy people. I mean people worth hundreds of millions or maybe billions of dollars. Note: I never asked them which they were, multimillionaires or billionaires, but it didn't matter. All I knew is that the more I got to know them, the more I did not want to be them. I found them to be generally less happy than me, who had a small fraction of their net worth. They were insecure about things you'd be surprised to discover, stressed over family stuff like everyone else, and had health scares like you and me, even if they had better access to the best healthcare. Their wealth had not given them a free pass from being human. At their core, they were indeed human and needed to belong and feel valued and loved (or respected and feared, as was the case for some). They suffered the same drains on their intrinsic happiness as everyone I know who lived paycheck-to-paycheck. And I know way more folks who live paycheck-to-paycheck.

I can remember the exact day when it clicked for me. I knew at that very moment that pursuing more professional success and money was not going to be my path to more happiness. In fact, I realized the pursuit of those ends (not the ends themselves) might actually drain my happiness.

I was a division CEO in a real estate company, responsible for a global P&L. I was in my early forties, feeling successful, and expecting that my next big achievement would be to serve as a public company CEO. I reported to the CEO of the company and had a good bit of facetime with our board chair. I had already had two division CEO or president roles prior to this one, where I had been responsible for more than $1 billion in annual revenues, six thousand-plus employees, and one hundred fifty offices. I had held these roles in companies that had successful IPOs or exits. I was feeling good about my professional momentum and trajectory.

On this day, my boss, the CEO of the company, and I were visiting a potential company that we thought might make for a good acquisition. The trip was planned at the last minute, and the only way to accommodate my CEO's schedule was for us to take his private jet. I had never been on a private jet before. I'd been on a company jet, maybe, but not a jet for an individual's exclusive use. The whole experience was mind-blowing for me, a kid from southwest Atlanta who had spent so much of his youth scraping to get by.

He and I boarded the luxurious jet, along with the two pilots. I settled into the cushy seats and tried to act unimpressed, checking email and texting on my phone, when inside, all I wanted to do was snap selfies and post on Facebook "Look at me balling, y'all!" But I did my best to contain my excitement. The pilots asked if we wanted snacks or something to drink before take-off. I declined, reflecting on how odd it felt to have the pilot, versus a flight attendant, offer us beverages. Seconds later, it occurred to me that this was probably the norm for an echelon of New York business elite who never had to deal with the headache of LaGuardia or John F. Kennedy airports. Here I was, proud of my diamond status on Delta Airlines. Sheesh, what a JV amateur I had unknowingly been. This was the big leagues.

We landed an hour or so later. The pilot asked my boss if he should wait for us and when we wanted to return back to NYC. *Wait a second,* I thought to myself, *the pilots are going to chill and wait for us to have our meeting?* My boss owned their time, their day, and the plane, so of course they would.

After a full day of meetings, we returned to the private airport and our jet, waiting patiently for us with engines humming ever so softly, waiting for the command to rev up and take us home. My boss was feeling good about our meetings, and perhaps about me, one of his many lieutenants. As we ascended into the clouds, he said to me, "This can be you one day."

I looked back with a look of slight confusion. "What do you mean?" I replied.

"If you play your cards right, you can sit in my seat one day," he said.

It hit me. I was on the cusp of being everything I had ever dreamed of as a B-school student and younger professional. I could be in the play for a public company CEO role one day. I just had to play my cards right.

My boss was likely in his late sixties. He was wealthy but still worked like a young analyst. He was always on emails and was early in, late out. He still hustled like he was scrapping for his first million, not his one-hundredth. His eyes sagged with a certain weariness and sadness that might have been genetic or the result of decades of this routine. He told me about iconic buildings he owned in NYC and deals gone bad with Donald Trump and why he'd never work with him again.

As I looked into his tired eyes and slouching and thinning body, I saw the ghost of Christmas future. Like Mr. Scrooge, my final visiting ghost had given me a glimpse into a future that I had always thought would be joyful and chock-full of happiness. But what I saw, at least in the man sitting across from me, was the image of a person for whom life was anything but joyful. It was a never-ending grind. Instead of bouncing his grandkids on his knee, he was here with me flying back to NYC in the middle of the night strategizing about an acquisition and moreover, how we were going to conquer more of the world of real estate.

I wouldn't be so presumptuous as to say I knew whether he was happy or not. I am sure he loved his life, was proud of what he had accomplished, and enjoyed the comforts of wealth, like flying on his own plane. And I realize his life might sound sexy and even appealing to most folks, as it still does to me, in some respects. But in that moment, I realized that it was the thought of it that was more appealing than "it" itself. I tried to imagine what the last fifty years of his life might have been like and what sacrifices he likely made to get to such a perch in life. I tried to imagine decades and decades of running the nonstop frantic pace of deal making, the constant prioritization of work over living, and maybe the paranoia that seemed rampant among the ultra-competitive types who organized their lives around so-called winning. I was exhausted just thinking about it. I realized, shifting my gaze from him to the airplane window, that I did not want to be him. I certainly did not want to pay that price.

THE LIMITATIONS OF MONEY

It was not corporate leadership or even serving as a CEO one day that was not attractive at that moment, it was the pursuit of those things for reasons I knew were not pure or sustainable that was unattractive. Pursuing money and status for the sake of having money and status seemed empty and unlikely to yield any real joy. Money was important and had a role, but it also had its limits in what it could do for my happiness.

My then-wife and I did well. We made a good living for NYC standards, had a Harlem brownstone, and traveled whenever we wanted. We were not consumed with money at all, but it bought us things, such as experiences, the ability to make meaningful donations to causes we cared about and, most of all, things that increased our net happiness. We bought ourselves time for when things, situations, and so on crept up that could drain our time and happiness. We accessed premium healthcare when we were on our fertility journey. We brought the family together for trips, summer home rentals in Cape May or whatever made convening our family easier for our hectic schedules. It was a net drain if we had to find a place and time that worked for everyone. We would just take care of it. We didn't haggle with friends and family over the dinner and drinks bill, which could be a net drain on an otherwise happy night. We always picked up the tab. Our brownstone was more than a hundred years old. Stuff broke, and when it did, it was expensive and timely to fix. We did not let those things drain us or our net happiness. Money solved some of it.

But for all the things that money bought and brought, the pursuit of money (in my professional journey) was starting to drain my happiness more than I had realized. Dealing with corporate politics was—draining.

The daily and nightly stresses from near impossible performance goals were—draining. The emotional agony that came when it was time to oversee layoffs or, as is a whole other topic, being a Black executive in a sea of whiteness that always left me feeling alone and fending for myself were—unexplainably draining. Few of my friends or family could relate to my life, much less comfort me when I felt like I was drowning. I had a few mentors, but mostly from a generation earlier where you just put your head down, leaned into it, and pushed forward like our ancestors had done for hundreds of years prior.

Money had brought reprieves from these moments and in doing so, my net happiness might have been better from time to time as a result, but my gross happiness was suffering.

Money was not enough, and perhaps the pursuit and objectification of it and the professional success that was its medium were actually undoing much of the happiness that I thought I was accumulating. In these times, even when I realized what was at play, I told myself, convincingly, that happiness would come in retirement. However, looking into the face of my boss on his private jet, I realized that happiness was not promised and maybe, it was even unlikely if I did not prioritize different things in my life. I knew before the plane landed that I would need to make some tough decisions in the months and years ahead if I were going to put *my* happiness first.

There are many factors that can contribute (or not) to our happiness, and money is but one of them. However, research, life experiences, and common sense remind us that there are limits to what money can do for our happiness. Moreover, the absence of money is not necessarily a recipe for unhappiness. Nor will lots of money keep all the blues away. But as it relates to finding work that can and should be a source of joy, we should be careful to limit the role of money in our selection of college majors, internships, jobs, and professional identities. In the Bible, it says "For what will it profit a man if he gains the whole world and forfeits his soul?"[8] The same is true for your happiness.

REFLECTION QUESTIONS

1. What minimum amount of money do you need to experience well-being and happiness? Are you working to attain more than the minimum? If so, why?

2. Can you reflect on roles where you made less money but felt a greater level of happiness? Perhaps the work was meaningful, with people you enjoyed working with, and stretched you in some way that made you better.

3. Have you stayed in roles that depleted your happiness but paid well? What was your rationale?

4. Quickly jot down the things that contribute to your happiness (you might refer back to your answer to the Intrinsic/Extrinsic exercise in Section One). For each, write down which cost money and which are free (or money is not a prerequisite).

5. When you imagine your next or ideal role, how much weighting will you give to money in making your decision?

CHAPTER 9

ENVY AND SUCCESS

"Comparison is the thief of joy."

—Attributed to President Theodore Roosevelt

When I graduated from college, I was relieved and proud to have an offer from Arthur Andersen Business Consulting (later Accenture) to be a consultant in their enterprise technology implementation practice. But a few months earlier, I had been stressed and depressed.

I had interviewed for the more prestigious consulting gigs at Bain, Boston Consulting Group (BCG), and McKinsey and failed to get an offer from any of them. Some of my classmates who did get offers were probably much savvier with the case interview method than I was and had options to work in the most attractive offices for those firms, such as NYC, San Francisco, Atlanta, and Chicago. Although anyone would have been elated to have my job offer, I was stuck in a rut from the comparison and what I thought it meant for me. The rut deepened when I learned what their starting offers were relative to mine. My starting salary in 1998 was $43,000 a year. Those with offers from the more prestigious firms boasted starting salaries of $50,000.

It seems silly now, but my twentysomething-year-old self thought the $7,000 difference was going to permanently set me behind my peer group and was proof that I was not as smart, not as capable, and trending towards not being as successful in life. I was on a failure track as evidenced by what *felt* like a massive head start my peers had on me.

How silly and sad my younger self was for allowing this needless and meaningless comparison to rob my joy. Ironically, shortly after starting with Arthur Andersen, I was invited to work on a client engagement in Europe for a year. I had never even traveled to Europe at that point in my life, much less lived there. The firm would cover my housing, car, and living expenses—and gross up my income to cover EU taxes, all while I lived and worked in Europe. It was a massive dream gig.

I spent the year working in Belgium but traveled to almost every European country and broadened my horizons and sense for what was possible more than with any other professional experience. I worked alongside and befriended colleagues in our Brussels office, worked on important client projects, and led key initiatives with teams of people many years my senior. I had a wonderful and transformative time. The $7,000 salary differential was not only immaterial relative to what I earned and saved in Europe but was irrelevant to the happiness the next year of experiences generated for me. The joy of those memories remains today.

THE COMPARISON MINDSET

So why do we allow comparison envy to steal our joy? Why do we not embrace our own happiness and its path? Comparison mindsets are totally controllable. I would have to remind myself of this many times again in the years to come—and even today. A few years ago, after living and working in NYC for twelve years, I moved back to Atlanta. I had a few practical reasons for doing so. I was going through a divorce, had left my NYC-based job at

WeWork, and was now in between jobs. It was also during the pandemic and hybrid work had lessened the grip that cities like NYC had on those of us who felt we had to be there to be in the game. This was no longer the case.

But there was also something more subtle but serious at work in my calculus. I loved New York and had been very active in my Harlem community, very visible in the real estate professional circles, and had even invested in a restaurant that brought me some sense of belonging and NYC street cred. I also had wonderful in-laws and family that made the city feel like home. But I had always been annoyed, if not resentful, for the dirt, grime, and anxiety that came with being a New Yorker. The crowds, the expense, the traffic, and everything else (that New Yorkers love and are proud of) seemed to undercut my southern sensibilities and happiness. I can remember being on a Zoloft prescription for a few years when my anxiety reached levels that made it difficult for me to take the train to and from work each day. The thought of walking through Grand Central Station made me tense up, yet I did it every day.

First, I opted to take an Uber to work every day or drive in order to avoid the train, the crowds, and the grime. But over time, I took to drinking more, eating poorly, and indulging in comforts that were not always healthy or sustainable. In time, these poor choices, which had long since replaced my love for working out, ran their course. I was prediabetic, not feeling great about myself, and was generally unhappy.

Therapy, Zoloft, and church helped. I also had a loving and very supportive wife, to whom I am forever grateful for her partnership in that season of my life. But deep down inside, my lack of happiness (and maybe depression) was coming from things that were in my control.

One of the things that some of you can relate to is the "striver" mindset. My peer group of young execs in NYC were strivers too. And although I was not fully aware of it, I was in a constant state of comparison and competition that made me pursue things that did not bring me happiness.

New York can do that to you. It is a city where you go to hustle, win, and win big—or go home. I wanted to win and win out loud. Until I realized it was not serving me or my happiness. It was around this time that I realized I needed to pivot in both my career choices and priorities, but also in the life choices that contributed to or drained my happiness.

So I moved back to Atlanta, Georgia. Not because I couldn't be happy in NYC, which I could, but because I knew that removing myself mentally and physically from the rat race would help me affirm to myself that my priorities had shifted. I thought it would also help to not be in a community where I was tempted to compare and benchmark myself as much as I had. It was like the movie *The Gladiator* when Russell Crowe's character, who had been a champion gladiator, longed to simply return home to his farm, run his fingers through the grains growing in his fields, and embrace his family. That was me.

I no longer cared or wanted to compare myself with the other gladiators in the great coliseum of competition. I just wanted to be happy. I knew that it would have to be a singular, individual journey without regard for what brought *someone else* joy. I had also forgotten how important my environment was to my happiness. I needed to see more trees, more clean sidewalks, and less dirty snow caking up on sidewalks for months at a time. I also wanted to see more Black and brown faces every day. I wanted a bit more space to breathe, literally and figuratively. But most of all, I wanted time and space to embrace a slightly less hectic and intense professional life.

I would look for both structural and nonstructural ways to create more balance in my return home. I would spend more time eating healthy, scuba diving, and working out, and professionally I would find joy in coaching and advising business leaders versus needing to always be the business leader. My ego and its need for validation and comparison would need to be left behind in NYC, and that I did.

Our careers and professional peers can be important sources of motivation and achievement, as part of our overall happiness calculus. However, when the ambition and comparison get to a place that is either unhealthy or drains our happiness, we have to take a step back. We don't necessarily need to always relocate, quit our jobs, or leave our friend groups, but we may need to change our mindset. And if a change of mindset leads you to change your job, environment, or community, then chances are you are doing it for the right reasons—or are on the right track.

SUCCESS DOES NOT EQUAL HAPPINESS (NOT EVEN CLOSE)

You're not a big deal until you are. Countless of our most admired and successful leaders, creators, executives, and startup founders did not find the success that ultimately made them famous until later in life. Not that their lives were not remarkable and meaningful beforehand, but that which we celebrate them for (and ultimately use as a comparison measuring stick for our own success) often comes later.

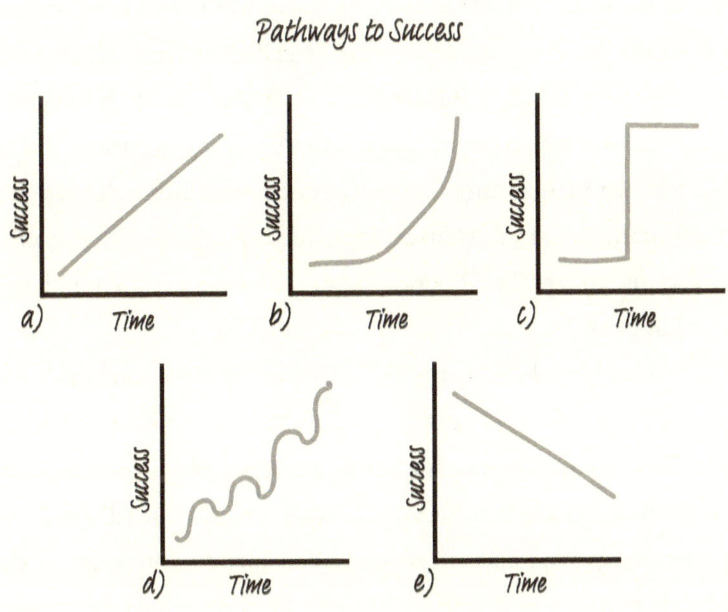

There are many paths to success, however one defines it. Let's assume we could plot it, with time on the x-axis and "success" on the y-axis. Over time, our success might be reflected graphically with a linear line, assuming a steady slope from the bottom left to the top right (a), exponential with some major turning point when things really start to take off (b), or a step-function that happens after some single event, like winning the lotto (c), or perhaps bumpy but generally from the bottom left to the upper right (d), or finally, declining over time like a one-hit-wonder performer who starts off with success in their career but tapers off over time while still remaining "successful" in their own eyes (e). There are perhaps endless permutations of how we might experience success over time.

You have probably heard of some of the ones that came later, such as Colonel Sanders at age sixty-five (KFC), Vera Wang at age forty (fashion designer), Samuel Jackson at age forty-six (actor), Ray Kroc after age fifty-one (McDonald's), Sam Walton at age forty-four (Walmart), and Toni Morrison at age thirty-nine (Pulitzer Prize–winning novelist), just to name a few.

One of my closest friends, who is a successful investor, once reminded me that wealth is often created in what he called "balance-sheet moments" or "balance-sheet events." The idea that material wealth is created every single day you show up to work or buy a stock is horribly misleading, misinformed, and just plain wrong (for most people who aren't already wealthy). There are moments after an investment (of capital, time, talent, etc.) and during the investment "hold period" when something big could happen, if in fact it happens.

These moments could be the IPO, or a merger, or successful sale/exit of a company in which you own equity. A balance-sheet event could also happen when the fixer-upper house you bought twenty years ago happens to now be in a trendy and highly desirable neighborhood. And one day, you get an unexpected and unsolicited offer during a super-hot real estate market that makes you wealthy overnight. While the investor might (and likely) plans and hopes for such an occasion, it's more likely that a window opens, an opportunity emerges, or you get lucky.

In his book *Fooled by Randomness*, Nassim Nicholas Taleb takes it a bit further. He makes the compelling case that most successful investors are just lucky. Just as less-successful investors might just be unlucky. The outcomes are a distribution of probability, and less so the compounding benefit of skill, unique insight, and the ability to see around a corner. When the investor gets it right, he or she credits their success with their brilliance. When they get it wrong, it was the market's fault, some unforeseen condition, or anything but their lack of brilliance.

So why do we spend so much time and energy comparing ourselves to those whose luck finally hit triple sevens? What does it say about the pressure we put on ourselves to be a big deal or to be wildly successful by some arbitrary point in time, if at all? I would not go so far as to say that what we accomplish in life is purely a matter of luck, because it's not. However if we're really looking for a significant, unnatural thing to define us and ultimately generate happiness, we should be a bit humbler about the role of randomness and time.

While we have already examined the relationship (or lack thereof) between happiness and success, I will spend more time emphasizing that success does not necessarily get you happiness. Success, if it is tied to our contributions, our impact, and our sense of purpose, can be strongly correlated with happiness—as well as fulfillment. Contrary to what many people would assume, some of the most successful musicians, actors, and executives have disclosed how they suffer from depression, drug abuse, and insecurity. Many are unhappy despite having fame, enormous success, and financial security.

Of course this is not always the case. Just because you are successful does not mean that you will be unhappy or vice versa. And just because you are not successful does not mean that you have better shot at being happy either. The relationship between success and happiness is a bit more nuanced.

I once had a conversation with a friend who said she had not accomplished what she imagined she would by this time in her life. She was in her mid-thirties and largely compared herself with what she had always dreamed she would have accomplished by this point in life and with the accomplishments of others in her friend group. I shared with her that the anxiety that she was feeling was understandable but perhaps misplaced. Her best and potential years were likely just ahead (notwithstanding the gratitude, honor, and pride she owed her past years), and the fact that she felt something steering inside was actually a good thing. Assuming, of course, this feeling to do more was coming from within and not from outside. I have heard from some pregnant mothers that they knew they were pregnant only weeks into the conception. Though it would be months before it would be visible to anyone on the outside, they knew very early on that something was brewing inside.

I believe success can be similar to the feeling that expecting mothers sometimes have. You may feel the potential for something great inside even when it's not yet obvious or showing. Like life at the conception stage, your calling could be microscopic, cellular, or even embryonic for a long time before anyone can appreciate or see what you have to bring forth in the world. In keeping with the metaphor, during this incubation period, a mother has to be patient, nurturing, and loving with her body to create the right conditions to birth life. The same is true for your potential. Just remember, there's no guarantee that the perceived success, fame, or wealth you associate with your calling will lead to happiness. It is likely that you will not realize true happiness unless you take action steps toward fulfilling your purpose and calling.

Money, success, and fame can be best enjoyed when they are the byproduct of your professional journey and not necessarily its primary goal. This is particularly the case if and when we're solving for our happiness. We may experience happiness with the support of these things, but there are serious limits. In fact, our happiness is likely short lived and fleeting (remember the hedonic treadmill and our Intrinsic/Extrinsic quadrant, specifically the lower left quadrant) when we rely on money and status to generate it. Moreover, we have illustrated how some of the most enduring forms of happiness can come when we don't have money, fame, or success as measured by others.

REFLECTION QUESTIONS

1. What role do outward signs of professional success play in your happiness?

2. Go back to your earliest memories of when you first began to imagine the life you wanted for yourself. How does your current reality compare?

3. Can you recall a specific instance in your life (professional or personal) where a seemingly small difference in status, income, or achievement compared to peers significantly impacted your emotional well-being? What was the context, and how did it make you feel?

4. If you were to completely detach your definition of "success" from external metrics like money, fame, or a linear career path, what would "success" truly mean for you right now? What would it look like in your daily life?

5. How can you practice patience and trust in your own internal development, even when external pressures or comparisons might tempt you to rush or doubt your process?

KNOWING YOUR SEASON

"Be the change that you wish to see in the world."

—Attributed to Mahatma Gandhi

A message to senior and seasoned professionals about the "second half": Hopefully by now, you are seeing the critical need to intertwine your work with your joy. Do what you love. As the esteemed poet Maya Angelou once said, "Making a living is not the same thing as making a life."[1] If you don't prioritize making a life over what you do for a living (if they're not one and the same), chances are you will struggle to be fulfilled in life. There are not enough time and space left outside of your 90,000 hours of work to have a fighting chance otherwise.

While much of the earlier chapters dealt with figuring out what the best career path might be for you (young professionals) or pivoting if you're off a bit (mid-career professionals), this last chapter assumes you've done all of that and are now looking toward your final act, second half, or whatever you, a more seasoned professional, might be wrestling with as it relates to impact.

Just because you are seasoned does not mean you no longer need to have purpose, belonging, and growth. These needs for fulfillment don't stop. They just look different as we get older and move through life. In this chapter, I offer a framework for thinking about the season you are in and what goodness looks like therein.

THE FOUR SEASONS (STAGES) OF YOUR CAREER

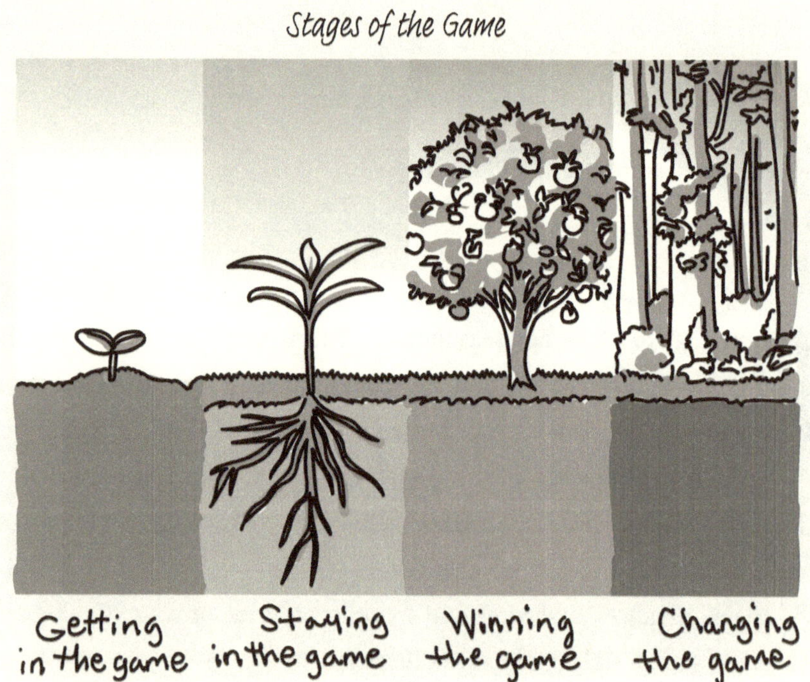

My "Career Seasons" use the metaphor of a game to describe how we can have increasing levels of impact (and fulfilment) in our careers over time.

I believe there are four seasons or stages that you will generally move through in your career.

Getting in the Game

The first season is about getting in the game, or the career and professional life you want for yourself. This can be difficult. After you've gone through your G.E.L. exercises and potentially found the need to pivot (P.P.P.), the work of getting in begins. It may require a sponsor, as it did for me when I tried to transition from tech consulting into commercial real estate. A sponsor is someone in the room that you are not in, who has permission to advocate for you being in the room. You might have to network, take classes, or pivot one "P" at a time to eventually get in the right role, company, or sector you desire. But developing a strategy to get you into the game is your first priority.

Staying in the Game

Once you get in the game, your next priority is to stay in the game. Roughly 1 percent of first-year lawyers make partner. Similar stats can be found in other competitive spaces. Somewhere between 5 percent and 10 percent of first-year consultants will make partner in firms like McKinsey, Bain, and BCG. Same for investment banking. The National Association of Realtors (NAR) found that 75 percent of real estate agents fail within the first year of being in the industry and 87 percent after five years. While some of this yield is structural and intentional in "up or out" organizations, some of it is manageable. In the book *The First 90 Days* by Michael D. Watkins, which should be required reading for anyone taking a new, big role, we learn that there are some common missteps we unknowingly make that impact our potential to be successful—and stay in the game.[2] Without the right game plan, mentors, and circumspection, we run the risk of not staying in our role, company, or industry for too long. I failed and failed miserably in one of my first executive roles. I knew how to do the job, but my emotional intelligence quotient (EQ) and soft skills left me extremely vulnerable when it came to building trust and followership and ultimately being successful. Fortunately, my mentor at the time made time for me on nights and weekends to help me course correct. Still, I had to be humble, ask for help, and be willing to make changes to stay in the game.

Winning the Game

After you've been in the game for a while, you've proven that you deserve to be there and can perform. Now you need to play a slightly different hand. You are not playing to stay in the game; you are playing to *win* the game. Winning may look different for each of us. For some, it means consistent promotions, increasing compensation, and more responsibility. For others, it means they have a seat at the proverbial table and a voice in the rooms that matter. This may require taking some risk, putting yourself in situations and positions that feel uncomfortable, and anticipating where the hockey puck is going when others don't.

In the book *Strength to Strength*, Arthur Brooks describes this transition as going from liquid to crystalized intelligence. Forbes contributor Avivah Wittenberg-Cox, in her article "How to Age Happily: Surfing From Fluid to Crystallized Intelligence," describes Arthur's grand insight: That first-half-of-life "fluid" intelligence (the kind that is fast and innovative, à la Elon Musk) morphs in the second half into "crystallized" intelligence (more insightful and integrative, à la Dalai Lama).

To win the game, you will need to leverage your crystallized intelligence to rise above those still relying on their liquid intelligence. At some point, you will have to trust your inner wisdom like the Dalai Lama in moments when the stakes are highest. This will be the moment, like in the movie *The Matrix*, when the bullets fly by in slow motion and you say to yourself what Neo said: "I got this." Once you do, you will be winning the game. This might be evidenced by your accelerated career growth, the performance of your business or team, or however you define winning.

Changing the Game

Winning is not enough. Winning is also often self-centered. You are winning, but what about everyone else? Once you've earned the respect, political capital, and maybe even economic capital, what are you going to do with it? This is the final and most exciting season. This is the season when you get to *change the game*. Changing the game might mean giving back and pulling forward the next generation. It might be to change the rules of the game (in your field or company) so that they are more fair, inclusive, and supportive of people who might not have had the fair and unfair advantages that you and others had. Or it could be something much bigger.

In her book *Different: Escaping the Competitive Herd*, Youngme Moon chronicles the many companies and their leaders who looked at the landscape and saw that everyone was competing on the same dimension, doing more of the same, and looking for incremental ways to win the game.[3] Her book challenges leaders to look for ways to "tilt the plane" in a way that is contrarian and counterintuitive to exploit an unseen advantage. I loved this book and took her call to action to heart.

Perhaps you might not be in a position to transform the Internet browser world the way Google did when Netscape and Yahoo! were dominant or transform the way we think about phones and computing when Apple entered the market rendering Blackberry's dominant position obsolete. Your calling might be more modest but an opportunity to change the game nonetheless. As an example, I not only enjoy mentoring, sponsoring, and coaching talent in this season of my career, I also love advising founders and CEOs of companies that seek to challenge the status quo, unearth new opportunities, bring forth innovation that can make life better for others, and so on. I can play a role in changing the game by supporting those who I think can and will. I love this season in my career. I serve on boards of companies I admire. I advise executives and investors who expand and extend my reach into multiple businesses and sectors. I also enjoy coaching young professionals and being an adjunct B-school professor.

In your final season, the greatest of them all, you have an opportunity to really level up your happiness by finding an impactful and lasting way to make a difference. As we've explored, work, career, and profession can play important roles in our happiness. Ensure that your work is fulfilling by making sure it aligns with your purpose, is a place of belonging, and offers growth. If it doesn't, look for strategic ways to pivot by using the G.E.L. framework as your compass. Remember that money and status can be correlated with your success but not necessarily your happiness. Know that your path and timing is unique. It's not a race, and comparison with others will likely rob you of joy. Finally, once you have the wisdom and platform, look for ways to have impact.

REFLECTION QUESTIONS

1. Based on your current professional life, which of the four seasons do you feel you are in right now? What specific evidence (your goals, challenges, daily focus) supports your assessment?

2. Thinking back, can you identify when you transitioned from a previous season into your current one? What was the catalyst for that change?

3. Beyond promotions and compensation, what does "winning the game" truly mean to you personally? What would it look and feel like to be at the top of *your* game?

4. What does the idea of "changing the game" spark in you? In what area—your industry, your community, your company culture—do you feel a pull to make things more fair, inclusive, or innovative?

WHO DO YOU BELIEVE?

*"Faith is the substance of things hoped for,
the evidence of things not seen."*

—*Hebrews 11:1*, King James Version

The role of faith in your happiness is of immense consequence. Faith and religion cast a wide net on society. Religion affects almost every human either directly or indirectly, whether it's through associations with other people or institutions. Faith, religion, and the faith-based institutions that shape and define so much of our lives have an incredible influence on our happiness. Similar to your career, many religious scriptures encourage you to sacrifice now for a bigger payoff later.

Despite the similarities, it's far easier to discuss careers, because while personal, careers are typically not matters of the heart. Your work is important but rarely rises to the level of broad cultural identity. Nations don't fight wars over careers. Faith, however, is all of the above. It is one of the conversations, alongside politics, that we are advised to avoid if we want to keep the peace with friends and strangers alike. As a result, I wrestled with whether there was a respectful way to engage in a discussion on faith. I want to encourage independent thought rather than distract or possibly offend you with what I will say about my own beliefs. My religious beliefs are of zero consequence. In this section, I seek to spark your inner curiosity, if nothing else.

CHAPTER 11

FORBIDDEN (PLEASURES) BY RELIGION

*"Religion is regarded by the common people as true,
by the wise as false, and by the rulers as useful."*

—Adapted from Edward Gibbon

F aith in itself does not lead to unhappiness. In fact, faith can be positively correlated with joy, happiness, and fulfillment. Faith can lead to a strong sense of belonging, purpose, and even offer an explanation or comfort in the wake of life's unpleasant events and difficult circumstances. Viktor Frankl, one of the early and leading contributors to our scientific understanding of happiness, considered "self-transcendence," or a belief in something greater than yourself, to be key to finding meaning—and, therefore, happiness.[1]

Arthur C. Brooks, one of my favorite contemporary writers on practical happiness and the leader of the Leadership and Happiness Laboratory at Harvard, credits faith as a key ingredient (alongside family, friends, and meaningful work) to be necessary for happiness.[2] But long before Viktor and Arthur, the Bible offered similar advice when it said, "And the peace of God, which surpasses all understanding, will guard your hearts and your minds in Christ Jesus. Then you will experience God's peace, which exceeds anything we can understand."[3] But in the Bible, it also says that faith without works is dead!

Whether or not the thing you believe or are told to believe is actually true or not may in fact be irrelevant. The "works" that follow after the belief matter most, especially if this action impacts yours and others' happiness. Faith-based actions that impact your happiness and well-being may be limited, hard to generalize, or even identify when it's uniquely individual. You may notice and be concerned but not feel the need to panic when someone makes the decision to be a martyr for a cause they believe in or refuses a life-saving medical treatment because they believe healing will come from prayer. It may go unnoticed if someone quietly denies the pleasures of the flesh when everyone else indulges, even when these actions originate from an individual's religious teachings or the influence of culture and institutions. It's easy to write that individual off as misguided, an extremist, or mentally unwell (if you happen to not share their faith)—or a "God-fearing" person of faith (if you happen to share their faith). But when faith-based actions impact societies, generations, and the lives of many, they are easier to identify and examine with respect to their potential impacts on your happiness.

Let's use religion as a proxy. It is a convenient example of a faith-at-scale that impacts societies for generations. To be clear, faith is not necessarily religion (or vice versa). Faith is much broader than religion. You can have faith in your government, your cultural traditions, and even your individual understanding of the world. But I use religion and religious institutions, which often inform and shape government, culture, and individual biases, to help illustrate how unhappiness can be tied directly to faith. And, moreover, faith in religion can give rise to beliefs (in people, events, history, and so on) without any basis, expectation, or prerequisite for fact, science, or reason. That is, for many people, the definition of faith.

RELIGION

Roughly 85 percent of the world's population identifies with a religion. According to an article published in *Population Education*, over 75 percent of the population belongs to one of four major faiths: Christianity (31 percent), Islam (24 percent), Hinduism (15 percent), and Buddhism (7 percent).[4] As an agnostic (meaning, I am more comfortable saying, "I really don't know for sure, but I am open"), I belong to the balance of the population who identify as everything ranging from those who "believe in God but have no religious affiliation" to those who consider themselves atheist.

By the way, the number of folks who are like me and don't fit neatly into the big four religions appears to be growing year over year, especially in places such as America. But even in the US, 71 percent of the population still identifies as Christian, and it informs much of our current social and political infighting.

The four major faiths share commonalities in terms of what they encourage and discourage relative to our potential joy and happiness. In the following list, I have highlighted a sampling of faith-based rules and guiding principles from each faith. You will note the more common "thou shalts" shared between them are things such as avoiding fornication out of wedlock, drinking alcohol or taking drugs, and eating certain "unclean" foods. I should also note that some of the creeds, such as not killing or stealing, are just plain commonsensical and likely more about being a decent human. Some of these social norms likely predate formal religion and came with evolution of the *Homo sapiens*.

But there are some edicts that are less intuitive and a bit more questionable, such as the requirement to pay 10 percent or more of your wages in tithes and offerings to the church, seeking forgiveness for being homosexual, viewing minorities or women as lesser beings or requiring them to be subservient to men, or the requirement to fight in holy wars. There are countless others created over the ages (and even today) that are interesting at best. Examples of some beliefs that are embraced by a number of my friends who are Mormon, Jehovah's Witness, and Seventh-day Adventist include avoiding caffeine, hot beverages, social dancing, using birth control, receiving a blood transfusion, or pursuing higher education. While I may find some of these odd, those born into families who embrace these faiths find these practices perfectly normal and godly.

COMMONLY PROHIBITED ACTIVITIES ACROSS MOST MAJOR RELIGIONS

- *Murder:* All major religions condemn the intentional killing of innocent human beings. This is a foundational ethical principle.

- *Theft:* Stealing or taking what does not belong to you is widely prohibited. This includes fraud and exploitation.

- *Lying:* Deceit, false witness, and dishonesty in speech are generally discouraged, with an emphasis on truthfulness and integrity.

- *Adultery/sexual immorality:* All these religions have codes of sexual morality that typically restrict sexual activity to within the bounds of marriage (often heterosexual marriage).

- *Disrespecting elders:* Honoring and respecting one's parents and community elders is a common moral imperative.

- *Greed:* While not always strictly "prohibited," an excessive attachment to worldly possessions and wealth, and the pursuit of greed, are generally discouraged in favor of spiritual values, charity, and moderation.

- *Cruelty to animals:* While dietary laws vary, gratuitous cruelty or harm to animals is generally discouraged and is often linked to principles of compassion.

- *Pride:* Humility is often emphasized, and arrogance or excessive pride is generally seen as a negative character trait.

- *Intoxication:* While some traditions may have stricter prohibitions (e.g., alcohol in Islam and Mormonism), the use of substances that cloud the mind and impair judgment (leading to harmful actions) is generally discouraged.

RELIGION-SPECIFIC PROHIBITIONS

Christianity

- *Idolatry:* Christians cannot worship anything other than God.

- *Blasphemy:* Christians should not speak sacrilegiously about God or sacred things.

- *Envy:* Christians should not covet what others have.

- *Divorce (in some denominations):* While practices vary, some denominations strongly discourage or prohibit divorce except in specific circumstances.

- *Suicide:* This is generally considered a grave sin against God's gift of life.

- *Sexual activity outside of heterosexual marriage:* This includes homosexual acts, masturbation (often discouraged), and premarital sex.

Islam

- *Consumption of pork and alcohol:* These are strictly forbidden (Haram).

- *Gambling:* This is prohibited.

- *Usury (Riba):* Charging or paying interest on loans is prohibited.

- *Images/idols:* The creation or worship of idols or images of God/Prophets is forbidden.

- *Eating carrion (dead animals not ritually slaughtered):* This is prohibited.

- *Misappropriation of funds/corruption:* This is strongly condemned.

- *Backbiting and slander:* This is discouraged.

Hinduism

- *Ahimsa (non-violence):* Not harming innocent living beings (people and animals) is a core principle. This leads many Hindus to vegetarianism, and beef consumption is widely prohibited due to the sacredness of cows.

- *Adharma (unrighteousness):* Hindus avoid actions that go against righteous conduct and moral duty.

- *Sexual misconduct:* This includes adultery, exploitation, and often premarital sexual relations.

- *Disrespecting deities/sacred texts:* Hindus should not treat sacred things with irreverence.

- *Gluttony:* Excessive eating is frowned upon.

- *Sati (widow immolation):* This is the now-forbidden, obsolete practice whereby a widow would be burned alive on her husband's funeral pyre.

- *Child marriage:* This is an issue that continues to be discouraged and worked against.

Buddhism

- *Taking life:* The first precept is to abstain from intentionally killing any sentient being. This extends to animals and insects.

- *Stealing:* Buddhists must not take what is not freely given.

- *Sexual misconduct:* Adultery, sexual exploitation, and other behaviors that cause harm or violate rights are strictly prohibited. Monastics typically practice celibacy.

- *False speech:* Lying, divisive speech (gossip), harsh speech, and meaningless chatter are all discouraged.

- *Intoxicants:* Buddhists should avoid alcohol and drugs that cloud the mind and impair judgment, as clarity of mind is crucial for spiritual practice.

- *Excessive attachment/craving:* While not a prohibition, the root of suffering is seen as craving and attachment, so cultivating non-attachment is a key practice.

Judaism

- *Working on Shabbat (Sabbath):* A wide range of activities considered "work" are prohibited from sunset Friday to nightfall Saturday.

- *Eating non-kosher food:* Jews adhere to dietary laws (Kashrut), which dictate what foods are permissible and how they must be prepared.

- *Idolatry:* Worshiping other gods or idols is prohibited.

- *Blasphemy:* Cursing God is prohibited.

- *Bearing false witness:* Lying in a legal context or to damage someone's reputation is strongly prohibited.

- *Coveting:* Jews should not desire what belongs to another.

- *Mutilation of the body:* This is generally prohibited.

- *Frivolous activity in sacred spaces:* For example, disrespectful behavior in a cemetery.

It's important to note that these lists are generalizations, and the nuances of interpretation and practice can be quite complex within each religious tradition. It's also true that some of these, like not bearing false witness, stealing, or murdering, likely led to greater peace, civility, and potential individual joy. Those dictating what one can eat or drink or when one can have sexual relations or divorce likely encroached upon someone's individual joy.

CHANGING MORES

Occasionally, if a belief or practice is viewed over time by a large enough percentage of the majority (of believers and nonbelievers) to no longer be God's will, to be a misinterpretation of God's will, or to be just wrong, a religion may reform or evolve.

In some parts of Africa, Asia, and the Middle East, female genital mutilation was (and in some cases still is) considered not only normal but an important faith-based practice. Long before the majority brought attention to and demanded an end to the practice, there was emotional and physical suffering, even death, not to mention unhappiness on the part of women, that would have been considered normal and acceptable.

In some ancient cultures, human sacrifices are believed to have been common. Historians say Inca, Aztec, and Ashanti cultures might have regularly sacrificed humans—from prisoners to children. Today, in Central America, Africa, and the rest of the free world, no one would condone or tolerate human sacrifices. When I visited and toured some of the ancient sites in Tikal, there were still massive and impressive pyramids standing that might have been the place where these sacrifices were made. However, my tour guides did not feel comfortable even acknowledging that practice took place because it was too unpleasant for some proud descendants to even imagine that their forefathers could have done this.

Central Americans are not alone. Most modern-day cultures have practices that might have been common among their ancestors, or even a few generations earlier, that we'd find shameful today. Especially if those practices and beliefs resulted in needless pain, torture, and death. It is sometimes easy to see and judge the past, or to even see the oddity in another's belief system today, but it is often hard to see it on our own. I will offer some examples later in this chapter that are more personal to me and my cultural history in the US. But first, let's consider why we believe and embrace these practices.

Many believers subscribe to their religious belief systems and their rules because they expect (or hope) that their lives on Earth, in an afterlife, or if/when they return to Earth in another form will be better. The thought is they will be happy or at least they will avoid unhappiness such as going to hell, purgatory, or returning to Earth in a lower form. Many beliefs are executed by dutiful and loyal believers because they've done the math: "If I do XYZ, I believe ABC will happen."

Perhaps abstaining from drinking coffee or remaining a virgin until marriage does not meet your definition or level of self-inflicted unhappiness, but for someone it does. Moreover, I am guessing the avoidance of sex and coffee is easier if you believe your soul will be happier one day because of it. For others, their faith equates to an insurance policy. They are unsure whether the underlying premise of what they claim to believe is true or not, but they are fearful enough of the consequences of being a nonbeliever that they walk the walk and talk the talk. Regardless of how painful or immediate the sacrifice, the cumulative effect of the choices and freedoms that are removed can over time have a significant impact on your potential happiness. Worse, in the case of holy wars, human sacrifices, and female genital mutilation, it can lead to death.

If you find the aforementioned examples to be a bit extreme and perhaps unrelatable, let's use a few more contemporary examples and refer back to our four quadrants of happiness from the first chapter. You will recall that the four quadrants I offered for sources of happiness are: 1) high intrinsic sources of happiness, 2) low intrinsic sources of happiness, 3) high extrinsic sources of happiness, and 4) low extrinsic sources of happiness. Now let's use one of my own recent experiences with happiness to make it more personal.

MY OWN STRUGGLES

I grew up in the southern Black church in what I consider to be a typical southern Black Christian family. While my extended family in Atlanta had historically been members of the African Methodist Episcopal (AME) denomination, which was also my earliest church experience, my household moved around a bit during my teen years. I spent meaningful time in the Church of God in Christ (COGIC), Baptist churches, and later, as an adult, in AME Zion churches before finally returning to the Baptist tradition.

My last and most meaningful religious affiliation was with Abyssinian Baptist Church, a historic Harlem church where Rev. Adam Clayton Powell, Sr. and Jr., once pastored one of the largest African American congregations in America. Abyssinian was typical of many Black churches in its beautiful fusion of theology, civil rights, community service, and activism with cultural arts and redemption.

Although I wrestled with some of the theological concepts preached in the Baptist church, I found so much value in all the other aspects of the church and belonging in the community. Moreover, my pastor, the late Dr. Rev. Calvin Butts, was like the grandfather and fatherly sage I never had, whose sharp and insightful perspectives on everything from politics to Black people's socioeconomic liberation was food for my soul. But my search for understanding, truth and worldly leadership had always led me to places like Abyssinian, and ultimately, after Abyssinian, to places beyond the church and within. As a college student, after attending the Million Man March in Washington, DC, I even briefly attended a Boston-area mosque, believing at the time that the Nation of Islam offered more practical answers to the many questions I had about faith, God, and society—especially as a young Black man struggling to find his way.

Regardless of what church, denomination, or community I visited, my mother's strict and basic interpretation of Christianity was always looming in the background. I am sure she was only a product of her upbringing. My mother's family was equally religious. Her brother was an AME pastor, her sister was a minister, and even her youngest brother (now in prison) was the drummer at my childhood church. My brother and I were in church every Sunday and participated in the choir, usher board, camera staff, and every retreat and summer revival. Religion was all around me, all the time. My mother played gospel music every morning that I can remember, and prayer was a constant thing, from the mundane grace before a meal to the intervention to bind or release demons my mother thought might be occupying our house, my brother, or me. That's just how it was.

My experience with faith was largely a mystical and scary thing. I grew up with a fear and respect for God that ranged from being quiet during a thunderstorm (because the Devil was beating his wife, as the adults warned us) all the way to assuming my deliverance through school would only be possible if God showed me favor. I was mostly afraid of hell. The fear of hell, demons, and the Devil's power to destroy our lives was a powerful motivation. My understanding of the world was very black and white. You were either good or bad, favored or possessed, heaven-bound or hell-bound, on the right track or doomed.

My mother was harsh, fussy, and tough to be around when she was angry or annoyed, which was often, it seemed. Although she was very religious (she always attended church and was made a deaconess before she died), I struggled with all the contradictions I saw in her and the church more broadly. Although she was very functional, my mother suffered from various drug addictions during my youth that led to her being volatile, manic, and very unpredictable. There's no question she loved me and my brother. She was just a tough-love type of person who could curse you out and beat you for being disobedient and then make you a meal with love. It was confusing. Her husband, my stepfather, was equally conflicted. Both occupied high profiles in church but did drugs, fought each other regularly, and used the Bible to control and lecture me and my brother daily.

My mother was most critical of sex and sexuality, which would go on to be a source of shame, anxiety, and judgment for me. While some of my mother's strictness was typical parenting stuff and necessary, some of it ran deeper and darker. My mother always warned me about the Devil's ability to use women to trap me and ruin my life with an unwanted pregnancy or disease. The subtle association of women with the Devil, or as easy pawns of the Devil, was not only horribly misguided but created trust and affection issues for me in future relationships. She never talked about the potential love and affection one might experience with a partner or romantic interest, only the imminent doom. She was not just anti-girlfriend. She was anti anything that might draw our attention away from school and God. It was tough being a teen under her roof, and that led to me feeling depressed, suicidal, and confused. It also stoked a great deal of resentment and rebellion as I developed counterviews on such traditional dogma.

Faith was largely the source of all my shame, fear, and judgment. I would go on to be as judgmental of others as I was of myself. During much of my young adult life, and well into my twenties, thirties, and even forties, I wrestled with my faith in large part because of the way I came to understand it and how it made me feel. While it could bring intense joy during a praise and worship service or after a deliverance from a tough situation (a.k.a. "trials and tribulations"), it was just as likely to be a source of unhappiness. Faith was just as likely to lift me up as it was to condemn me.

I also struggled with the intellectual contradictions that were always apparent. I read the Bible often and found that a good bit did not make sense or was highly unlikely. I found intellectual weakness, if not complete nonsense, in many of the sermons but mostly kept them to myself. My fear of condemnation was the greatest advocate and defender of faith. I found the economics of most churches to be suspect at best—especially those churches that boasted big congregations, budgets, and pastoral compensation. It often seemed like a glorious hustle—hustling the downtrodden, poor, and folks who might not know better—or perhaps hustling folks like me, who might know better but feared the wrath of God and found it easier to overlook the contradictions in service of the greater truth.

If you were watching a time-lapse footage of my church engagement and devotion, you would see a zigzag effect, bouncing from faithful to faithless, from baptism to bedside Baptist, from being a fervent advocate of the gospel and faith to being its greatest cynic. The only thing that was constant was my confusion and unhappiness.

While there were and are meaningful differences between some of the denominations and faiths that I experienced growing up and later in life, some things were consistent: The church was more than a place for theology—it was a place for community and community service, politics and political engagement, and most of all, the place where you went to make sense of the world around you. For me and most Black folks who grew up in families like mine, faith was infused into everything. Our deliverance from slavery was God. Obama's rise to president was nothing but God. Racism was the Devil. The healing that our community needed would only come if God did it. Even my mother's healing from cancer, which never came, was possible if it was God's will. For me, faith and religion were so intricately tied to my happiness that it was unclear whether anything else really mattered or could lead to true and lasting joy—only God.

MY TURNING POINT

I would later learn that many of my friends had similar experiences to mine. "Your mom did that too?" I would say, as we laughed about what seemed to be normal, but rarely did any of us commit to ensuring that the next generation had a different experience. At best, my more progressive friends and I would find comfort in simply allowing our kids, nieces, nephews, and whoever else might have looked to us for spiritual guidance to find their own way. "We don't push anything. We just let our kids figure it out for themselves."

Even as we watched the rise of the evangelical conservative political movement that sought to introduce more extreme and theocratic laws, we generally chose to push back on the laws and those they impacted (e.g., LGBTQ and pregnant women who wanted the freedom to choose whether to give birth or not) versus the underlying premise of the belief system.

In Congress, we don't argue whose interpretation of the Bible is right or wrong; we just argue whether the proposed law is lawful or not. We avoid discussions of faith, although it is the silent puppeteer in so much of our society's norms and laws.

Like so many people I knew, I was largely quiet about my own internal conflicts on faith and uncertainty about what to believe. I tended to ground myself in the facts and leave the rest to the Bible-thumpers and ideologues. However, I was at best going through the motions by still attending church, celebrating Christian holidays, and remaining a visible and supportive member of the community. But at worst I was feeling increasingly cynical and hostile toward the didactic and judgy attitudes and the hubris of the Bible-thumpers.

Then something changed that forced me "out of the closet." During my early forties, I started being a bit more honest about my struggles, initially with myself then eventually with others. I was finding it hard to be happy in an authentic way while also subscribing to the faith of my mother, my family, and my community. I was growing tired of pretending to not notice all the glaring contradictions in the history of religion, mythology of religion, politics of religion, and theology of religion. They were all totally different things in my opinion. I started reading more and more books about the history and politics of religion, which gave me strength to push back on the theology and mythology of religion. I initially did all of this quietly and academically. I was mostly reading and reflecting and occasionally sharing my thoughts with my then-wife. But over time, I grew stronger in my conviction that I had no conviction at all.

Long before I understood the word *agnostic*, I felt a huge sense of release when I concluded after all of my reading that "I just don't know." Maybe some religious tenets were true, but maybe not. There was no way for me to be sure, and I didn't feel the need to spend a lot of time trying to figure out what was the truth and what was not. Although I concluded that most of the theological tenets were likely untrue, I didn't have enough facts to construct an alternative version of the stories I had been taught. I was comfortable that the man Jesus had lived and been a preacher in Roman-occupied Palestine. He was likely a Jewish reformer and Zealot, as Reza Aslan describes in his book *Zealot: The Life and Times of Jesus of Nazareth*.[5] There was proof of this, but I was less comfortable subscribing to his divinity and all the underlying subplots: God favors Jews over everyone else, Paul (who never met Jesus) was handpicked to save the Gentiles—a message that was counter to the teachings of Jesus—and so on.

I also found no basis for God being singular versus plural, or deeply involved in the lives, politics, and nations of his creations versus completely removed and indifferent. I found no basis for a god or God to be male, White, and preferential toward the same or even that he, or she, or they or it was the "original Black man," as I often heard in my "hotep" circles. There was no evidence that God favored capitalism, the West, and American supremacy. Everything I came to know about God, from his taking land from the Canaanites and giving it to Abraham's descendants in a series of battles fought by Joshua, to his insistence on us going through various men (Jesus, the Pope, and the like) to get to Him, all seemed to be of man's creation.

As Reza so rightly describes, we have been creating a god in our image—not the other way around. This was true for most faiths. The formula was pretty consistent: He knows (or we know) what is right and divine. Do what we say, and you will be happy. If you don't do what we say, you will be damned in this life or the next.

Of course, I am exaggerating to make the point about religion being a creation of man and a tool to promote man's interest in the world. Our rights, freedom, and happiness are collateral damage and to be expected. I decided to let all of that go, without any sense for what would or should replace it. I also let go of the unhappiness baggage that was judgment, shame, and condemnation that went hand in hand with the "thou shalt" formula. It felt weird at first but then amazing. I went from initially feeling fear that the Devil had finally tricked me into giving up my faith to embracing a more rational interpretation. I was rebooting my hard drive and replacing old programs with new ones, and if there weren't new ones, I allowed myself the grace to be curious and say, "I really don't know."

As an agnostic, I simply submit to not knowing. While I continue to believe in a greater power than me, which is perhaps the source of all things, I am okay leaving it there for now. I am okay waiting for a new truth to arrive in a way that feels authentic and real, and I am okay sitting still until then.

A NEW PEACE

A funny thing happened when I let go of some of these old faiths and beliefs. I found myself feeling lighter and happier. I was no longer afraid to do what I wanted, nor feel the need to please or answer to anyone, nor feel the need to judge anyone or myself, and certainly I didn't feel the condemnation that had ruled over my life. However, I also didn't lose the joy I often felt in church that came after a good sermon or gospel song. That remained.

In fact, I felt like I was experiencing joy more often and with greater impact. It came from feeling gratitude, purposeful, giving, and in touch with nature, as I always feel when scuba diving. I also felt more confident when I would interact with my close friends and family who continued to be strong believers and, out of love for me and my soul, would gently encourage me to return to the church.

I rarely felt the need to explain myself or debate with my loved ones because they were (and are) my loved ones. Further, I am primarily an advocate for free thinking and not of thinking like me. Live and let live is a motto that really resonates with me these days. To be clear, I am not without values or morals, nor without even a belief in a greater power and good. I'm just far more delicate and humbler with how I think about faith and its power for good, bad, and happiness in my life. I now find happiness in my faith or lack thereof. I also find happiness that my curiosity about life, people, and the world as I can comprehend it will lead to wisdom, truth, and perhaps to a god.

FAITH-BASED INSTITUTIONS (BEWARE)

Faith is a deeply powerful and necessary aspect of the human condition. I have faith in my own set of things, notwithstanding my agnostic leanings. Yet, I rest comfortably in the vast universe of things that fall into the unknowing and the unknown. I don't feel compelled to develop a story, myth, or theological framework to make sense of things that in fact don't make sense—nor are impossible with our current body of science to understand. Some will adopt certain faith postures, not so much because they believe but because they are afraid of not believing. Faith in this case feels more like an insurance policy. I once had someone say to me, "You're right, some of this does not make sense, but I would hate to die and find out it was true . . . so I am going to believe it just in case."

This is where institutions and society play a role I am deeply suspicious of and want to highlight. There are some institutions and systems that directly benefit from people's blind faith. In more extreme cases, some institutions intentionally promote falsehoods with the goal of exploiting people's faith. It was in the White slave owners' interest for African slaves to adopt and embrace Christian principles, especially if it supported a belief that slavery was ordained by God and the natural order of things. It was in the interest of the Catholic Church for much of European history to believe that the church was the authority on all matters of life, per God's will, or that all treasure, land, and life were owed to the church and its administrators. It was in the interest of ancient kings and queens who commissioned massive and costly projects, such as the building of pyramids, for the commoner who either labored or paid more taxes to believe in the divinity of the projects and their rulers. The pattern has repeated over the ages, across all cultures and faiths.

During the COVID-19 pandemic, I binged all six seasons of *Vikings* and admired the series' storied valor. Men and women alike (as the legend goes) would often serve with honor on the front line of an unwinnable battle, with full expectation of dying a glorious and honorable death that would ensure their seat at the table in Valhalla (the mythical place Vikings believed to be heaven for fallen soldiers). It would have been a great benefit to a Viking king, like Ragnar, to have an army of committed soldiers and shield maidens to believe such a thing when the king stood to gain lands, riches, or fame from raiding distant lands.

Even on a less-bloody scale and closer to home, I always found it convenient that megachurch preachers preached to their church members that God wanted their pastor to be wealthy. It was in their interest for their church members to believe that God wanted their pastor to be wealthy as proof of God's blessing and favor. Our faith in other institutions that often lead and engage its followers using "core values," though not religious ones, are no different.

For example, it is in the interest of politicians for constituents to believe that by voting, making political donations, volunteering on campaigns, and ultimately enduring a season of hardship (e.g., from increased taxes or sending troops to war), the country would see a brighter future. We have always had corporations, and the managers of those corporations have workers believe that if they were loyal to the company, at the end of their work tenure in retirement, they would be promised a pension that would give them a reasonable standard of living and happiness. Even in many of the companies I worked for, CEOs encouraged us to go the extra mile and work harder with the explicit and implicit promise that the equity we were granted would be well worth it.

But not all transactional relationships are bad and not every promise is made without caveats and disclosure of the risk. Further, not every institution that makes a promise does so with nefarious and scrupulous intention. Still, you should be vigilant and look for evidence that your promised happiness is assured when one side has a compelling and vested interest in another's suffering in exchange for an uncertain, distant future payoff.

I frame the argument as though it's binary when it's in fact not. We can have a very healthy faith for whatever suits us while also being careful when those beliefs creep into some of the most important decisions in life. Meaning, we can choose to believe in God and also take our health, wealth, and happiness into our own hands. In an ideal world, that would be my suggestion. Make sure your beliefs are not somehow at odds with your happiness in ways that you don't approve of or understand.

YOU DON'T KNOW WHAT YOU DON'T KNOW

I went scuba diving for my fiftieth birthday in the beautiful country of the Maldives, in South Asia near India. This small island country is known for having some of the most beautiful waters for scuba diving (one of my favorite sources of extrinsic happiness). Its oceans are warm, clear, and full of an array of vibrant ocean life. I spent two weeks there, scuba diving and photographing as much of the marine life as I could see and experience. I captured special moments with manta rays, a variety of sharks, countless coral reef fish, sting rays, and turtles. The experiences brought me joy in so many ways, but I also learned a bit about the country and its people.

The Maldives has a population of just under half a million people, who live mostly in its capital city island of Malé. It's a traditional and conservative country of mostly observant Muslims. Most of the women wear *hijabs*, even when swimming, and alcohol is strictly prohibited. You won't find a bar, store, or hotel that offers beer, wine, or spirits to even the millions of tourists on whom the country's economy depends. Its only meaningful export is fish, and it depends heavily on trade with nearby countries, including India. During my time there, I found the people, though largely working poor by US standards, to be extremely warm, friendly, and respectful. The average household spends upwards of 30 percent to 50 percent of their income on rent, making multigenerational homes and apartments with kids, parents, and grandparents common.[6]

Their simple pleasures appeared to come from drinking coffee at all times of day in one of the numerous modest cafes on any given street. In Humamalé, where I stayed for a week, many of the locals swim in the morning or just sit at the shore watching their loved ones swim. The kids' faces seemed to light up as they rode shotgun in between the legs of parents or grandparents on the thousands of Vespas that are the country's most common mode of transportation. The building and housing infrastructure is of relatively low quality, except for a few ornate mosques that I found sprinkled throughout the city. And despite some climate outlooks that project that the Maldives could be as much as 80 percent below water by the year 2050 due to rising sea levels,[7] no one seemed worried or visibly unhappy. In fact, most of the people I saw seemed relatively content with life in the Maldives.

I was happy there because I was doing what I loved in a place that was lovable. But I often wondered if the people I met and got to know were as happy as they could be. I often wondered how much their faith, and specifically the religious policies governing the hundreds of thousands of people who call Maldives home, might be limiting their happiness—whether or not they were conscious of it.

I tried to imagine what it might have been like to live or grow up there, based on my happiness quadrant and the happiness quadrant of my scuba companion who was with me for part of the trip. She is also African American and indulged me on many thought exercises about happiness. But I did not limit my curiosity to hypotheticals, I also asked a number of the locals I had a chance to meet and get to know about their happiness experiences. I wanted to make sure I was not projecting too much of my Western lens onto people who, by definition, were different from me in their lived experiences and what might be in their happiness quadrants.

I met a number of people who expressed a great sense of pride and joy from being a fisherman, father, and provider, or belonging to a local community of friends who met regularly for coffee and fellowship. These felt like solid sources of both intrinsic and extrinsic happiness. I also witnessed the joy visible on the faces of parents and grandparents when they were with their young, not unlike the faces of parents and grandparents around the world and at home where I grew up. It was a kind of happiness that felt timeless and able to transcend culture and geography. But I also met some folks who offered a look into some of our important cultural differences and how faith was potentially limiting their happiness.

There was one man I met in particular who was once a professional Maldivian athlete, but who was now a middle-aged father living on a modest salary in a two-bedroom flat, with his extended family largely depending on him for room and board. We will call him Shaheed (not his real name). Though proud, Shaheed expressed regret that he had not had an opportunity to do more with his life. He had had enough exposure to other cultures and lifestyles to know what was possible elsewhere but understood that those other paths were not to be his reality. Perhaps his chance encounter with me, an American tourist, might have reminded him of this other life outside of the Maldives.

He shared that he never seriously considered moving to another country to really pursue a career and better life, even when he was younger and had a chance to do so. He was quick to acknowledge that it would have been difficult, even if he wanted to. It was culturally unthinkable to leave your family and country. It was something few ever did. His culture, society, and faith had largely already shaped his sense of purpose, duty, and identity. The script of what was possible and what he should do had been running on autopilot. It was the default software program, and it was only now, in his later years, that he was more conscious of it. However, it is not clear that his consciousness would have been enough.

The country's population is nearly 99 percent Sunni Muslim.[8] Sunni Muslims make up nearly 90 percent of all Muslims around the world[9] and have a more rigid interpretation of the faith. They believe that the Quran, as an example, is the literal word of God. The country's constitution requires one to be Muslim in order to be a citizen, and should a person leave the faith, they could jeopardize their citizenship. It goes further, according to the US State Department. The Maldives's law states:

> Non-Muslims living in or visiting the country are prohibited from openly expressing their religious beliefs, holding public congregations to conduct religious activities, or involving Maldivians in such activities. By law, those expressing religious beliefs other than Islam face imprisonment or house arrest of up to five years, fines ranging from 5,000 to 20,000 rufiyaa ($330 to $1,300), and deportation.[10]

The UK government also warns its travelers visiting the country:

> It is illegal to bring in anything deemed contrary to Islam, including "idols for worship," Bibles, pork and pork products, and alcohol.[11]

Despite the fairly strict religious laws governing their citizens and visitors like me, more than two million visitors poured into the country in 2024.[12] Our conversation was candid and authentic. I was surprised how comfortable he was reflecting on the role of his culture in his potential happiness (my words, not his). Given the strict code of conduct, I was sensitive not to put him in moral or legal jeopardy by sharing views that might be risky if overheard by others. So I cautiously ventured a bit further, probing what his reflections might mean for the future. I asked him if he thought his kids might pursue or at least consider lives and careers for themselves beyond the island. He paused, reflected on the question, and replied, "Probably not."

Though tempted, I resisted the urge to probe further into what seemed odd. Why would he not insist on encouraging his kids to think beyond their cultural traditions if it meant a chance at greater happiness? I then felt sadness and dread come over me as I imagined how just being born here might limit someone's potential for growth, purpose, or the ability to realize their full potential and be their authentic self. He then abruptly ended the conversation and said that he needed to get going. I imagined that our conversation had drifted into uncomfortable waters or was maybe drawing unwanted attention to us as we stood chatting on the beach. I thanked him for sharing his time and thoughts with me.

Each morning, I saw young girls and women of all ages swim. It was a refreshing sight, especially as I reflected on how many friends back home never learned to swim. Even a number of my friends from Caribbean islands never learned to swim—despite growing up literally surrounded by water. *This act of encouraging women of all ages to swim was pretty progressive,* I thought, *especially for a country that is fairly conservative, and in some cases violent, in its treatment of women.* Women make up less than 5 percent of Parliament, and some parts of the country still practice female genital mutilation.[13] Progress has been slow. Before 2021, for example, marital rape was legal. These structural aspects of life for women and girls put this small glimmer of hope and joy in context.

Further, the women and girls swimming reminded me of this deeper and darker reality. All the women swimming were fully clothed from head to toe with hijabs. And though some of the men wore shirts as well, none of the women wore traditional bathing suits—not even a one-piece with shorts. The women all wore mostly black hijabs, black body suits covering their arms and legs, and they were always draped with some type of dark-colored dress that hid their body contours. The temperatures were hot—in the low- to mid-eighties by 6:30 a.m. and humid. I was even hot and sweaty in my loose-fitting shorts and T-shirt.

But they swam as though this was not only normal, but natural. And after swimming in the ocean for a while, they would rinse off together in the public outside showers—still in all their clothes, including the hijab. I badly wanted to snap a pic with my iPhone to capture the moment but sensed how creepy that might look to anyone who might be watching. So I just mused and watched as they washed the salt water off with their clothes on and then watched them, one by one, hop on to their scooters or simply walk off in their wet clothes.

As an avid swimmer and scuba diver, I tried hard to imagine if I could enjoy swimming with all those layers of clothes on my body, even if it were my choice. I wondered if I would feel the coolness of the water on a hot day or the freedom of gliding aerodynamically through the ocean if I had to wear long pants and a long-sleeve shirt. I couldn't. I then thought about how much I love the warmth of the sun on my brown skin when I lie on the beach or play in the pool. Those simple pleasures bring me joy and make me feel alive, and it saddens me to imagine being born in a place that could take those pleasures away in the name of faith and religion.

The Devil's Advocate

Maybe there are other ways to think about what I experienced in the Maldives. Was it not this type of arrogance and patriarchal thinking that led to religious missionaries, imperialism, and countless wars over competing economic systems? Didn't all of those efforts, perhaps originally inspired by someone's belief that they knew better and should impose that way of life on others, lead to misery, pain, and death? There is still significant trauma in countries that were ruled and influenced by Western colonialism, from the loss and depreciation of local languages, cultures, and norms to imported beauty standards that have led to self-hate and mutilation.

I felt hypocritical as I pondered these parallels. I also posited more abstract considerations: How do I know if they are not in fact happy? How can you miss what you've never had? How can I honestly assess another's happiness based on my values and experiences? The answer was obvious; I can't, nor should I try. However, I think it would be easier for me not to dwell on the plight of Maldivian women if it were merely a preference— and specifically, the woman's preference.

To be clear, I don't think encouraging women to wear skimpy swimsuits or swim nude necessarily leads to happiness. It is not about the clothes (or lack thereof), it is about the choice to self-determine and pursue your unique happiness—so long as it does not encroach upon another's happiness. There is also an important age-old consideration for when someone is able to be accountable for their own happiness. Thomas Jefferson once wrote that a well-informed electorate is a prerequisite to democracy. Freedom is powerful and necessary for happiness, but it also comes with responsibility and some measure of knowledge.

For example, should teens be able to drink and smoke sooner? Should Congress remove any requirements of social media platforms to protect minors from bullying or predators? Should politicians require people to get vaccinated if they have information that such vaccinations will save lives, even if it conflicts with individual beliefs? Should the elderly automatically lose the right to drive their vehicle after a certain age because the state decides it's best for everyone, including the elderly?

In each of these examples, the person for whom a privilege is withheld or removed could experience less happiness because someone else felt they knew better. Even when these policies and laws are democratically imposed (i.e., the majority votes to approve the measure), we are now subjecting the happiness of the minority to the happiness of the majority. And what would be a fair percentage to constitute a "majority" if in fact this was the best way to manage these trade-offs at scale? Is it 51 percent, 60 percent, or more? And what about the extreme opposite, when one's individual freedom encroaches upon the masses?

My favorite classic example of this reversal is someone exercising their freedom of speech by yelling fire in the movie theater when there isn't a fire, and it subsequently leads to everyone else in the theater being trampled. This is not an easy moral, legal, or even philosophical debate to win from either side. That said, in a landmark Supreme Court case of *Schenck v. United States* in 1919, the courts found that "shouting 'fire' in a crowded theater" was outside the scope of free speech protections because the primary purpose of the act was to create panic or cause harm.[14]

Maybe there is something we can learn and apply from this ruling as to how we think about these tensions elsewhere. We have to consider not only the intent (i.e., to create harm or reduce individual freedoms or protect them), but also the impact (i.e., it actually creates harm and reduces individual freedom). While far from being as easy as it sounds, it's probably directionally right. As Carl W. Buehner once said, people may not remember what you said, but they will remember how you made them feel. We can do a lot to make people feel seen, heard, and validated as individuals, even as we try to do what's best for all. And "all" can't mean one race, one gender, one religious group, one political party, or one of anything. All has to really mean *all*.

Race, Class, and Ethnicity

While wrapping up my last few days in the Maldives, I got to know the hotel servers and staff some. They were mostly lighter-skinned men from Northern India on some type of temporary work visa and rotation program. I found it odd that a country with as much poverty as the Maldives would allow labor from another country to take jobs in nice hotels such as the one I stayed at. I wondered what role race, class, and ethnicity, alongside faith, might play in societies like the Maldives. In India, as an example, being born into a certain caste (a longstanding cultural and faith-based tradition) can have a huge impact on not only livelihood, but happiness. The lowest of the caste groupings belongs to the Dalits, or "untouchables." If you are born into this caste, you might be allowed to have only the most menial jobs (e.g., cleaning latrines), be limited in who you can love and marry, and ultimately be limited in your life's overall socioeconomic outlook.

There is nothing real about the caste itself. There are no genetic, intellectual, or physical differences between people of different castes, only those imagined and believed. In fact, race itself is a manufactured concept. Humans of all races are genetically indistinguishable. Our genes might, over time, express differently under different environments, but our composition is virtually the same. Yet we create systems, including faith-based systems such as the Hindu and Indian caste systems, that manufacture differences for an end goal that benefits one group at the expense of another—and these beliefs matter. Your potential happiness would certainly be impacted if you are born an "untouchable."

In Isabel Wilkerson's book and later movie *Caste: The Origins of Our Discontents*,[15] she likened the Indian caste system to the discrimination practiced in other regions and different time periods, such as the enslavement and Jim Crow laws Black people suffered under in the US. In the landmark case *Brown v. Board of Education* that made "separate but equal" segregation of Black people illegal in America,[16] the plaintiffs used social psychology experiments with children to prove how the culture of discrimination directly impacted a child's sense of self-worth and was harmed under the Jim Crow laws of the South. Though simple, seeing a Black child, without nudging, consider a White doll the better doll was powerful enough to make the point that being born into this environment negatively impacted children. The values, creeds, and belief systems that a child is born into can have an undeniable impact on a child's self-worth, emotional health, and life outcome. That's before we even get into happiness.

Racial segregation, codified in both written and unwritten laws, was enforced with brute force in America. But it is important to remember that they were socialized and made respectable by Christian values and culture. I am sure many White southerners who embraced these racist beliefs (or felt no need to challenge them) considered the racial caste system of America to be not only a fact of life but something very natural and intended by God. They did not need proof, because this was a matter of faith. Even when presented with horrible images of lynched bodies, bloody encounters between police and nonviolent marchers, or innocent pictures of the little boys and girls who were murdered and mutilated in Money, Mississippi, or the Birmingham church bombings, White indifference was an example of collective cognitive dissonance at its best.

In the American South, God and Jesus were White, and it was clear to all that He did not like Black people—or Jews and gay people for that matter. For many generations after the Civil War, the KKK burned Christian crosses in the yards of anyone who might challenge these faith-based ideals. The KKK was still marching when I was growing up in Atlanta, and the Confederate flag, another symbol of this painful past, continues to be flown in many parts of the South today. Following the removal of Union soldiers from the Southern states by President Andrew Jackson, racial discrimination and violence was not only ordained by faith and religion, it *was* the religion. Even today, the evangelical right-wing agenda, viewed by many as the modern-day cultural equivalent of the religious segregationist movement of the early to mid-1900s, is not only politically conservative but advocating a social agenda with language that demonizes minorities, immigrants, and homosexuals in the name of their God.

Oppression, conflict, and genocide in the name of faith are not limited to the Christians, Muslims, and Hindus. Even Buddhists, typically associated with pacifism, peace, and nonviolence, have their share of blood on their hands, both literally and figuratively. The faith teaches its followers to not cause harm or injury to others and to largely live a life centered on achieving inner peace, but so do the main tenets of Christianity, Islam, and Hinduism. Most of the faiths, at some level, advocate for things that seem reasonable and certainly not oppressive and designed to undermine our happiness. However faiths are merely belief constructs that in themselves have no life or being without the humans who give them life. It is also humans who leverage systems of faith to drive their agendas, who make it hard to separate intent from impact.

In my experience with Christianity, it was not uncommon to see scandal after scandal in the church. The scandals could be fairly localized and seemingly insignificant in the grand scheme, like discovering a married church pastor was having an extramarital affair, all the way to abuses that were institutional and lasted generations, such as the sexual abuses of children by clergy in the Catholic church. Each time we find ourselves disappointed in the fallibility of faith, religion, or church, we seem to accept the excuse that the human, which is fallible, should be held separate from the faith, which is not fallible. This simple and well-worn answer allows us to kick the can down the road on interrogating the actual faith that conceals, conflates, and confuses the intent-impact relationship.

I had a chance to visit Myanmar a number of years ago. While there, I toured a number of ancient Buddhist temples, learned about the local culture and its traditions, as well as the country's own struggles with the role of faith in politics, ethnicity, and culture. Burma, now called Myanmar, was one of the earliest to embrace Buddhism when the faith arrived from India in the third century BCE. Buddhism as a national identity (and not just a faith) played a powerful role in unifying the country in the early 1900s against British colonialism and today represents about 88 percent of the country's population.[17] The country also has one of the highest percentages of monks per capita. And like we find in other faiths, their monks are not just spiritual leaders but important political and cultural forces. The Burmese monks played an important role as counterforces to the military rule that has defined much of the country's recent history but also incited violence and bloodshed in the name of their faith.

When I arrived in 2016, Aung San Suu Kyi, a national politician and activist who was awarded the Nobel Peace Prize in 1991 while still under house arrest, had a year earlier in 2015 led her party, the National League for Democracy (NLD), to a historic victory. The NLD was elected to power in Myanmar's first free and open election in twenty-five years. I remember people, like my taxicab driver, talking openly and excitedly about their hope for the future of the country. While there were very real structural challenges faced by many of the people I met, there was an overall sense of optimism and happiness that seemed common in my brief visit.

But just a year later, little did any of us know that the mood would change. In 2017, there was horrific and bloody violence towards Myanmar's ethnic minority community, the Rohingyas. Rohingyas are a mostly Muslim minority with cultural and historical ties to India. Despite the peaceful teachings and principles of Buddhism, a senior Buddhist

Burmese monk had been teaching and advocating violence against the Rohingya, which led to genocide and subsequent migration of Rohingyan refugees to Bangladesh. The monk, Ashin Wirathu, was so inflammatory in his hatred and rhetoric towards Muslims that his Facebook page was eventually shut down.

A TRICKY THING TO UNTANGLE

It's hard to imagine being born into any society or culture where faith and religion determine who you are, what you are free to do, and how you ultimately express your authentic self and experience true happiness. It's hard to imagine how someone can experience true happiness if and when their choices and abilities to self-determine, self-express, or just be are limited or preconditioned. And because faith can be a tricky thing to untangle (particularly its intent with its impact), you have to ask yourself a few questions when you find yourself subjected to faith:

- What is it that I am being asked to believe?

- Why and on what basis is this belief?

- Do I willingly and knowingly share and embrace this belief?

- Does it impact my or someone else's well-being and happiness?

I don't believe that the original intention behind most faiths (or religions) is necessarily nefarious. In fact, just the opposite. I believe that most people begin with good intentions and wrestle with the temptation and impulse to harm others over time.

However, we don't always fully understand or take time to consider the consequences of what we are asked to believe, its validity, and how it impacts our collective happiness. Sometimes, if the impact seems relatively small, such as not being able to have a cocktail for two weeks while traveling in the Maldives, we tend to dismiss it. Or if it is confusingly tangled and intertwined with a belief we do embrace (or the words used to describe the faith sound like something we might embrace), such as "family values," "decency," or "religious freedom," we might miss the potential dangers that could be lurking below the surface of a policy or religious edict.

And sometimes that is the intent. Sometimes the preacher, politician, or parent wants us to believe that the intent underlying our faith is good—and therefore its outcomes and impact are good. But as we have seen over history, from every geography, race, and creed, this is not always the case. When the impact of faith has destructive or harmful consequences, it's likely that we are well past happiness concerns and just maybe, the early and initial seemingly small encroachments on our happiness are the warning signal for a greater and more dangerous infringement.

EXERCISE: HAPPINESS FRAMEWORKS

I created two simple frameworks to help reflect on your beliefs, the basis of the beliefs, and how they impact your or someone else's happiness and well-being.

The first framework is an opportunity to reflect on a series of things you believe that potentially impact happiness and which of the beliefs are based upon known (or knowable) facts and knowledge, and which are not. Take a minute to populate each of the quadrants below with two to three examples of your own.

How the table works:

- Something unknown and important tends to be occupied by faith

- Something unknown and unimportant tends to be ignored

- Something known and important tends to be occupied by science or facts

- Something known and unimportant is considered common knowledge

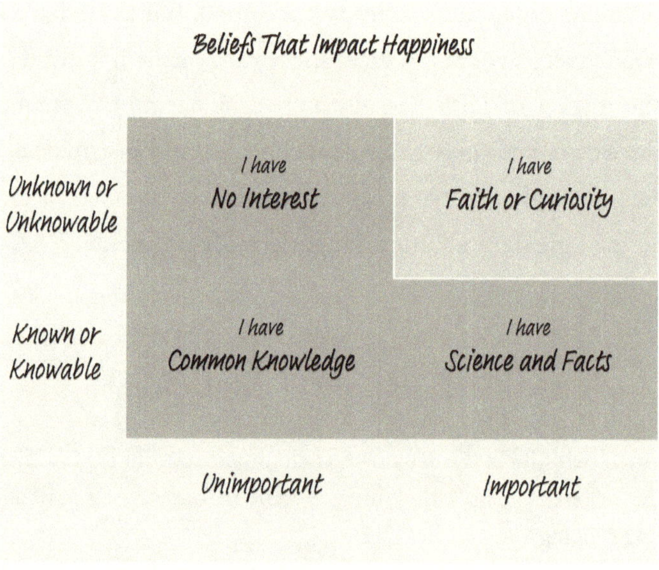

These four quadrants can help determine whether something is known or not known and whether it is important or unimportant.

I have populated each with a fictitious example to give you some sense for how you might complete your own version.

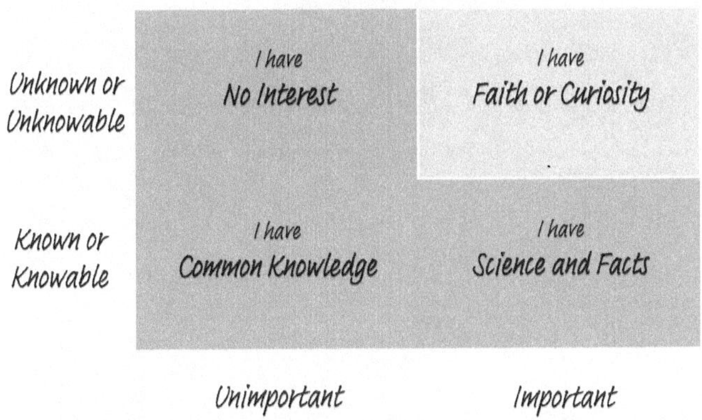

Here are the four quadrants filled in with examples.

After you have populated each quadrant with a few of your own examples, take those that you listed in the upper right-hand corner and jot them down on a clean piece of paper. We're going to take those in the Faith or Curiosity (top right) quadrant and analyze them further in the Reflection Questions at the end of this chapter.

Once we identify those beliefs that impact our (or someone else's) happiness that have no supporting evidence or it's unclear why we hold the beliefs to be true, we can use another framework to help us understand when and how to push back. For example, if we believe something that has little impact on our happiness, perhaps we can choose to ignore or tolerate it. However, if the belief has a big impact on the happiness of lots of people, we might mobilize a movement to resist or challenge the underlying belief system.

Beliefs without evidence that have a large impact
on my or someone else's happiness

	Unimportant	Important
Big Impact	Resist or Rebel	Encourage Others To Resist
Small Impact	Tolerate	Expect Others To Tolerate

Examples of how you might respond to beliefs that lack evidence
but have an impact on your happiness.

REFLECTION QUESTIONS

1. For each belief that sits in the upper right (Faith or Curiosity) quadrant, which impacts your happiness? Which impacts the happiness of others?

2. For those that impact your happiness or the happiness of others, which of the impacts would you consider small versus meaningful?

3. For those of your beliefs that have a meaningful impact on your happiness or the happiness of others, what if anything should you do with these beliefs? How does seeing the beliefs in this format make you feel about them?

CHAPTER 12

DEATH: THE TERMINAL VALUE OF HAPPINESS

"Everybody wants to go to heaven.
Nobody wants to die."

—Unknown

Christians and a host of other religions and creeds believe there is an afterlife. In this afterlife, if you are faithful and obedient to God's words (and his prophets, shepherds, pastors, preachers, and the like), you will be rewarded with eternal life in a magical and wonderful place called heaven. There will be no pain and no suffering, and you will dwell in a place of paradise.

The Bible says of heaven:

"He will wipe away every tear from their eyes; and there will no longer be any death; there will no longer be any mourning, or crying or pain." (Revelation 21:4 NASB)

"In my Father's house are many mansions: if it were not so, I would have told you. I go to prepare a place for you. And if I go and prepare a place for you, I will come again, and receive you unto myself; that where I am, there ye may be also." (John 14:1-3 KJV)

The Quran also describes heaven as a beautiful garden that is a place of eternal peace and comfort where the faithful will be rewarded. In Judaism, some believe that heaven is a place where the soul "experiences the ultimate presence of God," similar to the Garden of Eden.[1] Most of the major faiths offer up a reward in the afterlife for doing "good," whether the reward is a physical place or state of being.

Our beliefs in the afterlife and the promises it holds are powerful. It's not limited to just heaven, but everything ranging from an eternal life with seventy-two wives, to reincarnation into a greater or lower being, all the way to the ability to reap retribution on your enemies. Regardless of what you and many others believe, the assumption is that in death, you can find the potential for happiness. In exchange for this ultimate promise (that no one can prove or disprove), the faithful may be expected to live a life in which suffering, humility, service, and more is a reasonable price. As many modest folks are reminded in church, "the last shall be first, and the first shall be last" (Matthew 20:16 NIV). So perhaps it is good to be last in this life or less happy in this life, with the hope of being bumped to the front of the line in the afterlife.

We are also told stories about the rich to comfort the poor. One of the most famous is from Matthew 19:24: "Again I tell you it is much harder for a rich person to enter the Kingdom of God than for a camel to go through the eye of a needle" (GNT). Yep, we should rejoice in our poverty as it's our best chance for getting to heaven.

In exchange for the ultimate promise of happiness, we tithe, make offerings, and donate our time to the institutions of faith as ushers, choir singers, and volunteers of every sort. We will also resist our most primal human instincts to do what feels good and natural in the moment, turning the other cheek when slapped by an enemy, offering the other cheek for a second slap. This does not even begin to speak to the more routine host of daily sins that feel very normal and instinctive to our flesh but are often prohibited by our gods.

Of course, many religious teachings (of which there are countless) have evolved to encourage a broad and robust range of self-indulgences today, such as prosperity preaching, which posits that believers can and should prosper while on Earth, or more tolerant and moderate interpretations of old scriptures that seek balance. However, most of the traditional denominations preach something very different. They preach that those who would have the most happiness in the afterlife are those who are most likely to suffer today.

In some cases, our suffering is out of our control, in which case, the promise of having peace, joy, and happiness later is a comforting thought. But still others make very specific choices designed to maximize their chances of a heaven lottery ticket. Think about a vow of celibacy. This is self-imposed. Or imagine a person who avoids certain foods or careers because they believe that creating wealth is inherently evil. In some extreme cases, I have seen and heard of people declining medical treatment (e.g., vaccines, blood transfusions, or cancer treatment) because it conflicted with their faith or belief that God would save them through faith. The list goes on to include the range, from the more benign such as difficult or costly pilgrimages to the more maligned such as spouse beatings, self-mutilation, and suicide. All of these self-imposed choices are based on the beliefs and hopes of a god not seen and unverified promises of everlasting peace and happiness.

During the Dark Ages of Europe, these self-impositions and the oppression of the masses were common and brutal. This led to a time of misery, mutilation, and mayhem. Everything could be a sign of potential evil lurking about, and the carriers of said evil could be murdered, as was the case for heretics, witches, and others who believed something different. During the bubonic plague, some claimed that the source of the disease that wiped out half of the known population in Europe was an evil spirit, the work of Jews, or God's divine punishment. We now know the source was infected fleas carried by rodents.

BELIEVING IN YOUR OWN GOD

In *Sapiens: A Brief History of Humankind,* Yuval Noah Harari discusses the history of religion and how humans came to believe in God.[2] The need for understanding in things that were not understandable gave rise to belief systems and what Yuval calls "collective myths."

Long before we understood that lightning was caused by the buildup and discharge of static electricity within the clouds, we might have associated lightning and thunder with some greater presence (i.e., Zeus). If you were a farmer in early human history, a drought would've been devastating. It's not hard to imagine how early civilizations created fertility gods to help make peace and negotiate with the inability to control the weather and its effects on a harvest. Rain dances, sacrifices of animals, and everything else would've been our way, over time, to justify the belief in something greater that could make our lives easier.

Faced with lots of uncertainty, conflict, and risk, we adopted belief systems that give us the semblance of influence, if not control. It makes sense that in the face of uncertainty we created stories, myths, and gods with whom we could plead and negotiate our fate. If occasionally the sacrifice of a calf coincided with a hoped-for outcome, it offered proof of the deity or validated the myth. If the outcome didn't manifest, it was more likely that we sacrificed the wrong calf. Confirmation bias was likely a powerful force in forming our early belief systems. These systems are as varied and colorful as they are important in thinking about the root sources of our happiness calculations. If I do this thing, God will spare me pain or grant me happiness.

I am not arguing that these are not valid or justified beliefs, for I have believed many of my own as a Christian for most of my life. That's not really the point. I'm not interested in this chapter in debating the merits of one faith over the other or even in the existence of God. I am more interested in when, why, and how we develop belief systems that we believe will lead to greater happiness, even when there is no evidence to support the claim.

I was raised and lived most of my life as a Christian. More recently, my inability to find reason, evidence, or even probability to support many of my once-Christian beliefs has left me more in the camp of the agnostics. However, it was not reason and logic alone that led me on this journey. That alone wouldn't have been enough to veer me off the course my mom, family, and community laid out so well for me. It was the lurking feeling all along—of contradictions, tensions, and sometimes even shame between the things that I knew or felt to not be true but had heretofore quietly accepted on faith or duty—that changed me. There were so many things that made no sense, and I knew it made no sense, but I was willing to gloss over for the good of the bigger picture. I always struggled intellectually, as a kid, through college, and as an adult, but did so quietly. I allowed my emotional self, my cultural self, and my spiritual self to "let go and let God" so that miracles could happen in my life as they might have happened for my ancestors and all those who followed.

In recent years, however, the cognitive dissonance gave way to curiosity. I allowed myself to wonder a bit, and then I wondered a lot. I studied, devouring countless books on the history of religion and faith with an eye towards finding truth, not necessarily happiness. Books such as *Zealot: The Life and Times of Jesus of Nazareth* by Reza Aslan[3] were transformational in my journey. For the first time, I read the works of historians, academics, and scientists who articulated in elegant and objective prose the messy and confusing thoughts and feelings I had carried with me for decades. And while none of the books that I read led me to replace my old beliefs with a new set of beliefs or religion, they loosened the grips of the scripts enough for me to experience a kind of freedom. And with it came a new feeling of happiness and peace.

As an agnostic (as I define it), I am comfortable saying, "I really don't know any of these things for sure, but I am open." This unwillingness to simply accept something on faith alone has made my deeply Christian family—and countless friends and loved ones—a bit uneasy with my new faith, or lack thereof. I get it. I was once a hardcore believer, too, and worried about the souls of my nonbeliever loved ones. But I have since been willing to venture in uncharted waters in search of a greater truth that is my own. For example, I personally believe in a creator that was and is intentional, but I fall short of assigning that creator a gender, race, personality, or anything else that favors a human preference. Most of what I find in religion are our own human biases and preferences passed along as God to support our need for a theocratic basis for the world we believe exists, should exist, or will exist.

Reza makes the brilliant observation that over time we have created a God in our image, not the other way around as was written in the book of Genesis in the Bible. We've fashioned a God that cares about our unique interests. Perhaps your God wants you to be rich, get a certain job, or be married to a soulmate and have perfect kids. Maybe your God favors your race and detests another race. Maybe your God favors your nation and wants to see other nations bow at your feet. Maybe your God detests homosexuality while someone else's God has no gender and cares not for sexual orientation. One person's God could be Black while another's might be White. It all feels fairly subjective, if not random.

I stopped being overly interested in all the permutations of beliefs among eight billion people and what they need their God to be. However, each time I scuba dive and experience amazing and breathtaking interactions with nature, which seems anything other than random, I am humbled by the idea that there is something greater than me.

I had the opportunity to hear Dr. Neil deGrasse Tyson speak on the topic of "Is there life out there?" I was so mesmerized and captivated by the brilliance and common sense of everything he had to say. Though he is a world-acclaimed and celebrated astrophysicist, he makes all the complex, abstract, and wonderful aspects of the universe feel approachable and intuitive. As he did in the talk that I attended, he puts our planet and all life therein in the context of the greater expanse and realm of possibilities. Most of all, he uses facts, data, and a healthy curiosity when we reach the limits of current science to make blind faith and conviction seem idiotic.

After his presentation, I wasn't sure if and where there was life beyond Earth—but I was pretty certain that it was not only possible but likely. Moreover, I wondered how any religious fundamentalists who believed that the Earth was literally a few thousand years old, the center of the universe, and the only place where God created life could ignore the plain and undeniable facts supporting the contrary.

Like deGrasse Tyson, I approach the wonders of the world with greater bias toward science than blind faith. I accept what we can know from science, am comfortable being agnostic about those things we cannot, and there is a small bit left over that I choose to believe. But your faith, religion, and ultimately what you believe is a personal matter and not worth debating in this book. I am mostly curious about those things you believe that play a role in your happiness—or as is more often the case, your unhappiness. Your faith plays an important role in how you think about happiness and the suffering you are willing to endure because you believe a greater happiness is promised. Let me offer up two final and personal examples that may resonate.

THE GREAT PROMISE IN DEATH (AMERICAN SLAVERY)

When the Dutch, Portuguese, English, and other European people brought enslaved Africans to the US a few hundred years ago and forced them to give up their culture, language, families, and freedom, these enslaved people struggled to maintain any sense of humanity and hope. I am African American, and my ancestors were beaten, mutilated, killed, and made to work until they literally died. Everything you might associate with hell, here on Earth or in the life after, was what African people experienced in America for hundreds of years. Even after the Emancipation Proclamation in 1863 and the liberation of enslaved people from institutional slavery, African Americans continued to experience lynching, humiliation, terrorism, and a host of horrors—some of which continue in practice and haunt this nation even today.

In the traditions of African American beliefs, faith in God helped us endure these horrific times. It was not just the benevolence of Quakers or abolitionists, or even the heroic efforts of freedom fighters and civil rights leaders such as Harriet Tubman, Frederick Douglas, and later, Dr. Martin Luther King, Jr., that saw us through; it was our belief in a true and merciful God. The same God who delivered the Jews out of Egypt brought us out of the cotton fields of Georgia, where my ancestors were enslaved and toiled. As enslaved people, we appropriated the God of our enslavers, the Christians, and found comfort and resonance in many of the stories, such as the deliverance of Jewish slaves from bondage. It gave us hope and made meaning of the meaningless.

Similarly, those who enslaved my ancestors also found comfort in the Bible's description of master and slave relationships, as a way to justify enslavement as normal and even ordained by God. Everyone found what they needed to find in the stories to justify their own ends. Everyone could sleep a bit better at night knowing that God favored them, now or in the future, and that happiness was promised.

But the most powerful belief system was rooted in the idea that, although in this life I might not see freedom or happiness, in death I would. In death, I would be reunited with my family, my dignity, and my God. It was this belief that brought the greatest hope, joy, and maybe happiness for enslaved people who had little elsewhere. This faith was forged out of both necessity and early African cultural and theistic traditions. We created a salvation and deliverance type of God and negotiated the realities of an unbearable life in exchange for a great promise in death.

It's powerful to imagine how valuable in day-to-day life the belief in the afterlife was to people who had no way to verify or validate its existence—until they died. I can't even begin to imagine. But while the thought makes me sad and angry, it also makes me proud that my ancestors could create something from nothing. They made hope from the hopeless and found comfort where there were only pain and discomfort.

In the more than 160 years since the Emancipation Proclamation, Black Americans continue to hold a powerful relationship with faith. Some of the traditions that gave enslaved people hope and comfort are just as integral to our culture and survival instincts today. "Won't He do it?" as we commonly say about God. We still believe that God, the one who delivered us from slavery, is capable of making us wealthy, healing us from cancer, getting our mortgage application approved, getting the falsely accused off death row, or getting our kids through high school and off the block. You name it. We believe God will do all the things that we ourselves are incapable of doing. I come from a community of people who, even today, say that God can make bills mysteriously disappear. God can move us out of horrible situations like He did Daniel in the lion's den. Of all the things we believe, the most powerful to me is the one that we reserve for the afterlife. Again, this is not to say it's not true. This is only to raise the question of "What if it's not? What might people do differently to ensure more of their happiness today?"

My mother believed in this future payoff. She saw to it that we did, too, as kids. We lived in church growing up. We were in church all the time. As youth, we were on the children's usher board, the children's choir, on the camera staff (we attended a large church that filmed and broadcasted sermons), and everything else you can imagine. We were in church during the weekdays for revival, at banquets for the pastor's appreciation, on every retreat, lock-in, and all the things.

Church and religion were also the way we spoke about everyday things. If something bad happened to us, it was likely a sign of the Devil at work. If misfortune fell onto someone we knew, it was either God's will or his wrath. My mother, long before society became a lot more open-minded to differ-ent lifestyles, sexual orientations, and the like, would say things I considered to be homophobic. I don't know what her deep feelings were about sexual orientation, but I do remember her saying homosexuality originated from a spirit. My mom would also say things in passing that suggested that a spirit could inhabit a host, unknowingly, and take control. Spirits could lead you to be selfish, greedy, or even gay.

I grew up in a world where God and the Devil could be the answers for anything. This included that my success in high school was God's grace. My admittance to MIT and ultimate graduation years later was because I was anointed and favored by God. I believed it. I also believed my mom, when I seriously considered dropping out of college, that the Devil was trying to trick me out of my blessings. I just needed to have faith and trust not into my own understanding, and I would be delivered. And voilà, whenever I was delivered (or made it through a tough period), I attributed such deliv-erance to God. If I ever was healed from a sickness, it was proof that God was at work. If I ever got a few extra dollars in my bonus, it was proof that God favored me. If my car narrowly avoided an accident, His angels were watching over me.

The opposite was also true. If I was struggling in my career or relationship,

I needed to submit it to prayer and draw closer to the Lord. If I was sick, I was lacking faith. If misfortune fell on me, it was a sign from God. You can probably imagine why it took many years, significant introspection, pain, research, soul searching, and therapy to make sense of and find my own truth in the universe. Truth be told, I am still searching.

However, my mom believed these things until her final days. When my mom discovered she had cancer, her faith kept her strong. Since she was a deaconess in her church, she had the benefit of preachers, ministers, and the bishop himself who would come visit her in the hospital. At the time, I wanted to believe in their prayers. They often brought oil and anointed her head, laid hands on her as they touched, agreed, and prayed to God. My mom believed in their prayers, and I did too. Her husband, against my and her family's wishes, declined a more aggressive chemotherapy for my mother because he believed that "she was in God's hands." Although the surgeons, oncologist, and doctors told my mother she had less than a year to live, she died just two or three weeks after the doctor's prognosis, and all of these churchgoers came and pronounced their faith and her healing.

After she died, I could not make sense of it. My mom had believed more than anyone I knew and so did all of the people who visited her. I later learned about something called confirmation bias. In confirmation biases, no matter what happens, we will look for the parts of the story that confirm the bias that we had. In the case of my mom, I realize that had she been healed, it would've been proof that God works. However when she died, it was proof of yet another thing that believers often share:

"We do not understand God's ways."

"It is His will for her to go home to glory."

"He wanted her to rest and not feel any pain."

"God works in mysterious ways."

Upon those reflections, I realized that it did not matter what actually happened, we were committed to believing what we want and need to believe to feel at peace. We needed to believe that the future happiness promise was true—even if it came after death.

I know it is deeply offensive to some to even suggest that these promises may not be true, but they do not need to be true or false for what I am advocating to make sense. My call to action as it relates to faith and your happiness sacrifices is quite simple: Think for yourself. Ask yourself if the future promise of happiness justifies whatever sacrifice you're making today. If it does, right on. If it does not, it is up to you and only you to figure out what makes sense.

REFLECTION QUESTIONS

1. In your own life, how has a belief system (religious or otherwise) functioned as a source of hope or comfort during difficult or seemingly meaningless times?

2. When facing challenges or pain, what specific "future payoff" of happiness—either in the afterlife or in a distant future—do you tend to rely on? How does this reliance impact your current approach to navigating hardship? Are there any specific sacrifices you are currently making in your life (time, energy, relationships, health) that are based on an anticipated future reward?

3. If you came to believe that the future payoff was either not true or unlikely, what actions might you take today if you shifted your focus from a future promise to maximizing your present-day happiness and fulfillment?

4. What is one action you can take right now to challenge a belief or sacrifice that no longer serves your pursuit of happiness, ensuring you are living a life of purpose and joy today, rather than deferring it for an uncertain future?

CHAPTER 13

IF ONLY WE BELIEVED WHAT WE SAY WE BELIEVE

"God works in mysterious ways."

—Unknown

Why is it so hard for us to shake some ancient beliefs loose even when they may not make sense to our modern sensibilities or there are little basis and evidence for its truth? Some of our religious beliefs have been with us so long that we don't even know when and where they originate. People view many of these beliefs as fact in part because they have survived for so long. It's curious how some ideas survive time in spite of individual and collective interrogation, not because of them.

It is likely that something you believe was long ago told to someone, who told someone, who told another, and which was told to someone generations later, and finally to you. No one even knows where it originally began or how to audit its truth. Just as we do with supposed truths shared over the Internet, we assume if everyone has seen it, reshared, and posted it on social media that it must be true. To that scary point, as became alarmingly concerning during recent US elections, more than 54 percent of Americans get their news from social media. According to the Pew Research Center,[1] about one-third of Americans get their news from Facebook and YouTube. Following the 2024 presidential elections and Donald Trump's return to office, Mark Zuckerberg, CEO of Meta, said he would reduce censorship of inflammatory or false news on Facebook and Instagram.

In an era where the mere mention of "fake news" makes us suspicious of things that could be easily verified, we are loath to believe facts that do not conform with our worldview. Moreover, we are willing to contort ourselves into believing things that are obviously not true. We are living in a time I refer to as societal cognitive dissonance. Still, there is a large swath of Americans and citizens of the world who seek truth, embrace facts and science, and respect, support, and value the role of the independent journalist.

For much of human history, however, we did not have objective sources to report world and local events, nor were we encouraged to be critical thinkers of what we learned or heard. In the past five decades, the global literacy rate among adults has grown from 67 percent in 1976 to 87 percent in 2022.[2] In Biblical times, however, numerous scholars reported that fewer than 2 percent of the population was literate. So the illiteracy rates in Jesus's world were somewhere around 98 percent.[3] Before 1500, when Christianity spread and held an iron grip on every aspect of life, fewer than 20 percent of the European population was literate.[4]

Unfortunately, the origins of many beliefs that started then still remain with us today. They were fashioned and proclaimed during periods when people were mostly illiterate, unempowered, and unable to challenge the edicts that came from the top without risking punishment or death. The cement was allowed to cure and harden for centuries before the emergence of critical thinking, literacy, and a free press. High illiteracy rates mostly benefited the elite, wealthy, and powerful—at the expense of the commoners' happiness and right to pursue it.

Beliefs and their corresponding doctrines concerning everyday life and the pursuit of happiness were handed down from the powerful, political, and elite priestly (and papal) classes who were driven as much by their strategic and economic expansion motivations as they were by theistic ones. The Palestinian Sadducees and Pharisees are great examples. They were notorious for using their access to God and the temple, and backroom dealing with their Roman occupiers, to keep control, exert influence, and maintain a privileged existence over their mostly illiterate and poor Jewish subjects.

Imagine if the events of these ancient times happened today—but this time with the benefit of independent journalism and objective news sources. How might you view them? Imagine a *New York Times* investigative journalist exposing the money laundering, backroom deals, and hypocrisy that might have happened (according to the Gospels of the Bible) in the Hebrew temples of that day. How might people, who were already suspicious of their rule, have felt empowered to protest their religious leaders? Or what if investigative journalists, such as Bob Woodward, who famously broke the story of Watergate and went on to write numerous books on the inner workings of many administrations, had been alive when these sacred events were happening? How might his articles and books validate or invalidate what you believe?

According to the book of Genesis, Abraham left his home in Haran—just north of modern-day Syria—around 2000 BCE because he believed God called him to found a new nation in what was then Canaan, modern-day Israel/Palestine. The story goes on to describe how God instructed Abraham's descendants, specifically Joshua, to take possession of an occupied land and to kill all the people who lived there and to take their livestock, treasure, and homes. So the God of Abraham, Jesus, and Muhammad—lest it is not clear to anyone—called for explicit genocide, destruction, and theft.

It reads in the New International Version:

Joshua 11

⁶The Lord said to Joshua, "Do not be afraid of them, because by this time tomorrow I will hand all of them, slain, over to Israel. You are to hamstring their horses and burn their chariots."

⁷So Joshua and his whole army came against them suddenly at the Waters of Merom and attacked them, ⁸and the Lord gave them into the hand of Israel. They defeated them and pursued them all the way to Greater Sidon, to Misrephoth Maim, and to the Valley of Mizpah on the east, until no survivors were left. ⁹Joshua did to them as the Lord had directed: He hamstrung their horses and burned their chariots . . .

¹¹Everyone in it they put to the sword. They totally destroyed them, not sparing anyone that breathed, and he burned Hazor itself.

¹²Joshua took all these royal cities and their kings and put them to the sword. He totally destroyed them, as Moses the servant of the Lord had commanded . . .

¹⁴The Israelites carried off for themselves all the plunder and livestock of these cities, but all the people they put to the sword until they completely destroyed them, not sparing anyone that breathed. ¹⁵As the Lord commanded his servant Moses, so Moses commanded Joshua, and Joshua did it; he left nothing undone of all that the Lord commanded Moses . . .

²⁰For it was the Lord himself who hardened their hearts to wage war against Israel, so that he might destroy them totally, exterminating them without mercy, as the Lord had commanded Moses . . .

²²No Anakites were left in Israelite territory; only in Gaza, Gath and Ashdod did any survive.

²³So Joshua took the entire land, just as the Lord had directed Moses, and he gave it as an inheritance to Israel according to their tribal divisions. Then the land had rest from war.

How might this passage, which is the foundation of the three major faiths and their countless wars, be viewed if it happened today? I imagine Anderson Cooper's TV show *Keeping Them Honest* might report God's promise to Abraham a bit differently than how the stories are told in millions of Sunday schools and temples around the world. The world might be a bit more critical of the events—if not outraged. Some might call it genocide (Joshua's unprovoked attack and murder of the Canaanites) or perhaps insist on a war crimes tribunal. Like today, when these types of incursions happen, country leaders from around the world might give impassioned speeches at the United Nations, insisting that the world intervene. Even if there was not legal or military intervention, Joshua would probably be called a madman for killing tribes of men, women, and children because of an alleged voice that he, and only he, heard. College students would protest and insist that their universities divest from the region and demand their governments place sanctions on the newly created nation. You get the point.

Why is it that because these events happened thousands of years ago, we give them a pass on being critiqued? While I could pick any number of ancient stories from the Quran, New Testament, or Hebrew Bible that would make this point, I chose this one because they all share this concept, and it has been the basis of so much pain, conflict, and unhappiness. It's also a story I once believed reflected God's will and accepted it as fact. Today, however, I for one have no idea what really happened and do not care to weigh in on ages-old holy wars. There is zero upside in doing so and only massive downside. But I posit it as an intellectual exercise.

Here's another example of a biblical story and how it might read differently if you were reading about it in modern media:

> Today we are reporting live from Damascus. Paul, the man formerly known as Saul, is recovering after suffering a heat stroke on his horse ride from Palestine to Syria, hospital officials say. The incident happened while he was en route to arrest followers of a new religious sect called The Way. Since Paul gained consciousness, he says he saw God, and more specifically the recently crucified Jesus, who inspired The Way's movement, according to early reports. You will recall that Jesus of Nazareth, who many say is the Jewish savior, continues to be mourned by his closest followers for suffering the execution at the hands of the Roman state. Paul says that his vision of Jesus told him to take a new message to the Gentiles of Greece, Turkey, and Rome, contrary to the firsthand accounts of teachings to his disciples and followers. Paul's self-proclaimed title of "apostle" is being met with hostility and rejection by James, Jesus's brother. We will continue to follow this story.

If this happened today, chances are the Internet would light up with memes and gifs about Paul. We would not take the word of a man who people heard suffered from heat stroke, dehydration, or a host of other illnesses. The fact that a man claiming to have visions and hear voices would become the basis for a religion with billions of followers is interesting, to say the least. People today would question his motivation at best or simply write him off as another crazy religious zealot. So why do we hold these stories with such conviction?

Today, we would probably need to see a livestream of Muhammad's ascension into Heaven before anyone would believe it. Even then, there would certainly be claims that someone rigged the footage or it was an AI-created reel. So why do many Muslims around the world believe Muhammad's ascension today?

How would people view a young New York boy named Joseph Smith, if he said God and Jesus appeared to him in the woods over the weekend and said all of the other religious beliefs were wrong and commanded him to start a new faith, The Church of Latter-Day Saints?

In current times, ironically, we are as suspicious of facts and science as we are vulnerable to untruths that are perpetuated via social media. Any proclamations from individuals claiming to possess unique knowledge and spiritual insights might be met with both criticism and fanfare, perhaps making us no different than we might have been hundreds or thousands of years ago. Perhaps literacy and free press would not have benefited our ancestors any more than they do those who prefer to get their news from Facebook. And finally, there might at least be some measure of critical thinking and analysis from a subset of the population, as I am sure there was in ancient times as well.

The question for you is: What would you believe, and why? Are your beliefs your own, or have you readily accepted beliefs of someone else's— perhaps someone who lived thousands of years ago—without proper interrogation? Of those beliefs, which inform, shape, and give rise to your happiness or unhappiness? Which of them contributes to world peace, and which contributes to world pain, conflict, and chaos?

REFLECTION QUESTIONS

1. What is a significant belief you hold about life, success, or morality that you've never critically questioned?

2. When you examine the origins of this belief, is it based on empirical evidence, personal experience, or inherited tradition? How do you currently verify information in the age of "fake news," and are you equally rigorous in applying that verification process to your oldest beliefs?

3. How does the potential widespread acceptance of this belief influence your own sense of its truth? Would you still hold this belief if you were the only person who did?

CHAPTER 14

PARENTS, PREACHERS, AND POLITICIANS

*"When God wants to speak and deal with us,
he does not avail himself of an angel but of parents,
or the pastor, or of our neighbor."*

—**Martin Luther**

Not everything we believe today comes from dubious, ancient, or distant sources. Many of the people and institutions that seek to give us instruction and guidance do so from a basis of good intention. Humans have accumulated wisdom and institutional knowledge in books, schools, and oral traditions. We don't start from scratch with each generation but rather build upon the experiences of generations and generations before us. The scientific method and the recording of peer-reviewed research allow us to categorize some things as fact until they can be proven otherwise. In areas where the scientific method is not practical or possible, philosophy and consensus can prove useful.

There are several people we typically turn to for wisdom in our communities: parents, preachers, teachers, and politicians. We generally look to these people for truth and assume they have good intentions. Further, the relationship we share with these people evolves from a "push" in our early lives to a "pull" as we get older. As children, we don't always seek out our parents' wisdom, in part because it typically means not doing what we want (staying up and out late, eating all the candy we want, and so on) or worse, the wisdom is reinforced with spankings and punishment. It's *pushed* onto us. Later, as we mature, teachers (and parents) are a hybrid source of wisdom. We are sometimes curious about classroom topics, while bored in others. It's both a push and pull relationship. Finally, as we become adults, we may desire understanding and seek out answers about the world around us from our preachers and politicians. We now have a *pull* relationship.

There is a term that the US Army coined "VUCA world." The acronym stands for environments characterized by volatility, uncertainty, complexity, and ambiguity. The more we experience VUCA, the more susceptible and open we are to preachers and politicians, who often make sense of economic recessions, wars, disease, and societal hardships.

Meanwhile, some of the beliefs that have been running on autopilot in our brains for years are those that came from our early childhood programming. They are like the default software that comes with hardware, such as those on your laptop and smartphones. We are vulnerable to the convictions that were placed in our heads when we were young because we do not have reason to reject them or do not have other lived experiences to offer contrary points of view. Sometimes as adults, we realize that we never revisited these default software configurations to make sure they are actually valid.

In the case of my iPhone, for example, I don't often revisit all the apps I downloaded (and forgot about) until the performance of the phone slows down and I need to free up space, or I happen to notice that I am paying a subscription for an app or service I don't even need. Although the GarageBand application has come preloaded on every MacBook I have purchased in the past decade, I have neither used it nor bothered to delete it. I literally just looked (as I was writing this) and realized that it was taking up 1.2GB of space on my Mac—delete!

Our beliefs are similar. It's not until we experience some discomfort, pain, confusion, or worse that we are compelled to do an audit of the belief apps we have on our hard drives. Sometimes it is easy enough to just delete them if they no longer serve us, while in other cases it takes therapy to find all the hidden apps and their reference codes and files hiding out of plain view.

The beliefs that we willingly download from the spiritual app store are those that we often get later in life as we seek out answers. But even those need to be more closely inspected, revisited, and audited as we learn and are exposed to new information.

I've designed this book to encourage you to scan your hard drive and identify the apps (beliefs) that take up the greatest amount of storage and processing capacity and delete the ones that are not useful. This is of course easier said than done. Some beliefs are tricky to undo because they have become so intricately tied to our identities, egos, and ways of life. Other beliefs are hard to shake because they continue to be reinforced by society and social media. Regardless of whether our beliefs were unknowingly or per invitation placed on our hard drive by someone we trust and love, we have a responsibility to do an occasional audit. These beliefs can not only rob us of our happiness but be harmful to others. Let's take a closer look at each source.

PARENTS

Your first understanding of the world around you was likely brought into focus by your parents. If not your biological parents, then perhaps your surrogate parents. Those who fed, clothed, and kept you safe likely earned the permission, and the responsibility, of arming you with the first dos and don'ts of the world you knew. It could have been as simple and necessary as instructing you to look both ways before crossing the street, not playing with fire and electricity, or not eating too much candy before bed. These were the type of lessons our parents were entrusted to imprint. In time, basic safety and care might have been replaced with more complex instructions and values. We often are first introduced to biases in race, religion, and gender through what is passively and actively discussed in our family surroundings. But we don't always know how to guard ourselves from ideas that may not serve us in the future.

Our parents often do what they do from a place of love and their own convictions, which were likely passed down from their parents. As an example, I can remember developing views of police officers from just observing how nervous they made my parents when we drove by them. I remember noticing how my parents' bodies would stiffen with nervousness when a police car happened to be behind us on the highway, even though we had no obvious reason to be fearful. I later in life found myself doing the same.

Previously, I reflected on how my mother, in her strict religious orientation, passed on her biases to me, which I later found to be a source of blind spots and ignorance in my own life. Similarly, I never even considered a political party other than the Democrats, because that was the only party ever discussed in my household, family, and community. Today, although I generally affiliate with the Democratic Party, I consider myself to be a moderate or center-left (seeing some value in both center-left and center-right policies).

Similarly, as a youth, it never occurred to me that there was any other pathway to God outside of Christianity, as that was the language, culture, and worldview of my household. Today, I consider myself to be agnostic and more spiritual. I had to intentionally replace my default political and faith applications with newer, more appropriate apps of my choosing. However, let's take a closer look at some of the mental apps that are installed by our parents and early communities.

Race Apps

I grew up in a Black neighborhood, school, church, and community. I never had much exposure to other races, ethnicities, and cultures until college. My mother grew up in the segregated South and instilled a fear of White terrorism, which was still visible to us, even in my childhood. My grandmother shared stories of the Klan burning crosses in her front yard as a child and her sister, my great-aunt, coming home afraid because she didn't give up her seat on the bus and feared retribution.

When I was young, the KKK still marched a few miles north of my neighborhood, the Confederate cross still marked our Georgia state flag (until 2003), and I remember watching on TV in high school, along with millions of others, as Rodney King was beaten to near death by the Los Angeles police. So I saw with my own eyes that my mother's nervousness about being Black in America was not an overaction. I did not have many personal experiences in my childhood that offset the ones that shaped the race-influenced worldview of my mother. Of course, TV shows such as *Leave It to Beaver*, *Family Ties*, and *Silver Spoons* offered counterviews of how joyful, happy, and loving White America lived, but those were clearly not the experiences that I knew firsthand. My first "Race App" program ran fear, anger, and hypervigilance. It still runs today, more or less, the way it was intended to fifty years ago.

Faith Apps

My aunt Brenda was a deeply spiritual person and like a surrogate mother to me. She spent countless hours having me read the Bible and sharing visions that she believed God gave her for me. I was shaped by her views that God was mystical and still moved in the ways of the ancients, capable of calling lowly people to achieve great things. She would pour positive messages into me for most of my childhood and young adult years, proclaiming that God had a mighty and important purpose for me.

For most of those years, I didn't feel so special. In fact, I suffered from extreme depression as a teen and attempted suicide at least two times, that I can remember. I was likely depressed because my father had left us, and my mother's misery had led her to take refuge in substance abuse for much of my childhood. Despite her love and insistence on us having a good education and strong spiritual foundation, my brother and I struggled with the volatility, verbal abuse, and chaos that often filled our home. We sought our own refuge in school, art, and music. We couldn't physically get away, so we went inward.

Faith, an early app on my hard drive, gave me what would become my first understanding of resilience in the face of suffering. But this app would later cause me issues and create shame, guilt, and internal conflict. I discussed this strife in greater detail earlier in this section, but suffice to say, this was an app that I more recently found difficult to tweak or just update, as I tried to do in my thirties and early forties. I had to delete and load a new app that encourages curiosity over conviction.

Love Apps

My mother remarried and had a tumultuous relationship with her second husband, which added to the craziness my brother and I experienced as kids. My mother's love language was service. She would cook, take us to school, and make sure we had what we needed for school. However, I do not recall experiencing as much of the other love languages, such as touch and affection, words of affirmation, or significant quality time. Later, I struggled to show up whole and healthy in my own romantic relationships given what I knew to be normal. Of course, it was only later that I learned from my aunts and uncles that my mother was only showing up the way her mother had shown up for her. This "love app" was generations in the making—and it needed to be updated. I now feel like touch and time are as much my love languages as is service.

Our parents mean well, and they are responsible for installing the initial apps on our hard drive. However, not all of it is healthy, even if it comes from a place of love. It would take me years of therapy, introspection, exposure, and a curiosity for other views to inform, if not undo, much of my early programming. In other cases, I chose to deepen my embrace of the ideas and values I found worthy of cerebral hard-disk space.

I once did a ten-day retreat where the attendees were asked to cut themselves off from the world—no phones, email, or contact with the outside. We were secluded in the forests of northern California for nearly two weeks of difficult and intense self-work. I won't go into much detail about the program, but the basis of the work centered on our "negative love patterns" that we developed as young teens. We learned that many of our most consequential challenges as adults stemmed from the unmet needs of our childhood and our need to resolve, forgive, and heal the wounds from our relationships (or lack thereof) with our parents. At the conclusion of the program, we participated in a ceremony where we forgave our parents and fostered compassion for not only our inner child but the inner child of our parents. We learned how these patterns recycle in our lives and, if we're not careful, get passed down generation to generation.

I am convinced that so much of our unhappiness comes from not deprogramming some of these early patterns that took root in our lives as children. Whether you engage in self-work on a retreat or simply begin with simpler reflections and introspections on your convictions, the path to happiness begins with first making sure your belief and value apps are yours, and not your parents'.

TEACHERS

My most formidable experiences, outside of those first and most impressionable ones in my household, were in school with my teachers. Teachers are some of the first adults we give permission to download apps onto our hard drive. Some of it comes in the way of basic educational instruction, such as math, science, history, and the like. Others come in the way of values, modeled behaviors, and even how they treat and see you, which shapes how you see yourself. The most powerful teachers are likely the ones who felt their calling was to do more than teach.

I attended a Black Catholic school from first to sixth grade. I was fortunate to have teachers who really cared. I can still remember my first-grade teacher, Miss Rivers, who would tell my mom she thought I was special and had potential. She was also my first crush. I can also remember Miss Mitchell, Miss Crawford, Miss Rouse, and Miss Lyons. Miss Lyons, my sixth-grade teacher, stands out because of her insistence on teaching the horrors of the trans-Atlantic slave trade. I am quite sure this lesson was not in our textbook, but she felt it critical for a classroom of young Black boys and girls to know this history. I can say for sure that her teachings would go on to instill my deep and lasting love for history and truth, even when I had no idea that was happening. Our teachers can also imprint us with ideas, views, and values that may not serve us later. These ideas are likely buried deep in our subconscious.

I was in the "gen pop" class with students of all types when I transitioned to a public middle school in the seventh grade. It was still an all-Black school. Like most public schools, mine had some of the most gifted, upwardly mobile, solidly middle-class kids, while other kids in my school sold drugs, got into fights, or were rudderless. They were just there. When I first transitioned to this school, I was just another kid with a slightly troubled home life. I might have looked more like the kids in the second batch than the first. I got into my fair share of fights, had a bad temper, and was not particularly good in school. I can even remember one fight that led to me having a gun put to my head by another kid in my class. I was probably on a one-way street to being another statistic, and I did not realize it.

But then it changed. I had a teacher who thought I had potential (unbeknownst to me) and insisted that I be transferred to the "smart kids group." I don't remember whether it was Group 5 or Group 1, but these kids were different. They played board games, read books, and were kind of nerdy. I liked them and made friends that would last me for decades to come. The following year in high school, I went from being one of the most unremarkable kids to making straight A's each year for all four years. Well, I did earn one B in trigonometry that cost me the valedictorian seat and, instead, landed me a co-salutatorian honor.

My high school teachers required excellence. They were tough and demanding but also nurturing. It was my calculus teacher, Mrs. Turner, who suggested that I attend a college briefing in the cafeteria with a Massachusetts Institute of Technology (MIT) recruiter. I had never heard of MIT. But a year later, that's where I went. My high school teachers made me proud of my inner nerd and encouraged it, celebrated me (and many others like me), and would heap my accomplishments onto the growing pile of other high school alums who made it to Harvard, Brown, Stanford, US military academies, as well as our finest HBCUs such as Spelman, Howard, and Morehouse, to name a few. From that point, I had confidence in myself and knew I could succeed at whatever I desired. That in itself brought me happiness.

But there were limits. My happiness was largely wrapped in the idea of being one of the "talented tenth" and successful. I was a casebook example of someone living with the "Golden Child Syndrome." We were hardwired for the success/validation self-worth loop, but we suffered from a deep fear of failure and inadequacy. I thought only about pleasing and succeeding, not about happiness or fulfillment.

Plus, there was a practical aspect to this app that our teachers dutifully placed on our hard drives. I might be able to escape the rough life that I experience every day, if I could leverage my academic talents for a one-way ticket to a better life. I fantasized about living like the characters on the popular 1980s sitcoms, *The Cosby Show* and *A Different World*. Happiness, if that's what it was, would come from being the African American dream: Getting an education, a "good" job, marrying a beautiful woman who, too, was successful, having two-point-five kids, and living in a picturesque upper-middle-class neighborhood.

In her book *Respectability*, Boston University professor Saida Grundy, PhD, chronicles how institutions such as Morehouse helped manufacture this image of the mainstream, assimilated, "perfect" Black man that we sought to be. I had never devoted the slightest thought to anything else—and for good reason. Anything above and beyond that was gravy. Our teachers loaded this program onto our hard drives like Morpheus did for Neo in *The Matrix*. They were building the future saviors of our race—not happy individuals. Perhaps because they, and we all, assumed that the two were one and the same.

Shortly after arriving at MIT, I realized that I was less interested in math and science, like I had been primed by my teachers to believe, but rather I was drawn to economics, political science, psychology, history, and people. I was a class president, deeply involved in my fraternity, and a bigger-than-life socialite. I was more likely to organize a student trip to the Million Man March in Washington, DC—which I did—than stay up late studying statistics—which I did far less. I pivoted majors from engineering to business, with plans of ultimately doing something in consulting, law, or politics.

I had no idea which path was best for me, but I knew it wasn't engineering. MIT professors taught STEM better than perhaps any other college or university—but they were ill-equipped to teach how to pursue your authentic path or happiness. In fact, I often felt inadequate because I chose not to major in engineering or a hard science (MIT had an unwritten hierarchy for the easiest to the hardest majors that earned you respect). I was Course 15, a management of information science major, which was viewed as a fluffy major by most other MIT students—myself included. My advisor, who I thought might have been either racist or very unenthused by my potential, cautioned that I was not a strong enough writer to make it in law school. *Damn,* I thought to myself. *What advisor discourages a student like that?* So I figured I would graduate, work, and figure it out later.

Note: I never considered being a lawyer ever again. I would have to figure out my path mostly through osmosis and observation. Despite being left alone to discover my professional path, my teachers and professors had done their job. Their app was basic and well-intentioned but significantly limited in terms of connecting me to my calling, my authentic self, and my happiness.

PREACHERS

When I was a little older, I graduated from "children's church" to actually attending Sunday service as a young teen with my mom and all the adults. This was actually not a good thing. In the children's church, housed in the building annexed to the church main sanctuary, I could goof off and expect that the Sunday school teachers would serve us kiddos cookies and juice to keep the inmates from getting restless. In exchange, all I had to do was occasionally demonstrate that I could remember Bible verses, play Bible trivia games, and recite the Lord's Prayer. But I did not have to sit still under my mom's gaze, doing my best to keep from falling asleep.

As a young adult, however, I was surprised to find that I enjoyed the sermons in the adult church, even if it was just a form of entertainment. I could expect the preacher to go from a slow and methodical introduction of a story in the Bible, graduating to repetition, emphasis, and with an elevated voice, on to stomping, hollering, and sweating, every so often wiping his brow with a hand towel. It was also around that time when the music corner knew to chime in with punctuated snare drum taps and perfectly pitched organ chords, almost to summon people from their seats for the weekly Holy Ghost dance.

I would watch in awe and often do my best to suppress giggles as elderly women might run around the church and then suddenly collapse while the ushers raised white sheets around the scene and fanned the women's brows as if to protect their last bit of dignity from onlookers like me. However, most of the sermon was less exciting. The predictable call for tithes and offering, announcements, and an invitation to join the church was formulaic, and I knew it like the back of my hand.

Later, as an adult, I looked for and sometimes found wisdom and value in the sermons. My mind would drift into daydreams that mirrored the stories that were being told of plots in the Bible that somehow lined up with the plight of my own life. As a teen and eventually a young adult, I had reverence and respect for my preachers and pastors. I imagined they had a unique access to God's wisdom, which they found ways to share with me in easily digestible stories and parables. As was typical of most Black churches, my church was as much about social, economic, and political ideas as it was theology.

It was on Sunday that I first learned and thought about the world outside of my home. Any major event, globally or locally, might be interpreted on Sunday in a way that made sense to me. I did not initially allow much of my own thinking to compete with the easily laid-out revelations from the preacher. I didn't focus as much on their own fallacy, hypocrisy, or shortcomings (although I was aware of them). I also willingly accepted their interpretations of race, politics, gender, and class. I welcomed and downloaded their apps.

Like teachers, I believe most of my preachers had the best of intentions and chose to believe most of what they preached. Many preachers struggled with their own human conditions, sins, and limitations in private, but I believed that most pushed through their internal conflicts to be vessels of a word they thought to be true. That was also how I initially dealt with my own internal conflicts. Focus on the part that was (or could be) the truth and ignore the rest.

But this would change over time. As I grew older, I wrestled a bit more with the apps I had either accepted from childhood or sought after as a young adult. The preachings that most impacted my happiness are the ones that led me to feel shame, guilt, and an obligation to do things that ultimately I either did not agree with or did not desire to live out. The conflict and tension between what I once believed without question and those things I later questioned in my core led me to read, research, and think critically about supposed truths from different angles and ultimately rest comfortably with the apps I chose to leave and those I chose to delete. The preacher apps have been some of the ones I have deleted in batches. It's been easier to start clean (as an agnostic) than to try to tease out the truths from the untruths. Of all the areas where I have felt unhappiness, faith and parent apps have occupied the lion's share of space.

POLITICIANS

I have always been intrigued with politics. Perhaps because I grew up in Atlanta where many of the politicians were former Civil Rights leaders, from the community, and relatable. I had a reason to pay attention. I vaguely remember seeing President Ronald Reagan when I was young, during his live, televised addresses to the country, but did not think much about what he was actually saying or what it meant for me. I had no sense for tax policies, Iran, or Mikhail Gorbachev and the dismantling of the Berlin Wall.

My life was still being shaped by parents, teachers, and preachers at that point. Politicians had not emerged as the source for answers to the complex questions of my day. That would come later.

President Bill Clinton was the commencement day speaker at MIT when I graduated. He was perhaps the first president I truly noticed, starting with his appearance on *The Arsenio Hall Show* when he played his saxophone before millions of people. Like me, I think Americans saw something and someone relatable—and cool. Those early days of his campaign would help establish a persona of a president who was one of and for the people, in poor White working-class communities and Black churches alike. That grace would serve him well in navigating a messy and public extramarital affair with Monica Lewinsky, which clouded his presidency.

President Clinton was like many of our best politicians who earned a special place in our hearts and minds. That place gave him permission to explain the VUCA of our day in a way that made sense. He could ask us to pay more in taxes, serve in wars, or otherwise make sacrifices in service of a better America.

President Barack Obama was a game changer for me. For many, his remarkable ascent to power could only be of divine intervention. President Obama was more than brilliant, articulate, and immeasurably perceptive about the issues that mattered to millions of Americans—and the world. He was uniquely possessed with an origin story and gift to have the credibility to deliver it. We looked to our president for answers on the complex and messy issues of our day, such as race relations and policing, as well as the impossible challenge of providing healthcare for millions of uninsured Americans.

Most of us had not considered why the latter had been an unsolvable math problem before. However, President Obama broke it down in a basic and intuitive way that made his naysayers appear heartless and evil (or dumb) for denying the medical necessities that could save millions from dying from cancer, provide life-saving insulin for people with diabetes, or prevent suffering in other countless ways Americans without healthcare, such as my mom, suffered.

I not only voted for President Obama, but I also donated countless times and volunteered in Georgia and South Carolina, knocking on doors and working the phone bank. I was willing to sacrifice for a chance at a better future in a post-racial America. Most Americans voted for him. Twice. We all believed. Shortly after he and his beautiful family vacated the White House, in came a polar opposite and iconic family: The Trumps.

President Trump offered his own firebrand answers to a host of challenges that some Americans thought were existential. The sentiment among some Americans was the country and their way of life were being stolen by immigrants, minorities, gay people, and liberals. It was their opinion that nothing short of absolute force would be needed to beat back the forces of technology and globalization, demographic shifts, and threats to the White working-class male birthright to being supreme over all else.

Trump was entrusted by many to address their grievances, and he capitalized on the call to action with racist dog whistles, pledges to do things (to minorities) we hadn't seen in America since the 1960s and isolate the nation from everyone in the free world. Under Trump, we would join the global gang of autocratic dictators, tyrants, and strong men–ruled countries like Russia and North Korea.

But how were both Trump and Obama able to hold such sway over the country? We, the people, gave them the power. We willingly took on their ideas and chants, from "Yes, we can" to "Build that wall." Some Americans voted for both and likely chanted both sayings. Unlike the parents and teachers in our lives, preachers and politicians were invited and empowered by us. We paid our tithes and offerings or made political donations to fund their respective platforms. We looked to them to make the world understandable when so much made no sense. We gave them the power to activate our capacity to love and hope, or to hate and anger. Our willingness to sacrifice today, by risking life and freedom and storming the US capitol on January 6, 2021, as the Proud Boys did under Trump's direction, all in service of a future where some thought they would be happier and more secure. If not them, their kids and grandkids would benefit. They were manipulated and played like pawns—and the future happiness they were promised and expected has yet to be realized.

Whether the beliefs we hold dear are those deposited early in life by our parents and teachers, or later in life by preachers and politicians, they are there. I have voted Democrat in every election that I have participated in and made countless donations over the years. I have also been an active founding member of a nonpartisan group of business leaders seeking to encourage a more positive role of corporations restoring, protecting, and promoting our democracy. I am seriously vested in our country's democracy and future. I even wonder if I, a center-left and fairly independent thinker, sometimes allow old scripts to run on autopilot without much critique.

As of late, I have been asking myself more and more, "Why do you believe that (fill in the blank . . . policy, candidate, or description of the problem)?" Sometimes when I slow down long enough to run that "disk cleanup," I find that some of those old views no longer serve me or make sense. For example, I don't think market failures are a reason for the government to get involved in every problem, as some to the left of me might believe. I actually think the private sector and free-market forces can be incredibly efficient when properly directed. I also don't think wealth is bad, nor do I believe that being poor is a virtue or vice versa.

There have been some center-right Republicans who have resonated with me. I once met and spent time with General Colin Powell, who was the Chairman of the Joint Chiefs, the Secretary of State, and National Security Advisor under President Bush. He was also a Republican that many, like me, could have felt compelled to vote for had he run for president.

I asked Powell why he had not considered getting in the race when Trump was gaining in the polls. "You would be the first GOP president I'd ever vote for if you did," I told him. He responded politely in what was likely a canned response at that point, something to the effect, that he was grateful but did not want to subject himself and his family to that life. I remember him also remarking that he was no politician.

It was just me and the general in the room at that moment, and I thought to myself, *That's exactly why you should run. I would trust you with all the apps!*

We will trust you because you are *not* a politician. We were learning not to trust politicians. Ironically, Trump would make similar claims in coming months about his trustworthiness as a nonpolitician. He would go on to win the presidential election against former US Secretary of State Hillary Clinton in one of the greatest upsets in American history. He then returned to the White House years later in 2025, in a decisive win over the nation's only second female nominee and its first woman of color. Despite Trump being a felon, liar, predator, and cheat, Americans still trusted him to install apps claiming to make Americans great and happy again.

REFLECTION QUESTIONS

1. When was the last time you consciously performed an audit of your mental hard drive?

2. What is one core belief about success, relationships, or morality—installed by your parents or early community—that you realize you have never critically revisited as an adult?

3. How has this particular default app influenced your actions and decisions in recent years? Is it currently a source of happiness or unhappiness in your life?

4. What are some early biases or values you inherited from your parents or guardians that you later found to be inconsistent with your lived experiences or modern sensibilities?

5. What narratives or "apps" have you willingly downloaded from preachers or politicians to make sense of a complex world? What sacrifices of time, resources, and emotional energy have you made in service of these narratives?

CHAPTER 15

THE DECLINE OF INSTITUTIONS

*"The fall of Rome seemed unthinkable to people
at the time but inevitable to historians reflecting upon it
with the benefit of context."*

—Attributed to Mary Pilon

For much of human history, *homo sapiens* have been building institutions. According to Yuval Noah Harari in *Sapiens: A Brief History of Humankind*, our ancestors underwent a series of transitions and transformations, from developing "shared myths" that allowed for large-scale cooperation, to developing sophisticated languages during our "cognitive revolution" (70,000 years ago), to farming and harvesting food at scale which significantly increased our population (12,000 years ago), which ultimately led to the "unification of humankind," which came from creation of universal money, religion, and political structures. Since some of the earliest kingdoms, scripts, and money some 5,000 years ago,[1] we've been giving our power, our riches, and our rights to key decisions (and even our lives) for the sake of our institutions. Our institutions for much of recent history, in exchange for our delegated power, have watched over us, protected us, guided us, instructed us, and offered a promise of happiness.

Homo sapiens, who emerged out of Africa over 300,000 years ago, came after a six-million-year history *of Hominins, Homo erectus, Homo neanderthalensis,* and so on. In the earliest era of *Homo sapiens,* our most complex organization is thought to have been small bands and family units of hunter-gatherers. Wandering the plains of East Africa, we might have organized responsibilities in such families around key tasks such as hunting, raising young, or maybe making key decisions about where to migrate or look for food. Over time, we evolved to establish more complex organizational units like tribes and chiefdoms. With the advent of farming and the domestication of animals for food, more complex organizations to support the allocation of work, trade, hunting, and governance evolved. I can imagine tribes beget states and states beget empires and so on. With each greater level of organizational complexity and sophistication, we would have greater demands placed on the least of them, the working classes, to support the warring class, to support a governing class that ruled over them.

THE RISE OF INSTITUTIONS

While the ruling class (of states, empires, and so on) might have used force to codify the rules that cemented their power, there would have been some benefit that the poor and working class would have expected in return. It might have been to make key decisions regarding pleasing their gods, military planning, and provision to protect the people from neighboring invaders—or maybe storing and allocating food to ensure their future. Perhaps more aggressive rulers sought to expand their reign and organized campaigns to conquer near and far lands, as did the Vikings, Mayans, and Yoruba nations, as an example. The least of the nations might have benefited from the plunder and loot that would have been returned to enrich not only the ruling class, but those closest to them in their nation's caste system.

The Romans were a great example of how effective and ruthless one nation could be at expanding its reach, rule, and revenue receipts. Roman citizens benefited from the Romans, sophisticated governance systems, transportation infrastructure, aqueducts, and access to goods from conquered lands and trade partners. Roman citizens might have also been expected to pay significant taxes and suffer penalties or death for noncompliance with Roman laws. If you happened to be a slave or lowest class of citizen, you perhaps wouldn't have enjoyed many, if any, perks at all.

In the time of Jesus, Palestinian Jews might have detested seeing their lands, temples, and the like occupied by Romans. However, Herod and some in the priest class might have enjoyed certain protections and access in exchange for their cooperation with Roman governors and Caesar himself. The institution would have been made possible and sustainable by the explicit and implicit cooperation of its citizens—from the elite to the peasant class.

These institutions only grew larger, more complex, and more expansive with Spain, the Netherlands, Great Britain, and ultimately (through imperialism), America. The methods might have evolved, but the end results were the same: Larger and more powerful entities that derive their power from the common people, either willingly or unwillingly. In his book *Age of Revelations*, author and CNN host Fareed Zakaria describes the patterns that gave rise to each of the empires—as well as their fall. For much of my life, America has been the de facto empire of our day. But it is not clear, as of this writing, if America is in a relative decline or a complete free fall. But it's hard to argue that it's not one of the two.

Setting aside the topic of rising and falling hegemony, I believe there is a broader trend at work concerning our institutions that transcends country. Within the American empire are a series of enabling and benefiting institutions, such as the government, military, church, corporations (large employers), universities, and so on. Each of these institutions have defined life as we know it in this country: Our laws, our values, our traditions, and our happiness. This can easily be said for other nations as well.

People pay taxes so that the government can provide for the well-being of the people. We work in corporate plants, factories, farms, and office buildings in exchange for wages, healthcare, and a sustainable shot at middle-class living. We pay tithes and offerings to the church for safe passage of our souls and to provide guidance around key decisions, such as family formation, sex, and maybe which humanitarian causes to support. We pay tuition to schools in exchange for education, work permits (diplomas, degrees, and certificates), and access to the workforce. None of these institutions would exist if we did not work for them, pay taxes to them, serve them, donate to them, and even, in the case of the military, give our lives for them. Likewise, we would not enjoy many of the benefits that we've come to expect from them in return.

The other big benefit of institutions to people has been stability, continuity, and identity. Our belonging to an institution empowers and informs our identity as individuals. Many in my family, on my father's side, were union workers in Detroit. Being a union worker and belonging to a work institution was a source of pride as much as it was a source of leverage in negotiating with corporations for fair wages and better work conditions. Being American has been a big source of pride for most citizens as it was a source of envy of onlookers in other countries who watched TV and marveled at our way of life, our wealth, our innovation, and, ultimately, our self-proclaimed supremacy. Belonging to the American institution was and is a major identity. Being a Marine, a Harvard alum, an Irish Catholic, and so on are all examples of institutional identities that have and continue to, in some cases, carry significant meaning.

In recent years, however, I have noticed an interesting trend. The power and influence of these institutions are waning. They are becoming less important to younger generations and are seemingly less capable of demanding as much of us as they once did easily. They are less effective at extracting dues, service, loyalty, and new members than they did for generations prior. You don't need to look further than the declining membership in churches and unions, the rise of gig work versus traditional work tenure, and the decline of trust in government.

It is possible that I am living during a time of a relative decline, and not an overall secular decline that will be sustained. Had I been an elite Roman citizen at its peak and subsequent decline, I might have imagined the end of society and a different and more dreadful future than the one that emerged in the following centuries.

More recently, in the 1970s, the American youth (Baby Boomers) were antiwar and antimilitary and suspicious of their government. That season was defined by a weakened US autocracy, as reflected in prior key events such as President Nixon's resignation and President Kennedy's assassination. African Americans shortly after 1865 might have held great hope and respect for the US government as the Union soldiers occupied the South and helped usher in the Reconstruction era. This hope and respect for the institution would have been short-lived and declined as the Union troops left the South, President Andrew Jackson replaced President Lincoln, and Jim Crow and KKK terrorists put in place new institutions that replaced slavery.

There are also examples of isolated civilizations and empires that disappeared in what seems like a flicker of the eye. In *Collapsed: How Societies Choose to Fail or Succeed*, Jared Diamond describes with great clarity the fall of the Viking and Mayan civilizations as examples. Had we been Mayan or Norse citizens, it might have felt as if the world was coming to an end . . . even if humans in other parts of the world experienced just the opposite. This is all to say and acknowledge that the power and influence of institutions might rise and fall like sea levels.

However, just as sea levels are rising because of climate change, it is hard to argue that some trends are persisting beyond normal cycles and patterns. There was once a time when the Pope of the Catholic Church would have issued an edict or made a big statement on something during a televised speech or prayer. Catholics and non-Catholics alike would have listened, respected, and maybe incorporated the Church's pronouncement on issues such as birth control. Any news from the Pope would have been breaking news. Not today. The church is largely a shadow of its past in many respects. The same is true for churches in general. Few look to church leaders for answers to the world's biggest problems, or even their salvation. I am not suggesting that the church is irrelevant—far from it. But its size, influence, and command over its subjects is shrinking. According to the Gallup organization, "Americans' membership in houses of worship continued to decline last year, dropping below 50 percent for the first time in Gallup's eight-decade trend. In 2020, 47 percent of Americans said they belonged to a church, synagogue or mosque, down from 50 percent in 2018 and 70 percent in 1999."[2] Prior to 1999, the percentage had hovered around 70 percent since 1937 when Gallup first measured it at 73 percent.

Even as many still consider themselves Christians, they are more likely to look for a church, denomination, or preacher who preaches what they want to hear, rather than suffer their happiness to an institution that does not reflect their beliefs or has lost credibility in some major way.

THE FALL OF CORPORATIONS

Corporations were once places where some people worked, retired, and collected a pension—or perhaps hoped to—but the average tenure has been trending down with each generation according to public sources. Whereas Baby Boomers, born between 1946 and 1964, tend to stay at jobs an average of ten to fifteen years, Gen Xers average five to ten years, Millennials average three to five years, and Gen Z average the least, at just one to three years.[3] Likewise, less than 15 percent of private employers today offer a pension compared to 45 percent in the early 1970s when Boomers were first entering the workforce.[4] And union membership has been declining since its peak of 35 percent in 1954, to 22 percent in 1980 and 9.4 percent as of 2022.[5] Of course, it is possible that generational cohorts may evolve in their needs and preferences as they age, have children, and approach retirement age or climb in seniority, but what seems to be clear is the changing attitudes toward work.

Today, in an era defined by "the great resignation" movement during and after COVID-19, many of our best and brightest are free agents—working as gig workers at one extreme or simply job hopping every two to three years to maximize their earning potential. According to UpWork, in the United States, more than one-third of the workforce, or sixty-four million in 2023, were gig workers.[6] And according to E-Solutions, the percentage of people engaged in gig work was 50 percent of the US workforce in 2025.[7]

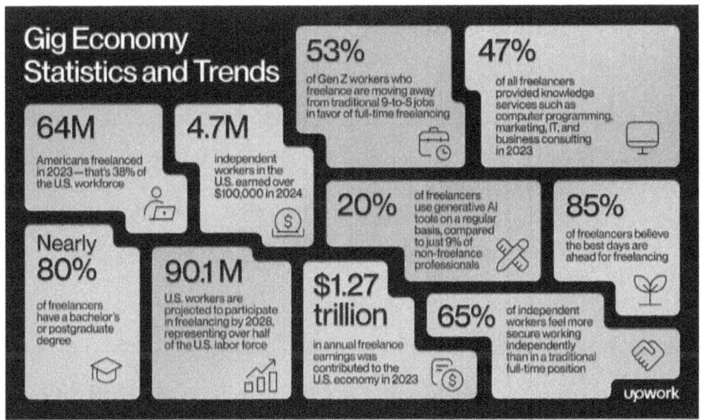

Diagram from Upwork[8]

THE FALL OF AMERICA

America is perhaps the saddest of all declines. I say this not because of the decline in its relative standing in the world, which is a different discussion (and the focus of great historical insights and books by Ray Dalio[9] and Fareed Zakaria[10]), but rather in its inability to hold together its citizens under a single and coherent identity. We've long had partisanship and the forefathers of the country warned that partisanship had the potential to undermine our democracy. According to the Library of Congress:

> Political factions or parties began to form during the struggle over ratification of the federal Constitution of 1787. Friction between them increased as attention shifted from the creation of a new federal government to the question of how powerful that federal government would be. The Federalists, led by Secretary of Treasury Alexander Hamilton, wanted a strong central government, while the Anti-Federalists, led by Secretary of State Thomas Jefferson, advocated states' rights instead of centralized power. Federalists coalesced around the commercial sector of the country while their opponents drew their strength from those favoring an agrarian society.[11]

The ensuing partisan battles led George Washington to warn of "the baneful effects of the spirit of party" in his Farewell Address as president of the United States. The full quote reads, "Let me now take a more comprehensive view and warn you in the most solemn manner against the baneful effects of the spirit of party generally." [12]

While we've continued to debate states' rights versus federal rule since the founding days, and especially during the legal battles over contentious topics, like Civil Rights, healthcare, and immigration, the level of tribalism, even within parties, is at a level today we have not seen before.

Even during the years leading up to the Civil War, one could imagine that issues defining the states that joined (or remained in) the Union or the Confederacy would have been fairly clear. Today, it is hard to see the United States as united in any meaningful way. Today, the tone and tenor of America feels as though we're on the cusp of another civil war, and not the willing subjects to a powerful, unifying institution and identity.

I am not ready to say that we are reverting back to tribes, clans, and family groups of hunter-gatherers—far from it. The complexity and agility of organizational formations crosses borders, race, class, and otherwise makes a clean sweeping narrative far too easy and simple to capture the realities of what's happening—or could happen.

Why Institutions Are Declining

It's important to note that the reason behind the decline of various institutions is varied and offers different implications for the future. I believe there are at least four examples:

1. *The Institution Is Less Effective.* Some institutional powers, such as governments, are declining because they are viewed as less effective at offering a bundle of goods that are still very much needed by individuals. These institutions are considered less effective than other emerging alternatives that offer a similar bundle of goods and services. You don't have to look far for your best example. Perhaps it was Flint, Michigan, and how the local and regional government handled the lead water crisis, or my favorite, the inability of Congress to pass important legislation. Regardless, these are just a few of many examples where and how our government is growing less effective at providing basic goods and services that people expect in exchange for their tax dollars. There is growing distrust

in the government's desire to accumulate more power and collect more taxes, as the track record appears to be worsening in the eyes of most taxpayers.

2. *The Bundle Is Less Valuable.* Other institutions are declining because what they offer is less desired or needed than in the past, even if the institution is just as effective at delivering that bundle of goods. The church is a great example. There is less demand for an institutional source for forgiveness (the confession chamber) or an interpreter of God and His will. Most churches are no less effective at administering communion, baptizing babies, marrying couples, or offering understanding and comfort for the realities of a cruel world. It's just that there is less demand for their services and other substitutes have emerged that cost nothing and require less commitment (e.g., cohabitating life partners versus religious marriages). Another example is the questionable value of a college education, particularly as it relates to the skyrocketing costs of four-year degrees. As young graduates struggle to pay their student loans with average starting salaries, many are seeking and finding a greater return on investment (ROI) in trade schools, certificate programs, and community colleges. There is still great demand (and "artificial scarcity," as Scott Galloway often describes[13]) for elite education in our Ivy League schools. However, it's hard to justify saddling oneself in hundreds of thousands of dollars in debt for a liberal arts degree from an average state school that could take decades to pay off.

3. *The Institution Is Less Interested in Offering the Bundle.* In some cases, there is an unwinding on both sides of the supply and demand equation. Corporations and labor are a great example. While it is true that labor has less interest in lifelong employment evidenced

by average work tenures getting shorter with each generation, it is also true that corporations are less loyal to labor. Layoffs are seemingly more common and inevitable, as is the spirit behind the Great Resignation. The same is true for vendors and supply chains that have links in every corner of the world that can easily be rerouted, replaced, and reduced to mitigate risk and lower cost. So the days of a corporation having a deep and undying loyalty to a neighborhood of plant workers, such as the ones in Detroit, where my father's family settled after the Great Migration, are as done as the son who goes on to work in the same plant as his father.

4. *Revolt.* In some cases the decline comes suddenly and not from any apparent change in the supply demand dynamic. It comes from a philosophical, political, or power shift that gives rise to an opposing force to the institution. The decline of British colonies, South African Apartheid, and US slavery and later Jim Crow laws are great examples of this. The decline of the institution fell after wars, intense political lobbying, and changing moods and social views. The Overton Window offers a great illustration of the latter. Something that was once thought to be a radical view can over time become not only policy but the norm (e.g., African Americans participating in the US political systems). A quote from the movie *The Fall of the Roman Empire* (1964) sums it up well: "How does an empire die? Does it collapse in one terrible moment? No. No! But there comes a time when its people no longer believe in it. Then, then does an empire begin to die."[14]

It's not clear yet if some of the key institutions that have held sway over our existence and happiness are declining with a net benefit to our individual empowerment or if we are simply channeling that power to other emerging institutions elsewhere. We will have to watch and see if old institutions get replaced with new ones, or if we revert to the older and perhaps more reliable organizational units of our ancestors.

We will also be watching for another trend, where an institution that long protected individual rights (and happiness) is intentionally dismantled from within or in collaboration with powerful minority interest groups who are quasi-institutions in and of themselves. One recent example is the recent overturning of *Roe v. Wade*. Today, a third of all women live in states where abortion is illegal or not accessible.[15]

Regardless of how we interpret these societal changes, the power we've given and the faith we've held in God, gods, and god's institutions for ensuring our happiness deserve the scrutiny that many are applying to them.

REFLECTION QUESTIONS

1. What are the key institutions (e.g., your employer, religious organization, political party, or country) to which you have given significant power or loyalty in your life?

2. What is the "cost" of your allegiance to these institutions (e.g., taxes, service, adherence to rules, emotional energy)? And what are the specific "bundles of goods" you expect in return for that cost?

3. Have you ever felt that your happiness or autonomy was sacrificed for the sake of an institution, and if so, what was the circumstance?

4. What would it look like to reduce or modify your expectations from the institutions that you look to for happiness?

WHO DO YOU LOVE?

The final leg of my happiness trifecta is "relationships"—our need for deep and meaningful connections. This is the only part of the equation that is both nature and nurture. The nurture side, shaped by culture, society, and faith, often clashes with our nature, which is where true happiness resides.

Unlike work and faith, relationships have a few other unique qualities. We often choose our spouses and serious partners well into adulthood, after we've already formed strong ideas about our beliefs and careers. We also deal with relationships individually, not in groups, as we might in a workplace or a religious setting. This makes it difficult to get objective data on how people truly feel. We can't rely on church enrollment or employee turnover figures to tell us if a relationship is working.

Because of this, our unhappiness in relationships—and the source of it—often remains hidden, even from ourselves. Unless we are truly introspective, we might be afraid to face painful truths. Love is a deeply personal concept, and we often suffer in silence when our relationships are not working.

CHAPTER 16

WHAT YOU WON'T DO FOR LOVE

"Marriage is not a noun; it's a verb."

—Attributed to Barbara De Angelis

There is significant research supporting the health benefits of humans having meaningful human connections, relationships, and love. According to research conducted by University of Pennsylvania researchers and Michael Platt, PhD, "People who have more friends or deeper friendships live longer, healthier, happier lives, and they make more money." According to another study conducted at Brigham Young University, the implications are more existential. They found that individuals with strong social relationships have a 50 percent greater chance of survival than those who do not, and lonely people are more likely to suffer from inflammation and weaker immune systems. The cumulative effect of loneliness is more damaging than smoking a pack of cigarettes every day. So relationships serve a purpose that extends well beyond our happiness. They are critical to our health, wellness, and maybe even our existence.[1,2,3]

While I imagine the need for community and strong-tie connections are just as powerful for apes, dolphins, whales, and most other social animals, there are likely some aspects of our need for relationships that are uniquely human. We are hardwired to seek and thrive in both one-on-one and community connections, and they need not be romantic. We can experience happiness in familial, platonic, and fraternal relationships, to name just a few. At an emotional level, our receptors receive, process, and convert those moments, experiences, and exchanges into happiness.

In an earlier chapter, I pointed to research that showed that we have a less than 1 percent chance of being fulfilled in life if we are not also fulfilled in work. According to this research, fulfillment in work requires community and belonging (read: relationships) in order for it to materialize.[4] So even in our work, our relationships matter. Those who are most adamant about post-pandemic efforts to pull everyone back into the office point to the need for human physical interaction to not only be productive and build culture but to build relationships and trust, which are necessary for high-performance organizations to thrive.

According to Harvard Business School professor Leslie Perlow, we also experience more happiness from doing activities—such as eating, drinking, and volunteering with others—than we do from doing them alone.[5] So our relationships and connections can be both the source of happiness and also a significant amplifier of the happiness we already experience in our day-to-day activities.

We not only need to feel connected and in community but we also need to love and feel loved. While this is a very natural and beautiful thing that has the potential to generate boatloads of happiness, we sometimes allow institutions, traditions, and everyone but our authentic selves to hijack our romantic relationship agendas, thereby undermining and even robbing us of our full potential for happiness.

Instinctively, we know we should love and befriend who we naturally connect with—and not according to social expectation scripts—if we want to be happy. So why do we allow these forces to influence if not force us to form, sustain, and even evangelize relationships that *may not* generate happiness?

While I want to begin this section with a discussion on romantic relationships (i.e., the institution of marriage), I will also explore the social pressures that we feel within family relationships and in our decisions to have or not have children. These are all sources of potential stress that are never noted in the Hallmark greeting cards that signal how we're supposed to feel about all these connections in our lives.

First, a disclaimer: None of these relationships are bad. In fact, they are all beautiful and can be amazing sources of joy and meaning—when it's on your terms. However, as I explain and explore, these connections can be sources of pain when they are not on your terms, and oftentimes, they are not.

Humans have the ability to build complex organizational connections that allow us to coordinate across space and time. The ability to form trusting bonds and organizations at a significant scale is one of the ways that makes us different from other apes. Humans have a unique cognitive capacity for social bonding, allowing us to share experiences, form voluntary friendships, empathize, cooperate, and love. According to Summer Allen, a research fellow at the Greater Good Science Center, we are "wired" for reaching out, interacting, and being empathetic.[6] We are also intentional. Relationships can have the purpose of creating a family, establishing a business, or mounting a defense against a potential threat. But when the goal is happiness, we should revisit our expectations and approach differently.

WHAT DOES A ROMANTIC RELATIONSHIP LOOK LIKE?

Most marriages end in divorce. According to the American Psychological Association, 40 percent to 50 percent of first marriages and 60 percent to

67 percent of second marriages end in divorce.[7] I fall into the second batch, as a twice-divorced person. Ouch. Further, the marriage rate, statistically defined as the number of marriages per 1,000, has fallen from its high point in 1946 of 16 annual marriages for every 1,000 people in the United States to 5.1 in 2020, and somewhere between 2 and 7 for many countries, both rich and poor.[8] According to the same study, more folks are also marrying later, decoupling marriage from having kids, and divorcing at greater rates than generations prior.

There are perhaps many factors contributing to this, including the increased optionality that both men and women now have to not only have kids outside of marriage, build and sustain single-income households, prioritize their individual career momentum earlier in life, and also—surprise, surprise—be happy in other relationship types (e.g., ethically nonmonogamous, same-sex., etc.) or choosing not to couple at all.

So why is there a lingering narrative that goes something like this: Meet your perfect person, get married, have two-point-five kids, buy your dream home with the white-picket fence, and live happily ever after? The End.

Many adults know this outcome is unlikely, even if they hope (or hoped) it was possible. Our institutions, specifically churches and government, alongside other cultural and societal forces work hard to continue promoting this dated myth, which has lost steam in followership and legitimacy. While we know this to be true, many people struggle to move past these social norms—or feel judged and guilty when we do.

NONMONOGAMY

Many are surprised to learn that for much of human history, humans were likely not monogamous, and love was certainly not originally the most important consideration for marriage. In the Netflix documentary *Monogamy, Things Explained,* leading researchers in the field point to the nearly 90 percent of human history (nearly 270,000 of the total 300,000 years *homo sapiens* roamed the Earth) when we were hunter-gatherers and likely had more open and communal approaches to mating and family creation. Biologically speaking, humans are much closer to the nonmonogamous chimps and bonobos, and we share a sexual physiology that favors multiple sex partners.

Many researchers say that humans evolved to embrace monogamy for practical reasons (e.g., certainty of heirs and property rights) as well as the evolution of various religious and social norms. But regardless of the "why," the migration from nonmonogamy to monogamy was an unnatural choice, and not necessarily by design or nature. Likewise, the decision to enter into marriage was a means of building alliances between families and lands, protecting and expanding wealth, and ensuring the survival of the family. The original intent wasn't solving for happiness. That came into play a few hundred years ago and has mushroomed into a $70 billion commercial industry (e.g., weddings, jewelry) that is as far removed from its origin story as Santa Claus and the Easter Bunny.

Even with the normalization of monogamy and marriage, the applications have been uneven and inconsistent. In traditional patriarchal culture, monogamy was largely expected of women, who were thought of as man's "property" in some early and backward traditions. Society generally turned a blind eye toward—even expected—infidelity from men but scorned women for doing the same. In some cultures, particularly where Islam is the primary religion, adultery is not only illegal but punishable by death. In 2023, as an example, an Iranian court sentenced a woman to death for adultery, which her husband alleged.[9] In Iran, adultery can be punishable by stoning. However in many cultures, even today, infidelity is so common that it is expected.

While it's hard to pinpoint the exact numbers around infidelity, several surveys help paint a picture (albeit inaccurate) of just how common cheating might be among monogamous couples. The self-reported cheating is probably the most difficult to triangulate, in part because of who is likely to participate in a survey of such a taboo topic and who is likely to be honest due to potential shame and fear of being discovered. For example, research published in *The Journal of Family Psychology* found that women in a survey were six times more likely to admit to cheating in an anonymous computer questionnaire than an in-person interview.[10]

I also imagine there to be differing definitions for what constitutes "cheating" (e.g., kissing someone other than your partner, emotional affairs, etc.). According to the American Survey Center, 88 percent of women believe "kissing" is cheating, while only 73 percent of men reported the same.[11] Whereas in another survey by the same group, 90 percent of respondents believed that having sex or sexting (sending nude selfies and other suggestive photos of yourself) was cheating.[12] Despite the disparity in honest self-reporting and definitions, various surveys report the number to be somewhere between 21 percent (Techopedia)[13] and as much as 50 percent of married couples in the United States (World Population Review).[14] But significantly more (75 percent of men and 66 percent of women) in the World Population study admitted they *would* cheat if it was guaranteed they wouldn't get caught. Go figure.

Regardless of what the actual infidelity numbers are, Americans are likely not unique (see the following table for countries leading in cheating rates), and most people perceive cheating to be more prevalent. For example, a 2023 survey found that 46 percent of women and 34 percent of men reported that their partner had ever cheated on them. Another survey by YouGov found the number to be much higher, with 58 percent of women and 50 percent of men reporting that their partner cheated.[15] And when it comes to what people expect at a societal level (outside of their relationships), the numbers are even more telling. Just under 60 percent of young women (57 percent to be exact) and 44 percent of young men believe that infidelity is either extremely or very common in America.[16]

Infidelity Rates by Country[17]	
Country	Percent Who've Cheated (2022)
Thailand	51 percent
Denmark	46 percent
Germany	45 percent
Italy	45 percent
France	43 percent
Norway	41 percent
Belgium	40 percent
Spain	39 percent
United Kingdom	36 percent
Canada	36 percent

In the West, the socialization of sexual promiscuity is cultivated long before a couple says "I do." For example, many young men are encouraged by parents, friends, and social media to "sow their wild oats" before getting serious. Meanwhile, young women are encouraged to do just the opposite, warned to guard their chastity so that they will be taken seriously by a suitor one day. All of this leads to confusion, contradiction, and conflict in the world of love, where truth and reality are casualties of the marriage myth.

MARRIAGE AND HAPPINESS

The conflation of love and marriage as we know it today began in the 1700s, according to the Women's History website. In their article, "The History of Romance,"[18] they report:

During the eighteenth century, society encouraged young people to select their marriage partners based on their romantic attachments.

> This was a decided change from past practice when marriages had been arranged to cement relationships between families or clans and to consolidate fortunes. Brides' and grooms' feelings were not of paramount consideration. While love and respect might be a byproduct of marriage, young couples had not entered into marriage with that expectation. That changed in the eighteenth century . . . Courtship requires that prospective lovers reveal their feelings and that they do so more creatively and sincerely than their competitors.

According to the Pew Research Center, a 2022 survey found that roughly 30 percent of Americans were single. And if you break this cohort into age groups, the percentages are more interesting. For example, 47 percent of adults under age thirty reported being single, versus 21 percent for those aged thirty to forty-nine and 30 percent for those fifty to sixty-four years of age. The singles rate is also higher than the average in certain demographics, like Black adults (47 percent) and lesbian, gay, and bisexual adults (51 percent). And while this may not be by choice for all, a number of singles are breaking with tradition and finding happiness in singleness. For example, in the same study, Pew found that 56 percent of single adults were not looking for a relationship at the time and most of them (72 percent) said they enjoyed being single. Further, a record 25 percent of forty-year-olds have never been married, up from 6 percent in 1980.[19]

Social scientists have explored factors contributing to a decline in the marriage rate. They point to shifting public attitudes towards cohabitation, increasing acceptance of singledom, difficult economic times, and women's increased economic independence. Romantic love in modern times has a different feel when women no longer see marriage as an end goal but rather a partnership between equals.

While I don't feel the need to reflect on any of these trends as good or bad, I do see them as a potential sign of a growing population that is making choices that do not fit the neat scripts they were likely given. Hopefully these choices are leading to greater individual happiness for those willing to try something different. And even when these choices do not lead to greater happiness (or just the opposite), perhaps there is some redemption in testing your own hypothesis and exercising free choice.

Regardless of the growing percentage of people who are single, unmarried, or just shacking up, the majority of adults still marry and are married. In the same Pew research study,[20] 51 percent reported being married (down from 69 percent in 1970).[21] The happiness research related to marriage is actually quite interesting. Yes, there is happiness that can come from marriage—but not a lot, research shows. According to the American Psychological Association, the increase in happiness from marriage is approximately 0.1 on an 11-point scale.[22] And some of this bump in happiness comes from the couple's reaction from their friends and family. The happiness levels return to their prior levels after all the smiles and hugs at the wedding reception and all the Facebook and Instagram "likes" begin to fade. So why do some of us continue to cling to this assumption that happiness will come if we can simply find our ever after?

A *Psychology Today* article written by Elyakim Kislev, PhD,[23] author of *Happy Singlehood: The Rising Acceptance and Celebration of Solo Living*, offered five common reasons for why marriage is still highly sought after, ranging from practical and reasonable to hopeful and imagined. Elyakim offered the following:

1. Love: For many people, the primary reason for marrying is love. They have fallen in love with someone and want to spend the rest of their lives with that person.

2. Companionship and security: Marriage can provide a sense of companionship and support. When two people marry, they become a team and can support each other through life's ups

and downs. Thus, marriage can provide a sense of security, both emotional and financial. It can offer stability and a sense of belonging.

3. Children: Many people choose to marry because they want to have children and raise a family. Marriage can provide a stable environment for raising children.

4. Social norms: In many cultures, marriage is seen as a societal norm and a way to establish oneself as an adult. Some people may marry for this reason, even if they are not in love with their partner.

5. Religion: For some people, marriage is an important religious rite and a way to fulfill their spiritual beliefs.

While each of the five drivers for marriage is reasonable and rational on face value (some in fact were my own when I got married—twice), each also follows a script that presumes the benefit—lasting love, security, a more stable environment for kids, and religious or social conformity—to be a given. Each of the five in and of itself is a script of sorts that we run, almost subconsciously. Moreover, I make the not-so-crazy leap that each of the sought-after benefits is expected to bring individuals greater happiness, despite evidence to the contrary. But the question is why?

The answer could be found in the stories we as a society continue to tell ourselves based on old myths and also the lack of alternative and widespread narratives to take their place. While there are some signs that this is changing, it's slow and often met with resistance for reasons we will explore.

THE GOOD OLD DAYS

There was once a time when society might have actually appeared much more aligned with the happiness myths that society perpetuates in films, books, and pop culture, with earlier and longer marriages, fewer divorces, and more two-parent households. Except one major assumption about the good old days is less clear; were we actually any happier back then than we are today? Were your grandparents, or their parents, truly happy in those old black-and-white photos? Or do we stare at those pictures and fantasize about a world that might have never existed?

I once dated women whose parents had been together for decades but lived totally separate lives and slept in different beds. The optics were beautiful and inspired folks looking from the outside to admire their longevity. Yet, the reality was different. In many cases, these couples were representative and emblematic of an era when people married for different reasons—at a time and age when marriage was less about personal happiness and more about commitment, family, cohesion, and the realities of emotional and economic codependency. Yet we tell ourselves mythical stories about how beautiful and wonderful married life was back in the old days. While it was for some, it was likely not that simple for many.

My mother lived in a fairly strict southern household as it related to dating boys and her independence. In fact, I often heard her and her sisters say that there were some things that young ladies just didn't do in those days—regardless of whether they wanted to. One of those things was moving out before they were married. My mother would tell us how strict her mom was about boys and how eager she was to get a job, move out, and start her life.

Her chance soon came when she was attending community college (while still living at home, mind you) and met my father, who had failed out of Michigan State the year prior. He was a socialite like me, his oldest son and namesake. Craig was a handsome jazz musician, a newly inducted member of Alpha Phi Alpha Fraternity, Inc., and the youngest of eight kids in Highland Park (Detroit), Michigan, who had little interest in being a studious college student. So he was sent down south to Lithonia, Georgia, where his aunt

Jessie could keep an eye on him. Aunt Jessie, like my mom's mother, was a strict disciplinarian and a religious lady. Aunt Jessie was a strict Seventh-day Adventist who insisted on doing things God's way and clamped down on her hippie, sax-playing, blunt-smoking nephew—but it was not for long. Eventually, he and my mother saw the potential for freedom and happiness in each other that was synonymous with life in the early 1970s.

I would often look at old pictures in the year or so before I was born in 1974 and think how happy they looked. The operative word was *looked*. Marriage was perhaps the only way out for them both, and it was the most logical next step in life. My parents probably loved each other, as much as two twenty-two-year-olds were capable of loving. However, I believe it was more the case that they loved the idea of being free from their parents and surrogate parent households. Anything was better than that. Plus tradition dictated that marriage was the next logical step in life. Find your person and get on with life and happiness would follow. I came along two years later, after a simple at-home wedding and a reception at the local YMCA, but true happiness never followed for my parents. They were doing the things they thought would lead to happiness and validation, but they never succeeded—not for any of us.

Happily Ever After?

Before long, my parents' newfound freedom as newlyweds was replaced with new stresses typical of having kids, holding down jobs, and paying bills. Over time, the stresses begat bickering, the bickering begat estrangement and infidelity, and years of that begat a desire to be free once again. Before long, my father left us.

I can remember the day he walked out. He dropped me and my brother off at school and told us to tell our mom that he was going on a trip and would return. He never did. Nearly ten years passed before we would see and spend time with him again. I was nearly an adult, entering my senior year of high school, and my brother was a rising sophomore when we reconnected (after we reached out to him). We had already survived our most vulnerable years of being young Black boys growing up in some of the rougher parts of Atlanta, and we would have plenty of emotional scars and trauma to show for it.

My mother's pain was no less. The promise of happiness that marriage would deliver had failed her. In the weeks following my father's abrupt departure, I remembered her crying and being consoled by her siblings. While it was still mostly a blur to my nine-year-old self, in hindsight I guess I could have seen it coming even at that age. Years earlier, I remembered my parents fussing and fighting. It was mostly her screaming at him, which I once assumed was what drove him away—and I resented her for that. She would cry and complain to us in the wee hours of the night, often in graphic detail about my father's infidelity, saying, "Your father had a bitch in my bed."

My mother, the oldest of eight siblings, would sometimes confess that during her marriage she, too, wanted to leave and go back home after all those heated arguments. But my maternal grandmother, who had been born in the late 1920s and had gone to high school with Martin Luther King, Jr., had very traditional views on gender roles and insisted that a woman should stay by her man no matter what. Yes, my father had cheated, and while that was bad, she should go back home and "work it out," she said. Marriage wasn't about happiness—it was about obligation, prayer, and family. It was also practical, from an economic perspective. My grandmother was a widow with eight kids, after all. There was no way she could afford for any of them to stay in her home indefinitely or boomerang for something as trivial as unhappiness.

So this cycle between my parents went on for years, beneath a facade of Polaroid images of a handsome young couple that I would dig up later in life. But their marriage wasn't all bad. In fact, my aunts, uncles, and their friends would reminisce about how my parents threw some of the best parties ever. They were the cool couple that everyone liked to hang around. They always had the newest records and best jams playing, and I'm sure smoking weed played a big role in making my home the place to be. It was also true that after my brother and I were born, we became a new source of joy and heartbeat for the extended family. Besides, every couple had their ups and downs, and my parents were probably more the norm than not.

Both of my parents eventually remarried. My mother very quickly invited another man into our home, who we knew as a family friend. They eventually married and he became our stepfather. Their relationship, for the most part, seemed void of true love and based more on codependency. They needed each other more than they loved each other. In fact, I do know that neither of my parents' subsequent relationships brought them deep or meaningful happiness. My father, as of this book's writing, is separated from his third wife.

Although my mother remained in her second marriage until her death, my brother and I later learned that our stepfather was having an affair with another woman as my mother was dying from cancer in hospice. That hurt me deeply, and I have not spoken to him since.

I have since healed and moved on from the pain that I felt for my mother in both of her relationships. But I still feel sadness that she never had a chance to live for herself. She went straight from her mother's house to the care of two men, expecting happiness. Not once did she try to seek it on her own or outside of marriage. Yes, she was smart, tough, attractive, and certainly capable. Yet for some reason, she didn't know or feel that she had other options. She left her home and ran the script that her mother gave her (and perhaps the only one available to many women during that time in society): Get married, stick it out, and make the best of it. However, while happiness may have been implied in the script, I am almost certain it never came.

WHAT WE LEARN AND OBSERVE FROM OUR PARENTS

It was once very common for someone to ask you during a date about the history of your parents' marriage, as perhaps a proxy for what you experienced growing up. If you experienced a healthy marriage in your household, it was more likely, some thought, that you would be able to envision and be able to live one out yourself. It was almost to say, if you've seen the script work for someone else, by osmosis it will work for you. Or at a minimum, you are more likely to believe in the fidelity of the script and advocate for it. But if by chance your parents' marriage was a hot mess (like in my childhood), your date might ask for the check a bit early.

You've probably also heard guys talk about women with "daddy issues," as though it's that simple. Can we really size up someone's potential to be a healthy partner based on what they experienced growing up watching their parents? I personally think it's more important that when we're ready to seek out companionship, we understand how these forces have shaped us, rather than spend too much time judging and comparing people based on their parents' dynamic. I am obviously biased.

Much of my goal with this book aims to encourage you to imagine a world for yourself rather than the one that was prescribed to you. This includes both direct and indirect prescriptions, such as the ones you pick up by watching your parents either fight and scream or show love and affection for each other. If we are all mindless machines running the program that was loaded onto us, whether that program is perceived to be good or bad, we are just robots. But we are not robots. We are sentient beings capable of thinking, assessing, and self-determining who and how we love and receive love.

If by chance you grew up in a household where you were encouraged to be a free and critical thinker, then I think you had a reasonable head start. But if you grew up in a household that required strict robot-like adherence to a program, then you probably have work to do and maybe this book will be the gentle nudge you need.

THE PRESSURE FROM FAMILY AND FRIENDS IS REAL

When I first finished grad school, I felt like I was on top of the world. Everything seemed to be going right. I had a great job, a cool condo in Midtown Atlanta, and was living what felt like the life I had dreamed for myself. Except for one thing. According to the societal script, I was missing the wife part. I was an eligible bachelor in my late twenties and feeling gentle nudges from family and friends at every turn to take the next step in life. They would say stuff like: "It's about that time. Who are you dating? Are you ready to settle down? Ain't nobody out here, you might as well pick someone. Don't you want kids?"

Whether I wanted to settle down or not, I certainly felt the *pressure* to. In time, I convinced myself that I wanted it too. So I felt both the push and the pull of the group-think social pressure. This is not necessarily a bad thing, but it wasn't the right mindset to have when I started dating. Rather than wanting the feeling of love and excitement to carry me off someplace very naturally, I felt more like the bachelor on a game show who just needed to pick someone—preferably the "right" one.

So it's not surprising in hindsight that I eventually met someone who I really liked but mostly felt pressure to date seriously. Although I never felt certain she was the right person for me, I convinced myself that I was over-thinking it. Further, I had always felt guilty when I was overly picky and scrutinized women in the past and decided this time that perhaps it was me. I was looking for perfection when that wasn't even a real thing.

Maybe deep down inside I was just afraid of falling victim to the types of marriages I had seen growing up. I was projecting all of my trauma onto the people I dated, I thought to myself. And although I had not yet had any serious therapy at this point in my life, I instinctively knew I had baggage and that it was far too heavy a burden for anyone to carry. So, like every other goal I had in life, I decided I could and would make it work with commitment and determination. That's how I approached my first marriage.

It's not surprising to anyone that my first marriage lasted only a few months and ended miserably in a hurtful divorce. I was married and divorced within the same year. And for this, I was deeply embarrassed. We had more than two hundred and fifty people witness and celebrate our wedding, and only a few months later they were now hearing rumors of our separation. I felt like a failure, and this was not supposed to be *my story*. A big public failure seemed off-brand for "Craig the ever-achiever." However, it was more than my ego that was bruised, I was hurt. I also doubted myself and my judgment for being so careless and cavalier in my approach to marriage. It took some healing, time, and therapy before I could forgive myself and move on.

FOLLOW YOUR TRUE NORTH

For most of the following year, I literally hid under a rock and tried to disappear. I left Atlanta and moved to New York City for a new career opportunity and to start a new life in a big city where no one knew me. I initially thought that I would never get married again—ever—and enjoy single life in NYC, which I did for a few months. But fast-forward to a little over a year later, and I married again. This time I believed my motivations were pure and my own, and that I had prioritized all the right things, such as friendship, shared values, and a belief that God Himself had orchestrated our union.

For the next ten years, I was married to my best friend, a beautiful and an amazingly talented woman. We dated only a few months before we decided to tie the knot, partly because we wanted to start a family and were already entering our late thirties but also because we had already known each other and been acquaintances throughout college and grad school. Our initial dating was anything but typical. We started off as friends, ironically giving each other dating advice. I had suggested that she get on the dating app, eharmony, which was popular at the time. I even offered to help her write her profile, not knowing that in the months to come I would suffer a near-death experience that would bring us closer in a way that seemed spiritual and cosmically ordained.

Although we divorced after nearly ten years together, our marriage was one of the best experiences and relationships of my life and one in which I grew and matured emotionally. Our divorce was as atypical as our marriage. We were kind to each other, respectful, and generous. We even gave each other separation gifts to mark the beginning of our respective philosophies and directives for the next chapter. I was in the early and sometimes ugly stages of trying to figure out my philosophy on happiness—which this book is the byproduct of—so she gifted me a compass with the engraving "Follow your true north." I gifted her a scuba-diving computer with the note "Keep going deeper." I believe we have both followed each other's advice and have been blessed and enriched because of our time together, but also because we were able to let go and reimagine a new future apart from each other with only our authentic truths to guide us.

REFLECTION QUESTIONS

1. What specific scripts or unspoken rules about finding love, getting married, or having children did you receive from your family, community, or pop culture?

2. How have these scripts influenced your past or current relationship decisions, even if subconsciously? Can you identify a moment where you felt pressure to conform to a relationship script, even if it didn't align with your authentic desires?

3. What would it mean for you to reclaim your "romantic relationship agenda" and pursue connections solely on *your own terms* for happiness?

CHAPTER 17

THE UNINTENDED CONSEQUENCES OF DATING APPS

*"I look great in my profile pictures. They were taken when
I didn't need online dating to meet people."*

—Unknown

In 2025, most single people looking for everything from soulmates to hookups will find that apps are not only the norm, but likely the most effective and efficient option currently available. There is an app for every dating philosophy that might float your boat, including Bumble, where women must message first, and Tinder—which most folks view as a tool for finding more low- and no-commitment connections. On OkCupid, you can sort yourself into dating categories that might have been considered taboo just a few years ago, such as "nonmonogamous." According to the Pew Research Center, roughly 30 percent of Americans have used a dating app or site. But that number jumps to as many as 53 percent for those under thirty years of age.[1]

Many of these AI and big data-driven applications are owned by Match Group, a tech company and house of brands that seems to have cornered the billion-dollar online dating and connecting market. As of February 2025, Match Group (MTCH) had a market cap of just under $8.5 billion. According to a 2024 report on the global online dating market published by Market.us:

> The Global Online Dating Market is projected to grow significantly, expected to reach USD 18.1 Billion by 2033, up from USD 9.4 Billion in 2023. This reflects a steady CAGR of 6.8% over the forecast period from 2024 to 2033. In 2023, North America held a leading position in the global market, commanding more than 40% of the market share and generating approximately USD 3.7 Billion in revenue.[2]

There are even a host of sites and apps, like Ashley Madison, which boasts seventy million members,[3] that create marketplaces to confidentially and discreetly connect married individuals (unbeknownst to their partners) with others who don't mind being a plus one in an extramarital affair. Finally, there are places such as Feeld and FetLife, where you can go to find, explore, and live out your sexual, kink, and fetish desires. A person could easily find themselves on one or more of these platforms, as the personas that these tech platforms target are not necessarily mutually exclusive.

I have certainly tried a few of them over the years. I discovered dating apps after my first divorce and was on eharmony when I started dating my second wife. Dating apps were fairly new at the time, and most of my friends (including me) would not have publicly admitted to being on one. Using a dating app was akin to saying, "I'm not cool enough, attractive enough, or *whatever* enough to meet someone in real life." Boy, has that changed.

Still, dating apps continue to get a bad reputation to those who stubbornly cling to the tradition of meeting their romantic interest the old-fashioned way. And while dating apps no longer carry the social stigma of years past and are certainly more ubiquitous these days, most people still long for the good old days when you met someone through a friend, at a cookout, in church, at a bar . . . as humans. I get it.

To those who believe dating apps have drained humanity of its romance, spontaneity, and opportunity for divine intervention, I think we should reconsider the facts and view this innovation through a slightly different lens. We have to ask ourselves, "What is the problem that this product seeks to solve?" and "Why is the Match Group, and the category, growing more broadly as opposed to shrinking?" Are we better off—perhaps happier— *because* of the apps, not *in spite* of them? Initially I wasn't sure, but now I am beginning to think that we are. Here is why.

THE PROBLEM WE ARE TRYING TO SOLVE

There was once a time when who you dated, loved, and maybe eventually married was limited to who was in your geographic proximity, the people who lived in your town or went to your school, or somehow existed in your social network. Before the rapid urbanization of America, the local population might've been a fairly small sample set for the average person.

Now let's refine that subset to those who possessed the attributes you desire in a partner: attractive, family-oriented, shares your faith, desires to start a family, and so on. Now let's imagine the subset after applying your desired attributes and adding to those people who were available and interested in you. The number of people in the remaining distilled subset of people who have all the things you want, and want you, at the time you are both available is likely small.

With how unlikely it is that your ideal person will emerge from this distillation process of sequential and compounding probabilities (i.e., where "p" is the probability of the previously mentioned sequence, the probability of meeting your soulmate could be mathematically described as p1 x p2 x p3 x p4 x p5 and so on . . . which equals a really small probability), most people will likely just pick the best possible candidate. Yet that approach might not lead to happiness.

Better Living Through Dating Apps

Here are some objective ways that dating apps can create greater happiness:

- *Abundance Mindset.* Dating apps have taken us from a scarcity mindset, where we are content with what is available, to inducing an abundance mindset, where we are excited by what could be. It is possible that too many choices may actually have a diminishing effect on our happiness, but let's venture to say that having more than ten choices is a good thing. If I have one hundred, one thousand, or even one million choices, that seems better than having only ten. Dating apps provide this great innovation.

- *Test the Hypothesis.* You can quickly and efficiently test different assumptions about what you think you might or might not want in a partner with dating apps. It sounds sterile, cold, and dispassionate to say this, but you need a volume of experiences (data) to test your hypothesis that you could date someone with any number of attributes. Perhaps you don't know if you would be happy dating someone with kids, someone who shares a different faith, someone who has a different racial, ethnic, social, or socioeconomic background than you, and so on. In the old days before the advent of dating apps, you simply might not have enough time, interactions, and feedback loops to really define who and what will bring you happiness (or not).

- *Time and Geography Are Not Limits.* A great aspect to dating app matches is that people don't have to be online at the same time and share the same geography as you because matching and app interactions are asynchronous. You are free to explore connections when you have time, which could be during lunch breaks, in between sets at the gym, or late at night after you've put the kids to bed. In the real world, you have to physically be in the same place at the same time to explore a connection. And it's unlikely you can explore more than one connection at a time if you're chatting with a love prospect at the bar.

- *Billions to Millions to Mine.* Abundance is not a good thing unless you have the tools to manage, filter, sort and ultimately go from millions or thousands of options to potentially engaging and dating one that has promise. I liken dating apps to a sales funnel. It's ideal for top of the funnel (getting a lot of leads) and maybe mid-funnel conversions (converting leads into opportunities), but you ultimately still have to close the deal on your own.

- *We Don't Have Time for Randomness.* There was once a time (and for some this is still the case) when randomness was your friend. If you didn't believe in randomness, you might have chosen to believe in the opportunity for luck or divine intervention. All three might have taken place at a bar, a cookout, church, or some place and time when you might have had a chance encounter with someone who had the potential to be your "forever-forever." That would require so many probabilities to line up that you'd need to go out every night, attend every social outing, and be constantly available for randomness to have a chance to work. Unfortunately, most of us have other things in life we have to do with our time, such as work, sleep, and eat. We don't have time for randomness. Apps give us that time back—and time is money (yet another unanticipated benefit).

- *No More Fear of Rejection.* This last one is one of the unintended benefits that I love. When I was a young adult and trying my hand at approaching women, I was awkward, nervous, and probably a bit nerdy. I still am, truth be told. Fear of rejection probably represented a bigger barrier to me shooting my shot than anything. I would over-think whether to walk up to someone at a party or club, assess the probability of success, try to read her body language from across the room, and perhaps wait for her to be alone for my window to step up to her. Assuming I could finally gather the courage, I might feel humiliated or crushed if she was dismissive, declined my offer to buy her a drink, or simply dissed me in a way where onlookers could see. This complicated thought process led to no good outcomes—for anyone. Apps remove the fear of shooting your shot. You just swipe. If there's interest on the other side, they swipe back. There are no embarrassing rejections, no sting if there's never a counter-swipe and, most of all, I get to present my best self (my dating profile) versus the nervous, clammy version that typically shows up in random encoun-ters at the bar. She also doesn't have to feel pressured to entertain my small talk or accept a drink (or feel guilty) if there's no interest. This is a win-win for everyone.

Dating apps take less time, money, and effort to get to the same out-comes. In fact, according to Pew Research, 10 percent of couples (married, significant partners, etc.) report meeting their person on a dating app or site—and 20 percent of those under thirty and 24 percent of LGB adults say they met their partner online. Because of the abundance factor, I believe that, mathematically, you have a better chance of optimal outcomes and, therefore, happiness.[4]

THE DARK SIDE OF APPS

Now, let me not paint apps as the panacea for love connections. They are certainly not. An efficacy rate of 10 percent (of people who met their partners) is not exactly the home run stat that will make everyone into believers. And outcomes aside, the actual experience users report is split down the middle. Roughly 53 percent report having good experiences while 46 percent report having bad experiences. Note, men generally report having better experiences than women. But the data and factoids are hardly what's driving the perception of online dating.[5]

My friends who are discouraged from dating remind me that there are no good people out there. Some of them say dating apps are a place where "the creeps hang out," and that "You have to be careful because dating apps seem to be filled with stalkers, predators, and bad guys." Others will say "Everyone is misrepresenting who they really are." This is what is referred to as "catfishing."

Let's be clear, technology does not create or remove people from the planet and, therefore, the dating pool. It only allows you to filter through who's already out there. There are good and bad people everywhere. There are not magically more bad people or fewer good people just because of technology. The technology only allows you to sort, filter, and connect. It does not remove the instinct a bad person has to do bad things. It may make it easier for them to do it at scale, but it's also easier to filter and block.

It is also true that if a person tends to misrepresent and mischaracterize who they are, what they do, and what they want, chances are they will do that in the real world too. So just as technology does not reduce the percentage of people in the world you will find creepy, it also does not increase the percentage of people you will find loving. It only makes it a little bit more efficient for you to sort through the pool of both good and bad prospects. But there are some negative things I believe are valid.

How Dating Apps Undermine Long-Term Happiness

- *Developing Weaker Social Skills.* Have you ever wondered if a lion born in a zoo and fed three times a day by a zookeeper would survive if released onto the Serengeti plains of East Africa? Maybe, but maybe not. Dating apps make social animals more like social *zoo* animals, and you may over time lose the instinct and ability to catch prey, so to speak, in the wild. (Please note this is an analogy and I do not think of dating as being predatory!) Social media in general can dull your ability to engage in healthy conversations, read body language, build the courage to approach someone, or have difficult but constructive dialogue with someone in real time. Dating apps can similarly decrease some of the social skills that are necessary for ultimately cultivating and building healthy relationship dynamics.

- *Having Too Many Options May Be Bad.* With the perception of endless options, it can be easy to pick over the smallest of imperfections in a dating prospect. It's easier to keep swiping than it is to engage, look deeper, and really get to know someone beyond what you can glean from ten nanoseconds of swiping. If there's always someone slightly better, there's likely never going to be anyone good enough to hold your attention. This numbing factor has the potential to drain your happiness over time.

- *Encouraging Gamification.* Similar to the aforementioned, swiping and app interactions can often feel more like video games than an authentic search for your person. The apps have the goal of keeping members on the platform, paying their monthly fees, and purchasing upgrades (e.g., Roses, profile boosts), which all feel like gamifying romantic connections. This, over time, can diminish and trivialize some of the value and happiness that comes from dating.

- *Creating Another Daily Chore.* Dating takes time and energy. Companies design dating apps to extract their fair share, if not more, of both. If you're not careful, apps can feel like another daily chore—another to-do to get done. If your profile is particularly attractive or popular, you might feel **overwhelmed** with the sheer volume of prospects (as some of my female friends complain). If you love the attention that comes from a large volume of prospects, you might find the potential for addictive tendencies with the app.

Even with the potential negatives just outlined, I believe that apps are generally a positive (or significantly positive) contributor to our dating experiences, outcomes, and potential for happiness. The more you feel you have options that align with your authentic self and are empowered to pursue them, the more likely you are to experience the joys that can come from finding and sustaining loving, romantic connections. Whereas when you feel limited, constrained, and forced to choose from options that are not ideal, you are less likely to experience true happiness.

REFLECTION QUESTIONS

1. Before the widespread use of dating apps, how did you (or people you observed) typically approach finding a romantic partner? What were the most significant frustrations or limitations of that old-fashioned approach?

2. How does the compounding probability model described in this chapter ($p1 \times p2 \times p3...$) resonate with your own experiences of trying to find a compatible partner in traditional settings?

3. Does the efficiency offered by dating apps truly make you feel better off—and perhaps happier—in your dating journey, or do you perceive other trade-offs that might diminish happiness?

THE LAW OF EXPECTATIONS

"In relationships, the more expectations you have,
the less you're open to what is."

—Thich Nhat Hanh

So much of happiness is based on your expectations. If you have high expectations, there is a greater chance for you to be disappointed. If your expectations are fairly low, you have a reasonably good chance of having them met. This applies to our romantic lives as well.

If you need perfection to be happy—which you don't, by the way—chances are you will find yourself in a miserable Greek tragedy, where everyone but you can see the source of your unhappiness. However, I do not think that the opposite is necessarily true in your love life, either. Aiming low does not ensure you will have a better chance at finding your person; it just means you will be complicit and a willing participant in your own unhappiness.

That said, some of us self-sabotage our happiness by mining low or aiming for perfection without being aware that this is what we're doing. Research conducted by Yale psychologist Robb Rutledge validates my assertion: "In a series of studies including over 18,000 people playing our smartphone game, we found that happiness depends not on how well things are going, but whether they are going better than expected recently."[1] This also reveals how nuanced the applications of having high, low, or more realistic expectations can be in our happiness. But perhaps we can use a few scenarios to flesh out useful insights.

"10 OUT OF 10"

Let's imagine that we conduct a fictional survey in which we ask all 7.8 billion people on planet Earth (or the 5.2 billion eighteen years and older) to list the ten things they want in their ideal partner. The ten attributes for everyone's ideal partner will vary significantly but likely have a few common traits. A hypothetical list of ten might include things such as:

1. Attractive

2. Gainfully employed

3. Healthy

4. Family-oriented

5. Has a good relationship with family

6. Educated

7. Easy to get along with

8. Loves to travel

9. Shares my faith

10. Wants kids

What would be in yours? Try listing a few.

Now let's take the list of ten for everyone and group our survey respondents based on their expectations of actually finding someone with all of their desired ten attributes all weighted equally.

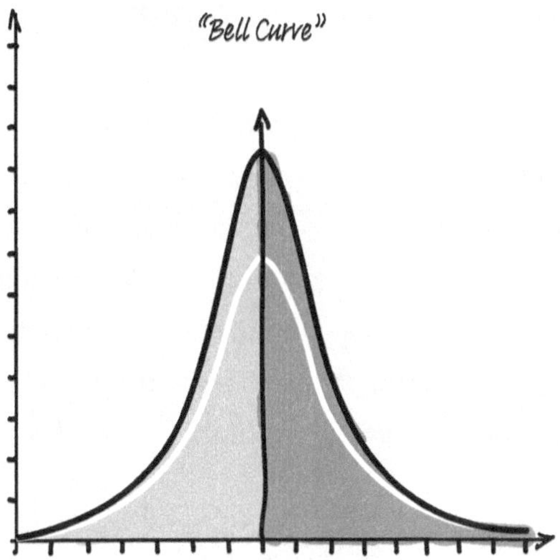

Typical "bell curve" distribution, which is a graphical representation of how data is distributed around its average. The bell-shaped curve reflects most data points ("the majority") clustering in the center and fewer points ("the minority") tapering off in the "tails" of either side.

I imagine that the population would largely fall into three groups based on their belief of finding and partnering with that ideal person with ten attributes; the three groups would neatly align with the shape of the classic bell curve distribution.

- *Group 1* (10/10). The first group are those respondents who believe that there is someone who has all ten attributes, meaning there is someone out there who is perfect for them, a "10 out of 10." They believe that they will eventually find this person if they're patient and intentional. They believe in unicorns despite the lack of evidence that they exist. You will probably recognize them by the language they use: Soulmate, godsend, dating with intention, faith, my journey will be different, and so on.

- *Group 2* (6/10). These are my pragmatic people. They want all ten attributes but are more suspicious of whether perfection actually exists. They are fearful of good being the enemy of great and will likely be happy enough with the right seven, six, five, or fewer. They won't think of themselves as settling but rather as being prudent and reasonable. They are also fearful of holding out for perfection and potentially passing over good enough and, thus, a reasonable shot at happiness.

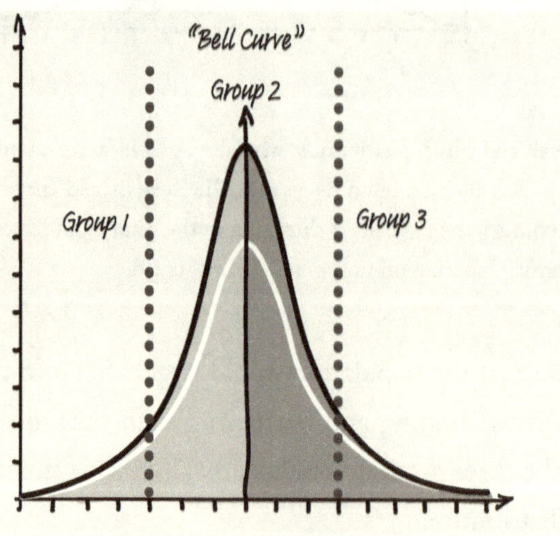

Theoretical survey response: Illustrative example of how the fictitious survey respondents might be distributed. Those in "Group 2" would theoretically be the average or majority, while those in Groups 1 and 3 would be in the minority.

- *Group 3* (5/10 + 5/10 = 10/10). The last group are my serial daters, perpetually single but dating folks and the full spectrum of ethically nonmonogamous people, where people are intentionally co-creating relationships with more than one person at a time. Whether by philosophy or resignation, these are people who want all ten qualities but are open to finding all ten in multiple connections, partners, or lovers—over time or at one time. They ignore the social pressure or have come to grips with the judgment they might feel from folks in Groups 2 and 1, but they are more driven by the perceived unhappiness they believe comes from being in Group 2 or waiting alone in Group 1. Perhaps they were once in Group 1 when they were younger, then spent time in Group 2, before ultimately embracing some form of Group 3.

I imagine the vast majority of our fictitious survey respondents are somewhere in Group 2 and a small minority are in either Group 1 or

Group 3. According to *Psychology Today*, somewhere between 4 percent and 5 percent of the US population identifies as "consensual nonmonogamous"[2] but as many as 31 percent (according to a 2024 Match Singles report[3]) have dabbled with one of the many relationship types and experiences on the spectrum, from swinging or having a threesome to polyamorous. Of those who engaged in consensual nonmonogamy, 38 percent reported that the experience helped them better understand their relationship needs and desires, 29 percent felt the experiences made them emotionally more mature, 30 percent said they became more sexually open, and 27 percent reported having sex more frequently. That said, 49 percent in the same study say that traditional monogamous relationships and sex remain their preference, but there is clearly a growing interest in choice—be it ethical nonmonogamy, the option to be alone, or something in between.

Crunching the Numbers

Let's consider a few more questions to make this exercise a bit more interesting.

Imagine you were fortunate enough to meet your perfect ten out of ten and were rewarded for sticking it out in Group 1. How would hedonic leveling (which assumes that regardless of the good and bad events you experience, over time your happiness eventually "levels out" and returns to its base point) impact you over time? Will that lead to you, upon finding the closest thing to a perfect ten, very quickly wanting more—now eleven, twelve, and so on? Or is it possible that despite all the happiness you initially experience from having all ten eventually fades, as it does for most novelty in life?

Let's examine those who say they can be happy in Group 2 with the "right eight," as a friend of mine always says. These people assume they can make relationships work and actually be happy for the rest of their lives. However, here's the thing that I have noticed from my friends who make this calculus: They are initially okay with the subset of ten that they intentionally decided to forego. They weren't perfect, but that was their person. They loved and embraced them until their focus shifted over time to the things this person did not have. Over time, my friends became not only annoyed and consumed with the things they did not have, but also perhaps began to slowly discount the things their partner did possess. Some of these folks will cheat to get some of what they want outside of their relationship, while others will secretly fantasize about those attributes in others but are careful not to act on them. Finally, others will ignore and maybe pray those thoughts away. All are eventually unhappy in my observations. Have you found yourself in any of these situations before?

Now assume we survey this group every ten years. How likely do you think it is that everyone's ten attributes will remain stable over time? Isn't it more likely that something that was nonnegotiable at one point might not even make the list ten years later? And vice versa—is something that wasn't even on your radar something that's now mission critical?

Finally, what if we asked our survey participants how their current partner would rank them against their ideal ten? Would the survey responder themself be considered a perfect "ten out of ten" to their partner? We tend to not only want perfection in our partners but also assume we are ourselves perfect. It's highly likely that neither of these assumptions is valid or leads to real happiness.

One of the insights that I draw from this fictitious analysis of the distribution is that our expectations have a direct correlation to our happiness. As is the case in hedonic leveling, our expectations evolve both up and down over time to find new targets for happiness. The other big takeaway is that we are likely horrible predictors of our future needs and desires in relationships. So what does this mean for how you think about picking partners today? What does this mean for your current and future happiness—as well as the happiness of your partner (or partners)?

EXPECTATIONS AND DESIRES CHANGE OVER TIME

My list has changed for sure. When I was younger, I wanted kids. I once believed with conviction that children would bring me happiness. This assumption led me to make it a requirement that whoever I was dating was not only willing but capable of having kids. In my twenties, I would've avoided dating a woman in her late thirties. The assumption would've been, right or wrong to my naive twentysomething-year-old self, that after a certain age, she would have more difficulty having children. So I arbitrarily removed any dating prospects over a certain age out of my consideration.

Boy, was I wrong. Today, I have no kids and do not desire to have them. I would not care whether the person I dated today was capable of having kids or not and would prefer to date someone for whom that's not a priority. But just ten or fifteen years ago, I felt very strongly that I wanted to be a father. What will I desire ten or twenty years from now? Who knows? But the assumption that I would meet a person today that will for the next decade or more of my life continue to be perfect seems statistically unlikely. So why should it be my expectation that either a person could be my life partner or that I would not have more than one partner over the course of my life? Or even that I might not have more than one partner at any given time?

The point is not so much what you think you want at this moment, but rather your ability to imagine how your desires might change in the future—and what that might mean for your choices and behaviors today.

THE "80/20" RULE

Notwithstanding the exercise we just did above, which did not make Group 2 sound all that attractive, I do think there are some practical ways to think about looking for perfection versus "good enough" in a mate. The Pareto

Principle states that roughly 80 percent of outcomes or results come from about 20 percent of inputs or causes. We call this the "80/20" rule. In our case, however, the 80/20 inspires a different calculus.

Let's assume that a person with 100 percent of everything we want is statistically, philosophically, and perhaps psychologically impossible for all of the reasons we outlined already. What we desire changes over time, a person who we fall in love with changes over time, and we ourselves change as well. That's before we even get to the question of whether or not there will ever be someone who initially (or at any point in time) is 100 percent, even for a New York second. So what would be "good enough" to get us as much of the happiness that is indeed possible? How would we even describe or quantify what is good enough?

Before we can answer that question, we have to be comfortable with the realization that true perfection is a fallacy. Out of seven days in any given week, there might be one or two days that weren't your best, but that would not make it a bad week. Five good days out of seven days would still be considered a good week for most. If your job offered you virtually all of the things you always wanted in your dream job, but you hated submitting monthly expense reports, doing end-of-year lattice reviews, or other administrative things that were required of the job, you would not consider it a bad job just because there were a few things you did not like about it. You can absolutely love and adore your siblings, parents, and family members, even if you bicker, have disagreements, or encounter any number of things that are normal in healthy social interactions.

This is the human condition, right? You would still love your family and not want to trade them for all the tea in China, right? The same could be true for your ideal partner. I refer to this minimum cutoff as the 80 percent. When you meet and eventually start dating a person, do you find them to have at least 80 percent of what you hoped and desired for in a life partner or are they closer to having 20 percent?

In the tech world, where I now spend a lot of time, there is a term called minimum viable product (MVP) that refers to the things a new and emerging product must have, at a minimum, before the marketplace will consume it and give enough feedback to guide further iterations in the future. When you are creating and launching a new product and want to quickly get it to the marketplace (before the competition) to begin testing and validating your assumptions about the demand, it has to have enough of the features people would want and desire for you to know whether or not there's a real marketplace for the product.

Some of the first buyers of the Tesla were willing to buy the car even though all of the promised features were not available at the time. They bought the car with its minimum capabilities they needed to fall in love with the product and brand. I bought my Tesla two years ago, after it had been around for two decades or so and was no longer considered new, but Tesla's full self-driving feature was still new and emerging. When I purchased my Tesla, there were some features that allowed me to experience what autonomous driving vehicles might feel and look like, even without all of the bugs and functionality being completely sorted out. The self-driving feature was still in the MVP phase. Still, there were enough bells and whistles to make me feel comfortable buying the car with the hope and expectation that the future innovation would continue to improve upon the basic MVP capabilities—and it eventually did.

The 80 percent we seek in a partner can be thought of as the MVP. What are the minimum things that you must see in a relationship to be willing to put forth the effort, commit, and maybe wait for future attributes to emerge? Of course, nothing promises that the other 20 percent will ever emerge, which is why you have to be comfortable with the MVP being the beginning and the end of your decision to commit. I believe we can be happy with give or take 80 percent of the desired attributes, so long as we do not obsess over the missing 20 percent. The minute you begin to fixate or compare your partner with another person who may have the 20 percent but not the rest of the 80 percent, your relationship is likely headed for a death spiral.

I am beginning to believe that identifying and being happy with your 80 percent gets easier with time. A few things happen as we age into our forties, fifties, and sixties.

1. We become more settled and clearer on who we are and what we want versus what we need. We have lived long enough to be secure in who we are and are less vulnerable to social pressure. We might also be more practical, having grown tired of chasing rainbows and unicorns.

2. Our life changes are perhaps less frequent. Our teens, twenties, and thirties are defined by major changes and expectations, such as going from high school to college, from college to the workforce, from the workforce to marriage, and from marriage to parenting. After a certain age, there may be fewer of these big milestones that impact what we need in a partner.

3. We have a more robust portfolio of happiness sources to complement the role of a partner. We may not need to burden our partner with all of our happiness needs, as we have hopefully developed meaningful communities to which we belong, hobbies and activities that we love, and a sense of purpose that transcends our partnership status. As they often say, we have to be whole and happy *before* we meet our person, not *because of* our person.

That said, there will be some who insist on finding perfection and believe that they themselves are perfect. I wish them well. For those who would rather find all 100 percent in more than one relationship (i.e., polyamorous), that is your choice, and I fully support it. If you feel that it is more practical and reasonable to accept something less than perfection, I encourage you to think practically and honestly about what is in your relationship MVP.

REFLECTION QUESTIONS

1. In your past or current romantic relationships, how have your expectations (whether conscious or subconscious) directly impacted your level of satisfaction or disappointment?

2. When you consider your "ideal" partner, what are the top five nonnegotiable attributes you would put on your list? Based on the chapter's description of the "10/10" group, do you identify with the belief that a "perfect" person exists for you, and what are the implications of that belief for your dating life?

3. How does the concept of "hedonic leveling"—where initial happiness from acquiring something ideal eventually fades—apply to your expectations of a "perfect 10" partner? What might you eventually seek beyond that initial "ten"?

4. The "80/20 Rule" (Relationship MVP) suggests being comfortable with finding 80 percent of what you desire. What are the absolute "minimum viable product" qualities that you believe are essential for you to be happy and willing to commit in a romantic relationship?

5. The chapter implicitly challenges the "find your person and get on with life and happiness will follow" script. What personal narratives or societal pressures might still be driving your expectations in love, even if they don't align with your changing desires or the realities of long-term partnership?

CHAPTER 19

DIVORCE: OUR LITTLE SECRET

*"Most people would rather be certain they're miserable
than risk being happy."*

—Attributed to Robert Anthony

In safe spaces, or perhaps after a few drinks, some of my married friends will confide that they would divorce if they could, but they stay married for very practical reasons. They have done the math and determined that the alternative (divorce, separation, splitting the kids, and so on) is likely more painful than their current unhappiness. That or perhaps the draw of the potential upside (freedom) is too uncertain to gamble.

While they might be unhappy, that's not the same as misery. There might not (yet) be enough pain or unhappiness to do anything different. Some learn to find joy and happiness in other places, almost to compensate for the void in their love life. They might throw themselves into their work, their kids, their volunteerism, or whatever suits them. The plant's roots will stretch, crawl, and eventually reach water elsewhere. Yet deep down inside, they know it's not ideal and it may be unsustainable to live this way.

In the interim, they may have very logical reasons as to why they should remain in less-than-happy relationships. These are some of the most common explanations I hear.

THE REASONS WE DON'T DIVORCE

1. *Good Enough.* "It's not any better out there. At least I know what I have." They've resigned themselves to the idea that they are not happy, but they may not find anything better if they were to try again. They take a sadistic type of joy in hearing the horror stories from their single friends dating. It secretly gives them some measure of comfort that they're not missing out. They will look for happiness in other areas of their life, such as their extracurricular activities, vacation, work, and so on.

2. *Cheaper to Cheat.* It turns out that cheating is more common than you think, as we explored in Chapter 16. Not just amongst men, but also women. Humans will be human. Not all cheating is sexual or looks like ongoing affairs. It can show up in any number of ways that range from emotional affairs to secretly desiring and fantasizing about other people. For some, cheating is a better alternative than what they perceive would be the massive penalty that comes from divorce. Economically, depending on how long a couple has been married, and what assets are involved, divorce could equal financial ruin for the breadwinner.

3. *We Stay Together for the Kids.* There is research arguing for (and against) the benefits of a two-parent household even when the two parents are miserable. I for one find it hard to imagine kids are better off in a two-person household where the parents hate each other. Assuming the two parents can co-parent and support their

child's well-being, I imagine that might be a better alternative than what I saw growing up. My parents argued all the time. It was more likely than not that something was popping off. Cursing, yelling, and seeing clothes thrown onto the front yard for neighbors to gaze at was normal. It had a massively negative impact on me. For years, I associated arguing with marriage and was consequently fearful of commitment for many years. It took lots of therapy to get past what I witnessed growing up. Couples stay married in part because they believe it's better for the kids. They hate the thought of their kids bouncing between households, being in blended families, and everything that typically follows the divorce. As best I can see, everyone involved suffers and is denied happiness when parents opt for this path.

4. *We Made a Vow.* Some feel a certain level of duty, honor, and obligation based on religion, culture, and other institutions to "do what we said we were gonna do." Notwithstanding the validity, reasonability, or even practicality of the creed to which they pledged, people may feel compelled to defer or deny their happiness because of their faith in something other than themselves.

5. *What Will People Say?* As social animals, belonging and acceptance by our chosen tribe is important. We are inclined to do a number of things that are counter to our happiness to belong, including clinging to the image of the myth that they and the tribe are working to uphold (i.e., the institution is working, even if in reality it is not).

None of the behaviors just mentioned lead to happiness. In fact, these behaviors are the antithesis of happiness. To be clear, the research and my own experiences show that marriage (or meaningful and loving connections) can in fact lead to happiness. This chapter is not arguing for or against divorce or marriage but rather examining what happens if you reset your expectations and, if possible, prioritize your own happiness over the desires and expectations of your friends, church, family, and the broader community.

ADAPT, EVOLVE, OR CONQUER

Humans are unique in some miraculous ways. In our short time on Earth as *Homo sapiens*, we've learned to do a few things that have given us a massive advantage over other animals. The first was to learn to collaborate with other humans over time and distance, beyond that of apes and other complex social animals. That allowed us to build empires, machines, supply chains, and institutions for extending our control and reach even further. We also learned to adapt to and control our environments. Adapting meant that we could live or learn to live with different food sources, in different climates, with different threats, and so on. We could also adapt to these changes more quickly than other species, giving us an advantage.

The second is "control," which is perhaps debatable as to whether it's a net positive or negative. However, as humans learned to domesticate animals, grow food, and shelter themselves from the elements, they, in effect, controlled and held constant their environment. This gave us the power to remove lots of uncertainty from our day-to-day lives that would have been a source of great stress to our ancestors.

We have brought these ancient natural selection and evolution skills into our relationships too. In the face of unhappiness—which is a far cry from being chased by a tiger or migrating to avoid a drought—we will find ways to adapt and persist or insulate ourselves from the source of discomfort or both. The net result is that we can endure being unhappy for much longer than we're sometimes aware, and maybe even over time, we convince ourselves we're actually okay because we've normalized our environments so that we can cope. When we do this numbing exercise in groups or normalize our unhappiness as a society, we slowly begin to accept that our unhappiness is actually a perverted baseline for our happiness.

Married couple friends know this well. They get together, commiserate, and find some measure of comfort in knowing their husband isn't the only one who does XYZ or their wife isn't the only one who does ABC. They all do it, and therefore it's normal, to be expected, and we learn to adapt. It becomes the new baseline for happiness—with a lowercase "h."

PUTTING YOUR KID'S HAPPINESS FIRST

One of my dear friends divorced a few years ago but had been married for nearly ten years. When she was dating her then boyfriend, and later her husband, during a window when they separated, she discovered she was pregnant. She did lots of research and found compelling evidence to suggest that her unborn child would be better off in a two-parent household, although she was not convinced her boyfriend at the time was the right person for her to marry. She convinced herself that the right thing to do was to marry this guy for the benefit of her future son. Her son would be better off in a two-parent household, even knowing she was marginally unhappy at the onset of the marriage.

Years later, she would find the unhappiness of her marriage wearing on her and debate the merits of leaving her husband. She would often leave him after heated arguments and return home to her parents for periods of time, only to find herself back with him. Practicality would always overrule her desire for happiness. "This is better for my son," she would tell herself. This back-and-forth went on for years before she ultimately decided that it was time to go—for good. She'd had enough, but she felt that it couldn't be her that asked for the divorce. She needed to find a way to nudge her husband to initiate it, because she feared if she had initiated the divorce, her son would hold it against her. He would view her as the culprit for breaking up the family. Her chance eventually came, and they divorced.

After all of these years, her son had been the reason she got married, stayed married, and, with much angst, manipulated her husband to be the initiator of the divorce. She had put her son's happiness over her own. And perhaps that was the right thing to do—maybe even selfless in the eyes of some—but was it rational? Was her son actually happier because she got married and stayed unhappily married? Was he better off because she, though obviously unhappy in the relationship, stuck it out? Did she and her husband model the best and right behaviors for their son: Be unhappy and stick it out? What will their son be inclined to think is normal when he's of age to date and eventually marry? There is research that suggests she was right in her instinct to stick it out for the sake of the child, but only *partially* right.

In his research[1] on the links between maternal happiness in marriage and children's outcomes, Dimitrios Nikolaou found the following:

- A 10 percent increase in the mean maternal happiness of the mother was predicted to increase a child's future social skills by an amount equivalent to ~$62,000 in income.

- Marriage had a large positive effect on cognitive skills and on select noncognitive skills. For instance, a change from single parenthood to marriage is predicted to increase cognitive skills by the same amount as ~$77,000, or just shy of the average US 2023 household income of $80,000 in household income.

- However, the results showed that marriage alone was not enough. It needed to be a happy marriage to get the benefits.

Today, my friend is finally an empty nester, with her son now in his first year of college. For the first time since she can remember, she gets to organize her life around what will bring *her* happiness. She's doing what brings *her* joy. She runs marathons, visits her nieces and nephews, and is enjoying her career. She's also thinking about what's next for her.

The temptation to put your children's perceived happiness and well-being ahead of your own is certainly understandable, and, in some cases, warranted. However, first be sure you are happy in the relationship if you hope to create a nurturing and healthy environment for the kids. An unhappy marriage is likely to do just the opposite—or best-case scenario, as I personally learned, lead to the child having to remove a lot of unhealthy default apps later in life.

REFLECTION QUESTIONS

1. Can you identify a significant area in your own life (whether romantic, professional, or personal) where you might be enduring unhappiness for perceived practical benefits or to avoid a greater perceived pain?

2. What is the math you (or someone you know) do to justify staying in situations that are less-than-happy but perhaps not misery? What is the potential long-term cost of this calculus for your overall happiness?

3. Some may compensate for unhappiness by throwing themselves into work or hobbies. Are there areas of your life where you might be overinvesting to fill a void from an unfulfilled relationship or other source of unhappiness?

4. A parent's *own* happiness in a marriage is crucial for a healthy environment for kids. What small, intentional steps can you take *today* to ensure that your happiness is not perpetually deferred or

sacrificed, especially if you are waiting for a future life stage (like empty nesting) to begin living for yourself?

5.   Ultimately, the chapter is not pro- or anti-divorce, but pro-happiness. What does it truly mean for you to "prioritize your own happiness" in your romantic life, even if it goes against traditional expectations or past decisions?

CHAPTER 20

FALLING IN LOVE AGAIN

*"Have enough courage to trust love one more time
and always one more time."*

—Attributed to Maya Angelou

f you have been so fortunate to have experienced true love in your life, you know it's one of the most magical feelings you can experience. It does not originate from the head, but rather from the heart. Technically speaking, social and neuroscientists may say that it *does* originate from something chemical in our brains, but let's not let facts get in the way of a good story.

You get my point. It does not come from a script handed to you from your parents, your church, or some institution. It comes from some place that is natural, not nurtured. Those butterflies in your stomach when you look into the eyes of the person you love are spontaneously and naturally created—not manufactured after debate, pressure, or duty. If and when you feel those loving feelings, I believe you should listen to them—or at least embrace them. Not that they are always infallible or without their own noise, but at least they likely originate from a clean, pure, or perhaps subconsciously primal source.

In Shannon Odell's TED Ed on the science of falling in love,[2] she describes how the brain experiences (and creates) the feeling of love. According to Shannon, there are a series of neurochemicals and brain systems that fire up when we fall in love—starting with infatuation (passionate love), which typically lasts a few months and generates dopamine-induced euphoric feelings, but later attachment (compassionate love), which generates pair bonding hormones. In the later phases, she describes our ability to potentially move toward forming deeper connections but also reengage some of our cognitive capabilities that will lead to a more sustained bond or determine that the fit is not sustainable (i.e., break up). But regardless, the entire series of activities is initially quite primal and natural. Not premeditated. I believe partnerships—and relationships more broadly—that have clean and pure energy sources have a better chance of being sustained than those that originate from the head—and especially someone else's head.

We can be motivated to seek out love because we feel pressure to get on with life, live up to the expectations of our parents and family, and even for professional purposes. My uncle Dale, who passed away at age eighty-five, was one of my favorite uncles. He was like a surrogate father to me, although he himself never had biological kids. Almost fourteen years older than his youngest brother, my dad, he was like a father figure to most of his nieces and nephews and a patriarch in our family more broadly. He was always the first on the scene if one of us needed school fees, a helping hand moving, or just life advice. He was wise, generous, gregarious, and ahead of his time. He was the first man I knew who collected art, hosted a book club—which lasted decades—and organized his shirts neatly in his closet by color. He was also handsome, charming, and gay.

When my uncle Dale was coming of age in the 1940s and 1950s, and then during adulthood in the 1960s, being an outwardly gay Black man was not only socially unacceptable but could also be dangerous. Dale would later share with me that he knew he was gay as a boy, and others throughout life, including his family, suspected it, but no one ever acknowledged it. Dale had a promising career in the teachers' union and was moving up quickly. He had female suitors at every turn who wondered why he never had any interest in them. He was handsome, gainfully employed in a white-collar career, and came from a respectable and close-knit family. It raised eyebrows when someone of Dale's profile was not married, which could undermine so much of his potential happiness in life, or so he thought.

Dale decided to marry a beautiful woman who was also a teacher and union colleague. My aunt Phyllis was a stylish, attractive, and ambitious woman from a middle-class Black family and community in St. Louis. She, too, looked the part in what could have been a 1970s-era precursor to *The Cosby Show*'s Clair Huxtable, and she knew it. Although I never talked to her about her motivations for marrying my uncle, Dale said they "had an understanding." He gave her a comfortable standard of living, social standing, and status in their community. He also kept her looking good in nice shoes, as he would say with pride. She gave him the appearance of what he needed to be by the standards and expectations of everyone else—his mother included, who was said to have cried with joy and relief when Dale announced his marriage: "He's not gay!" He would laugh as he imagined her reaction.

But he *was* gay. He belonged to a gay book club, a community of gay artists, intellectuals, and loving friends in Washington, DC. So he was effectively roommates with my aunt Phyllis and lived his real life as best he could, offline. They eventually separated, which was his first open step toward coming out, which he never officially did. He just telegraphed it loudly and proudly as he invited his loving friend and "roommate" to live with him for the next few decades of his life. He loved Edgar as much as anyone could love a wife, sister, or daughter, and Edgar loved Dale as much as anyone could love a husband, brother, or father. Although neither ever proclaimed their romantic love for each other, they didn't need to. We saw and respected the love and happiness they gave each other. And Edgar was with my uncle, by Dale's side, until he took his last breath. Dale was a prince among men and one of my favorite people. He unknowingly taught me a lot about what it meant to pursue your authentic truth and happiness.

Although I have divorced twice, I have loved and been loved. I love love. And though I don't feel particularly compelled to remarry for the third time, even if the third time is the charm, I do desire true and lasting love. In many of my uncle's last days, I reflected on how much his embrace of his authentic self and choices in love, romantic and otherwise, had allowed him to experience true and enduring happiness. As I had the opportunity to hold his hand many nights and mornings leading up to his death, I saw a man who had no regrets. A man who had loved and been loved. A man who was happy, on his own terms. And in so many ways, this is what I also want for me in my life and also for you.

PREREQUISITES FOR LOVE

There are a few ingredients that I think can make for a more enduring and happy partnership. These suggestions are of course debatable, totally subjective, and far from scientific. But here are the four that I came up with that I believe are prerequisites for the type of love I want, which I hope leads to happiness.

1. *Attraction.* Before you can decide to get to know someone and discover love, you have to *see* a reason to engage. There's so much science behind attraction that's deeply rooted in our reptilian brain,

the oldest part, both primal and natural. Some we might be aware of, like superficial preferences, while others, like height–width ratios and symmetries, are quietly at work scanning for genetic fit. Attractiveness is not just looks, it's other aspects of physical attributes such as smell, touch, and . . . wait for it . . . sexual chemistry and compatibility, which are huge. Anyone who tells you that you're being superficial with this initial and primal filter is already denying you an important ingredient of happiness.

2. *Intellect.* After you've assessed and found someone attractive, which I imagine might be the easiest of attributes to find, you need a reason to stay engaged. *Homo sapiens*, the thinking ape, generally engage through conversation and intellectual exchanges. This does not mean either you or the other person is intellectual or possesses a high IQ (which is not necessary at all), it just means that you find each other's interests, conversations, etc., engaging and sticky. You hit the ball over the net, and it comes back, with a back-and-forth volley that feels natural and unforced.

3. *Emotional Safety.* Now that you're attracted in all ways and intellectually engaged, you need to feel emotionally safe. You both need to feel seen, heard, and free to be your authentic selves. Can you disagree without being disagreeable? Can you be open to understanding and seeing each other's perspectives and respecting them, even if you see the world differently? I believe this is the most difficult attribute to find and test for and also the most important.

4. *Shared Experiences and Time.* Time is a curing agent that strengthens the first three requirements. Time offers experiences. Time provides perspectives. Time hardens the mortar between the bricks. You can have everything I just mentioned but crumble under the weight of your first trial. Time can build fortifications.

The aforementioned are foundational, though not comprehensive. I believe laughter, growth, partnership, and fun, among other qualities, are essential. However, these are useless without a foundation. Meaningful and lasting partnerships, either for a season or a lifetime, with a single, committed partner (or more if you're poly) can be a great source of happiness and lead to a better life overall. While the science and research back me up on this, it also just makes sense.

We're social animals and thrive best in community and connection. It's likely that we were also not designed to be isolated. We were made to love, and we were made for love. The four attributes are likely foundational for partners in most people's playbooks, but your list might be different.

One last point on the value of relationships in our life. The right, healthy partner possessing all the things we discussed above, at a minimum, can be a source of massive joy in your life, but the wrong partner can be a source of misery. The wrong relationship can destroy and undermine your happiness, which might be quite good in your base state of singleness. Meaning, you might be happier as a single person, with your intrinsic and extrinsic sources of joy coming from other places, versus allowing the wrong lovers in your life that deplete you.

What About You?

Regardless of what ingredients you believe are the most important for the "right" partner, the key is to ensure the following:

1. *You are self-aware.* Check in with how you're feeling in relationships, dating, etc. Is your energy being lifted or drained, and is it easy or hard? (There's a big difference between effort and hard work. Effort is healthy, hard work is not.)

2. *You are intentional.* Assessing, scanning, filtering, reflecting, and introspection take intentionality. Also, being clear on your "10" attributes and your "quadrant" helps you focus. Dating apps can be a great tool if you're intentional with how you use them.

3. *You are solving for your happiness and yours alone!* It doesn't matter what your friends, family, or colleagues think, if you're not feeling a connection with Mr. or Ms. Right, they're not *your* right. I don't care how good something looks in theory on PowerPoint; you can't love or make love to theory. Have the courage to do whatever you do—for you!

REFLECTION QUESTIONS

1. The chapter distinguishes between love that "does not come from a script" and is "natural, not nurtured," versus love influenced by external pressures. Think about a significant romantic connection in your life. To what extent did that love originate from a spontaneous, primal source (like those butterflies in your stomach) versus being influenced by expectations from family, friends, or societal norms?

2. Have you ever pursued or maintained a relationship more out of a sense of duty, pressure, or a logical "fit" than from a deep, authentic emotional connection? What were the long-term happiness consequences of that approach?

3. How do you distinguish between infatuation (passionate love) and attachment (compassionate love) in your own experiences, and how does understanding these phases influence your approach to long-term partnership?

4. If you were to fully commit to solving for your happiness and yours alone in your romantic life, what specific external opinions or internal doubts might you need to bravely disregard or challenge? What does having the courage to do whatever you do—for you—look like in your current romantic context?

CHAPTER 21

WHY HAVING KIDS MAY NOT BRING YOU HAPPINESS

*"Having children is like living in
a frat house—nobody sleeps, everything's broken,
and there's a lot of throwing up."*

—Attributed to Ray Romano

I once wanted kids, but after my ex-wife and I had a series of miscarriages and unsuccessful IVF efforts, we began to change our expectations of not only our lives but what was likely to bring us happiness. Although we were initially disappointed after spending five or six years trying to conceive, in the subsequent years following that pain, we directed our energy and derived joy from being amazing aunts and uncles, traveling to distant places, and supporting important causes.

With the benefit of time, I looked back on my younger self who, with his wife, wanted so badly to be a parent. I became curious about what my *why* was for wanting kids and what was behind this desire. Up until that point, I had never sat still long enough to seriously and honestly reflect on what I assumed was a natural and primal impulse.

For context, our path to parenthood was complex and required a lot of time, effort, and financial resources. Further, our fertility clinic was in a different state, and some of our miscarriages were ectopic and required surgeries for my ex-wife, who at the same time worked and handled all the stresses of being an Ivy League professor. After our fifth miscarriage, we were faced with the decision to keep trying with more rounds of IVF, as the medical team realized the source of the prior issues. We also wondered if we should consider surrogacy. We contemplated these options for several months, took some time to recenter, and put our dreams of a family on the back burner. Neither of us ever revisited that back burner, and we're actually both happy about that—but it took us time to get there.

The decision to stop trying was anything but clear at the time. It was a difficult season in our marriage and, I am certain, a far more difficult season for her. So I didn't have the emotional or intellectual capacity at the time to reflect deeply on my why. Why had it been so important to me that we try and keep trying? Although I didn't spend much time introspecting then, I did in the years that followed—and it was illuminating.

At some core biological level, I assume that humans are like every other species when it comes to reproduction. It's in our nature to procreate and promote the survival of the species, whether we are conscious of this or not. Research supports this assumption,[1] that humans are hardwired with hormonal and physiological drivers to experience "baby fever." Like the salmon, who pay the ultimate price (death) for the next generation, humans can be expected to compromise some of their happiness in exchange for carrying, bearing, and raising offspring. Although it's not clear that the salmon know that laying eggs will be their final act, humans know that the endeavor is an irreversible commitment for at least the next eighteen years, will be costly, and will likely limit some individual freedoms their childless friends will continue to enjoy. That's not even including the health risks and potential death that come for some mothers, which research shows[2] has not deterred women. So it's not a trivial thing to sign up for parenthood.

THE HAPPINESS MYTH

Most people who plan pregnancies likely consider the pragmatic factors in their calculus. What many also factor into their thinking—whether they know it or not—is a host of myths that are worth further inspection.

Some people expect that having kids will be a source of happiness. In his article, "What Becoming a Parent Really Does to Your Happiness," Paul Bloom[3] observes that not only do we not experience greater happiness but we also actually experience greater unhappiness. He reports a survey done by Harvard professor and psychologist Daniel Kahneman, where nine hundred mothers were asked about their happiness:

> They recalled being with their children as less enjoyable than many other activities, such as watching TV, shopping, or preparing food.
>
> Other studies showed that when a child is born, parents experience a decrease in happiness that doesn't go away for a long time, in addition to a drop in marital satisfaction that doesn't usually recover until the children leave the house.
>
> "[. . .] having children, particularly when they are young, involves financial struggle, sleep deprivation, and stress. For mothers, there is also in many cases the physical strain of pregnancy and breastfeeding."

The impact is also felt in the marriage, in which many experience a decline in happiness. He goes on to report:

"Children can turn a cheerful and loving romantic partnership into a zero-sum battle over who gets to sleep and work and who doesn't. Children provoke a couple's most frequent arguments—more than money, more than work, more than in-laws, more than annoying personal habits, communication styles, leisure activities, commitment issues, bothersome friends, sex."

More Parenting Myths

So why is the desire to have kids so strong for some of us? Aside from biological motivations, which could be enough, I believe there are a few social and happiness experiences that could be quietly at work. Here are a few:

- *The God Complex.* Some of my friends are fortunate to be well-educated, attractive by some superficial standards, and financially secure. They usually won't say it out loud directly, but some of them feel and may infer that "if anyone should have kids, it's us." They quietly imagine all the kids born in poverty, adverse circumstances, or to less-fitting parents and think it their duty to contribute their genes and lifestyle to the pool. They view themselves as gods of sorts, or vessels of God's will.

- *The Racial/Ethnic Motives.* The God complex can extend to racial and ethnic motives to have kids. Some people feel a duty to contribute their genetic, social, and economic resources to building and furthering their race, tribe, or cultural affiliation. This is particularly the case for oppressed, suppressed, and ethnic minority groups.

- *The Insurance Motive.* Who is going to love me? Who's going to take care of me one day when I am old? It was once a real and legitimate motivation for families to think about offspring as a source of financial and social welfare. Not only would it have been a concern of the parents' livelihood after their working years ended, but in some agrarian-based economies, offspring could be a more immediate source of economic support. Today, this is perhaps less the case—and in fact the opposite, except in the rare cases for parents of teen celebrities, athletes, and so on. Despite this motivation, there is not a lot of compelling evidence that kids want to grow up and take care of their parents. They might, but many would probably just as likely delegate that authority to assisted living, senior homes, or residential nursing resources.

- *The Biography Motive.* For some, this is the next most logical thing in their life narrative. They have carefully scripted and followed the playbook for success in every area of life, including education, career, and perhaps marriage. The only box left unchecked in the "golden child" narrative is producing a child: the *perfect* child. It's the way they've always envisioned their life, and they have been steadily piecing together all of the puzzle pieces and may feel the story is incomplete or lacking if they don't have kids.

- *The Cultural Motive.* Some people will feel an immense amount of cultural pressure to keep with tradition. My ex-wife came from a West African immigrant family, which gave me the opportunity to see and experience some of these well-intended pressures firsthand. Although she had accomplished every imaginable thing an immigrant family could want, including Ivy League degrees, a prestigious job, and all the awards and honors to boot, she had not yet had kids. This missing mother title was of immense importance to her family and cultural tradition. I am sure she initially felt awkward, maybe inadequate, and then ultimately annoyed each time someone in the family would inquire about our progress with conceiving a child. "When are you guys planning to try again? How's it coming? We're praying for you. We know that God can bless you if you have faith. I know someone back home who says this or that can help," they'd say. There was a very real pressure we experienced, and I'm sure many others do as well, despite the fact these comments were always well-intended and expressed with love and support.

If I am honest, I was likely driven a bit by all of these. I had cultural, social, and egotistical motivations that I was probably not aware were at work in my subconscious. If you have or want kids, can you reflect on what was or is your why? Again, there are no right or wrong answers. But of all the answers just listed, which do you think lead to and sustain happiness?

I still do not have kids, and I am pretty sure that I do not want any in the foreseeable future. I love my life as it is. I have the great fortune of being an uncle, a big brother, and a mentor to many. I have found many ways to pour back into the next generation as a surrogate parent of sorts. I sometimes still wonder if a future version of myself will wish that I had kids. But today, I embrace the freedom, mobility, and happiness that comes with not having kids.

My ex-wife and I had an amicable divorce and took a very thoughtful, intentional, and respectful path that led us to the decision. Today, we are not only friends, but each other's cheerleaders of sorts. From time to time when our paths cross or we have a reason to text or chat live, we sometimes reflect on how glad we are that we did not have kids. Although that was not always the case, our happiness quotient now comprises so many other things—traveling, scuba diving, making an impact in our professional communities, and pouring back into our nieces and nephews.

My and my ex's happiness expectations have evolved, and I am sure they will continue to evolve. But we are grateful that we did not allow any of the pressures, either from our own internal scripts or the external pressure from others, push us to do something that would ultimately have reduced our future happiness.

REFLECTION QUESTIONS

1. What is your core "why" for wanting children (or having had them)?

2. Which of the myths or underlying motives described resonate most strongly with your own (or others') desire to have children? How might these unexamined whys influence your expectations for personal happiness *after* becoming a parent?

3. How does the research presented by Paul Bloom and Daniel Kahneman align or conflict with your personal observations of parents around you, or your own experience if you are a parent? What unexamined assumptions about happiness might we carry into the decision to have children?

CHAPTER 22

THE JOYS AND PAINS OF KIN FOLK

"Families are like fudge—mostly sweet, with a few nuts."

—Attributed to Les Dawson

Family can be a great source of joy, comfort, and belonging. Some of my fondest memories are from family gatherings as a child during Christmas and Thanksgiving holidays. I used to love seeing all my family together, laughing, eating, gossiping, reminiscing, and loving each other. It might have been months or longer since we'd been together, but we'd pick up with hugs and love like it was just yesterday. Even today, I love my family and always look forward to our small and large gatherings alike.

It has been said that no one will love you like your own. Still, those who are closest to you in proximity and cultural obligation can also be a source of great strain and stress. Yes, families can be a source of great unhappiness. It is typically within families that you see long-standing feuds over money, property, and unresolved childhood grievances. The pain need not stem from something nefarious or preventable to be just as painful.

For some, caring for aging parents can be an immense source of stress and a financial drain. This compounds if you are caring for both young kids and your parents. According to AARP, an estimated 17 percent of adults in the United States care for parents and experience as much as $600 billion in lost wages as a result.[1]

In other cases, it could be the challenges that come from caring for a special needs child. My cousin and her husband had a son with severe autism, which required my cousin to defer her career ambitions in order to prioritize caregiving. In fact, her entire core family planned their life—from daily chores to family vacations—around the needs of their autistic son, until his unexpected death from a blood clot a month before he turned twenty-one.

But often our pain is preventable. For example, certain behaviors are tolerated within families much longer than they would be elsewhere. I can think of a number of people in my family who struggled with substance abuse, which placed a great strain and burden on the family. For these individuals in my family, we struggled to balance between loving and trying to understand their sickness while not enabling them or allowing them to cause harm to the rest of us. That balancing act is like teaching a circus bear to stand and walk on a ball.

Maybe it wasn't drug abuse but something else in your family. Some families have to also protect themselves from the drunk uncle who regularly gets angry and abusive after having one too many. Then there's undiagnosed and untreated mental illness, which might or might not be linked to a drug addiction. These things are tough but real, and I know them all too well.

I can also remember seasons when my mom's siblings did not talk to each other for months or years over what might have seemed insignificant to an outsider. Our love and pain were like a yo-yo, springing back and forth between the deepest undying love to an anger and angst reserved for complete strangers. That's family, and we love them just the same—but it does not mean we have to allow them to rob us of our happiness.

My father and I developed a loving relationship later in life, although he was absent for most of my and my brother's youth, and we typically only saw each other one to three times a year thereafter. He had a daughter, my half-sister Alon, with his second wife. Although he was much more involved in Alon's life, their relationship was bumpy and difficult as well. The four of us—me, my siblings, and father—never spent any meaningful time together, just occasional and brief gatherings at holidays. My father never supported my mother with child support or any financial support, for that matter. As adults, I and my siblings are now a financial resource for my father—and the irony is something I sometimes struggle with emotionally. However, there was an event that is a particularly painful example of what I hope to communicate in this chapter.

LOVE AND GROWTH

I wanted to give my siblings, my father, and myself a meaningful chance to bond and grow closer, so I offered to take us all on a vacation to Costa Rica for a week. I offered to cover everyone's airfare, hotel, and food. All they needed was their passport.

My father had never traveled abroad and had never needed or thought to get a passport. So this was a prerequisite action item we reminded our father to get done—every week. He's a procrastinator and needs constant nudging to get everything done from doctors' appointments to taking care of administrative matters. So we knew that our sibling tag-team effort was critical. My father learned during his passport application process that the government wouldn't issue passports to individuals with outstanding child support balances. My father had never paid our child support, so the balance was quite significant, and he had no funds to put toward it.

When my father shared the news, I was sick to my stomach and immediately knew what it meant for me. If I wanted my father to join us for our first family vacation, I would have to pay his child support, or enough for the government to release his passport. I was deeply troubled and cried when I thought about the irony and implications. I thought about the thousands I would need to pay, thousands that had been desperately needed by my mother when we were growing up without any child support.

I was also angry, disappointed, and resentful that my father, who is truly the nicest and most congenial guy you'll ever meet, would get off so easy in life. Despite having left his family and not supporting them in any capacity, he had benefited from us reaching out to him when we were young adults, visiting him each year to form and sustain a relationship, supporting him financially when it was necessary, and now paying down his child support balance so that *I* could take him on an all-expense-paid vacation to Costa Rica.

Regardless of how crappy I felt at the moment, I decided to let it go. There was nothing any of us could do to change the past. Those were all sunk costs of time and money. If we wanted to make the most of the time we had left in each other's lives, we would have to treat today as not only a new chapter but a new book. So I paid down his child support, and we went on to have a lovely and memorable vacation. I went from feeling sadness to feeling gratitude. We all had been given a second chance. It was perfect, except for one thing that hurt more and cut deeper than anything I had felt before.

When we returned to the US from Costa Rica, waiting for our respective connecting flights, my father motioned for me to lean over so that he could share something of importance with me. He shared how grateful he was for everything and reminded me how much he loved me. I know that he was. Then, without hesitation, he asked if he could borrow some money. I was crushed and had no idea how to even respond. *How could he even think to ask me for money after all that had transpired in the weeks prior?* I thought. *How could he love me and treat me like his personal ATM?*

I didn't speak with him for months afterwards. Although I would forgive him, have compassion, and shell out money time and time again, I never stopped loving him. But I would learn to keep a safe distance, emotionally and otherwise, to protect my joy and honor the boundaries I later learned to erect. I would also learn and be reminded that I could love and embrace my family, a source of pure love and happiness, while also being dispassionate when I needed to protect myself from feelings of guilt, shame, and obligation.

There are relationships in life that you choose and those that you are assigned at birth. Although you may not feel comfortable admitting it, we all sometimes find more happiness in nonfamily relationships. It's also the case that when we outgrow friendships from high school or college, as an example, we feel less guilty about bringing those relationships to an end. However, you may feel significant guilt and conflict over the decision to end a relationship with a family member or to care for (or not) an aging parent. You might feel conflicted about allowing a sibling who suffers from drug addiction to sleep on your couch, or even how to deal with a crazy uncle who spews racist, ignorant, or just embarrassing views at the Thanksgiving table. These are moments when your family can be a drain on happiness— and yet sometimes it feels taboo or inappropriate to admit it.

ESTABLISHING BOUNDARIES WITH FAMILY

When my mother passed, I felt a certain responsibility to step up and be a provider and leader in my family. I was only twenty-six, but I felt the weight as if I were a sixty-two-year-old elder in the family. I had not been asked to do this, nor had there been an explicit expectation I take on any such role. But I took some comfort in doing things for my family members that I could not do for my mother. My therapist later helped me to make that connection. My inner child had a pleaser complex and felt loved when I could be of service. But I also felt guilt that my mother passed before I had a chance to be the responsible adult and leader in the family that I had always wanted her to see in me, so I projected this onto my family.

Some of my friends who have enjoyed more professional and economic successes than others in their family feel a bit of survivor's guilt and consequently find themselves acting as the family bank. Even when they know it's unsustainable or wrong for the family to treat them as a money tree, the survivor's guilt and sense of family duty is too overwhelming to allow them to say no. That's been me for much of my professional life, and it has been a source of great distress at times.

At one point, I was paying mortgages, paying to have cars fixed, and even had some monthly expenses on auto withdrawal for some family members (and still do). I always picked up the tab, whenever there was one to pick up, and did so without hesitation. There were some in my family who would abuse it while others were gracious. I had one uncle, who has since passed, who would without hesitation ask for money and if I declined, might turn to more nefarious plotting and scheming to trigger my guilt.

Find Your Healthy Limits

These experiences have taught me a few important lessons about how to establish boundaries and protect myself from the people that have the potential to not only be a source of great love, but also of pain.

1. *It's Not About Loyalty.* I came from a tradition where you didn't talk about family business outside the home. It was an unspoken rule that some things, such as family secrets, you'd take to the grave. It's one of the reasons why it took me such a long time to open up in therapy, relationships, and important friendships about my

relationship with my mom. Being vulnerable in an authentic way meant I had to talk about her substance abuse. However, talking about something as potentially shameful as drug addiction, even for someone who's no longer alive, was very difficult for me. All I could imagine was how disappointed she would be that I was airing her business in the streets. But viewing everything through the lens of loyalty meant that I was not dealing with my own emotions in a healthy way. I also wasn't acknowledging what truthfully happened in my life and how those events have shaped me.

Further, not being fully transparent about my relationship with my parents and other people whose relationships greatly impacted me, both positively and negatively, meant that I was not being honest at all. That dishonesty was causing me unhappiness. I now realize that I can love my family and be loyal to them while also being honest about who they are *to me*. Sharing our lived experiences does not mean we're being judgmental or condescending, nor does it equate to being disloyal. It just means that this is part of healing, growth, and the desire to be happy. I am also coming to appreciate how my story is not that unique at all. Everyone thinks they are as unique as snowflakes. But in fact, we and our families are more the same than not.

2. *Tall Fences Make for Good Family Relationships.* Just as we establish boundaries at work and in our friendships, we can establish boundaries with our family relationships. Boundaries mean you have predetermined certain things you will not tolerate. There are certain spaces you intend to keep for yourself and not invite others to occupy. Those spaces can be physical and real or emotional and figurative. I have also found it sometimes helpful to communicate those boundaries in advance so that family understands why you are doing something and will hopefully respect that you've given it, them, and the situation principled consideration.

3. *Establish Rules.* Establish rules for when and how you engage with people and situations that have the potential to drain your happiness. Once you establish these rules, follow them and communicate them in advance. A good example of rules I developed that helped me mitigate moments when I felt drained were those for when and how I loaned or gave money to family members. There was once a time when I would just give money to whoever and whenever they asked. Now I have rules that are closely tied to things that I value, such as education, health and wellness, and opportunities for someone to help themselves. These rules also helped me when I was developing my estate plan for when I eventually die. It helped me think about how I want to continue to be a resource to my family when I'm no longer physically here to make those decisions for myself. Rules may sound callous and cold, but they're actually thoughtful and loving ways to ensure that you have the capacity to show up as your best and happiest self.

4. *Emotional Vampires.* There is nothing that says you have to spend time with family you do not want to. I once read a book called *Emotional Vampires: Dealing with People Who Drain You Dry* by Albert J. Bernstein, which goes through all of the various types of narcissistic profiles and ways in which those types of people can deceptively drain you the way vampires do their victims. Once you identify someone as a vampire (of your happiness) or any other thing of value such as money, time, etc., you can decide you do not want them in your life or keep them at a safe distance. There are certain folks that when I see their name pop up on my phone, I just don't answer. I know they are calling to tell me one of a hundred sad stories of how the dog ate their homework and they need a few hundred bucks to get through the month. There are times when I will choose not to engage in conversations with these types of

people and feel no guilt about it. Yes, you are my family, but you are also an emotional vampire. This is consistent with establishing boundaries and rules.

5. *Pick and Choose.* While I might sound a bit harsh, I am actually super close with 98 percent of my family and especially close to some, such as my siblings. My family on both sides have traditions of convening every year for holidays and special occasions. These are some of my favorite moments. I love my family, and I am deeply proud of our legacy, which I have spent considerable time documenting and preserving for future generations. I also have a wonderful next generation of nieces and nephews who I'm excited to see carry my family forward. However, I don't spend equal amounts of time with everyone. There are some family members who are a source of great joy, and I choose to spend more time with them versus other relatives. One of the reasons why I moved back to Atlanta, for example, was to be closer to my younger brother. My brother now has a three-year-old son, a beautiful wife, and a niece who is like a daughter. Being in close proximity to them gives me the opportunity to spend a lot more time with them—and thus more happiness for me. It's a choice I make.

THE FAMILY YOU CHOOSE

When we think about how the role of family has evolved from one of pure necessity and practicality to one of potential love, happiness, and belonging, we realize that the latter can be constructed in any number of ways. There will perhaps always be some level of connection that just comes from the people you've spent the most amount of time with since birth and have a historical, cultural, and genetic predisposition to loving you. It is also true that these people can be sources of immense unhappiness, as we discussed already. It is also true that DNA and genetics don't make someone family in the relationship sense. A person's *actions* make them family.

I have been fortunate to develop deep and lasting friendships with folks I met in college who I consider family. Some of them are my fraternity brothers (Alpha Phi Alpha), who I have known between twenty and thirty years. Many know me better than many of my blood relatives and vice versa. Most of all, we choose to be family to each other for reasons that are our own, and not out of duty or cultural obligation. In Leslie Perlow's research on the joy we experience when doing certain activities with others (over doing them alone),[2] she even found that some experiences generate more happiness when we do them with non-family relationships than they do when we experience them with family.

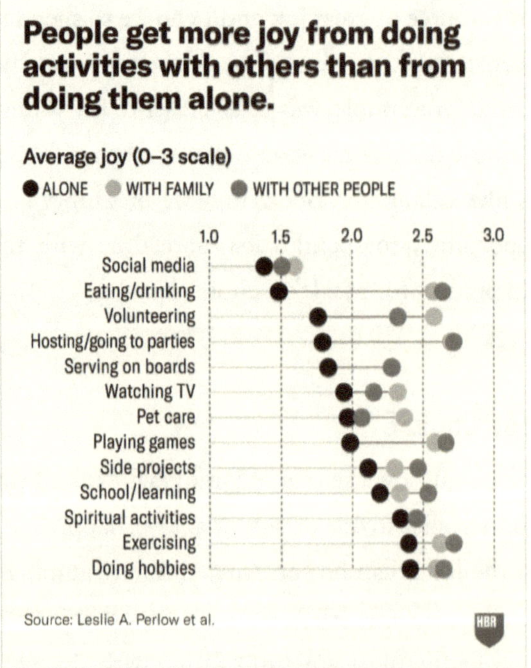

Joy in Activities Done with Others: HBS Professor Leslie Perlow documents the differences in joy experienced in doing activities alone, with family, and with others.

Just as we can choose to make and sustain deep bonds with nongenetic family, we can also choose to heal, redeem, and nurture our biological family relationships. When we were kids, my brother and I would fight, argue, and harbor resentment. Over time our relationship changed and evolved from petty sibling rivalry to more paternal, with me acting more like a father than a brother (which my brother resented but understood). Now we are men who have mutual respect for and learn from each other. Most of all, we choose to spend time, share articles, books, and music with each other, and we work through the things that arise between us—like how best to support our father.

Similarly, our relationship with our younger sister has evolved from a classical big-brother role to one of respect and equality. Although she is a decade or more younger than either of us, she has more experience being a mother and has managed to remain married longer than either of us. We choose to spend time together, learn from each other, and work through the tough times. While this seems normal and natural, it's not necessarily what we grew up experiencing. It was normal to write a family member off, assume that they were incapable of changing (or that we didn't need to change), and allow the narrative of "this is just how it is" to take hold. The three of us make a concerted effort to engage, support, and love our father, even when our instincts are to sometimes disengage.

Perhaps my best personal example of choosing to be family is choosing to be a Robinson in more than name only. When my parents separated, we lost touch with our father's side of the family, who we barely knew and saw as kids to begin with. They lived in Michigan, and my brother and I lived in Atlanta under the watchful eyes and isolation of our mother. Only our uncle Dale maintained an active relationship with us.

Although it's understandable how family can choose to avoid prying into the affairs of another (like my dad's messy and abrupt separation), my brother and I harbored some resentment for how it felt and appeared from our vantage point. It would take years of effort to mend and build new bridges—traveling to Detroit as adults, making time to get to know our cousins (and their kids) as well as our aunt and uncles, as well as inviting them into our lives. That was our choice. And I am so glad we did it.

My brother and I are deeply involved in every aspect of our Robinson family and enriched because of it. We help host family reunions, keep family history, and even serve as estate executives for our deceased uncle's estate. We love and are loved by our Robinson family—not because of genetics or duty, but because it's our choice to do so.

All relationships—those assigned by virtue of DNA and others that we choose over time, like I did with my fraternity brothers—have the potential to be great sources of happiness, belonging, and emotional safety, but they are equally capable of being sources of emotional distress and drain. We have more agency than we sometimes give ourselves credit for in terms of which relationships we want to keep and pour into and those we should let go.

One of my favorite sayings when it comes to relationships is "the grass is greenest where you water it." We have permission to decide which romantic, family, and friend relationships we want to water. The rubric should be easy: Water those that pour back into you! Happiness is just one metric, but there are many others. I pour into the relationships that encourage my growth, learning, exposure, and experiences. As for parenting, there are likely fewer joys than those that come from pouring into the next generation of life. However, whatever motivates you to want to be a parent, a spouse, or a beloved uncle, it's more likely to be a source of sustaining happiness if the reasons are your own.

REFLECTION QUESTIONS

1. When you reflect on your family experiences, what specific aspects of your family dynamics bring you the greatest sense of love, connection, or belonging?

2. Conversely, what specific behaviors, unresolved issues, or dynamics within your family have historically been (or currently are) a significant source of pain, stress, or unhappiness for you?

3. Can you recall a time when you felt a significant internal conflict between what you felt obligated to do for a family member and what truly served your own well-being and happiness? What was the outcome, and what did you learn?

4. Who are the individuals or groups in your life (beyond blood relatives) that you actively "choose to be family to," and what makes those relationships a source of deep fulfillment and belonging?

5. Ultimately, this chapter argues for more agency in picking which relationships to keep and pour into. How does embracing this agency empower you to cultivate greater happiness, and what does that look like in practice for your family connections?

HAPPINESS TRAPS

L et's assume that by now, you embrace the idea that there are forces at work that are reducing, delaying, or forfeiting your happiness. Some of these forces are silent and sneaky, while others are proudly on display and enjoying your collaboration to maintain. In the prior chapters, we explored our role in some of the biggest forces working to enhance or obliterate our happiness: work, faith, and relationships.

If you can start doing some of the hard work, even with small steps, to address these three structural decisions and forces in life, you will be well on your way to finding or reclaiming your happiness. But you will not be out of the woods just yet. You may very well find yourself a victim to what I call "happiness traps." These are moments and blind spots that, in spite of our best-planned efforts, can rob you of your gross and net happiness. In this final section, we explore how you can best safeguard your joy.

CHAPTER 23

PUTTING HAPPINESS FIRST

"Wherever you are, be there totally."

—Eckhart Tolle, *The Power of Now*

When I reflect on some of the things that bring me joy, there is one that jumps to the top of the list. I absolutely love scuba diving. While it's not the only thing that triggers the release of endorphins in my brain, it's one of the more uniquely powerful ones, and it requires some effort. It's also an activity that did not initially bring me any joy when I first tried it, but rather fear, anxiety, and a fair amount of insecurity.

But many years later and a few hundred dives logged, I now choose to organize almost all of my vacations around this single activity. I will light up anytime I have an opportunity to share dive stories. Besides the joy that I get from diving, I have also learned some important lessons about happiness in the process. There's one in particular that I learned from my dear friend, frat brother, and dive buddy, Dan Rodriguez.

QUALITY OVER QUANTITY (WHAT I LEARNED FROM DAN)

Just a few years before we decided to get scuba certified, Dan had learned that he had colon cancer. Although Dan was a few years younger than I (in his thirties at the time), he was already dealing with a form of cancer that typically shows up in men and women decades older.

But Dan wasn't any ordinary guy; he was an MIT graduate in computer science and an extreme sportsman. In high school, he was a champion wrestler; after college he committed to jiujitsu and eventually became a black belt and an instructor. Dan also had more than five hundred jumps out of airplanes and was a base jumper skilled in wingsuit glides from mountains and planes.

Dan was also odd in many ways you'd have to know and experience to love. He had lived a few years in LA, where he worked during the day as a computer programmer while auditioning and moonlighting as extras on Hollywood sets. But rather than rent an apartment stuffed with Ikea furniture like most newly minted grads, Dan lived on a sailboat for nearly three years.

Dan was carved up like a superhero, with muscles everywhere, but more closely resembled the shy and slightly nerdy Clark Kent. He was endearing and inspiring. Dan also held a number of life philosophies I initially found odd, later intriguing, and over time, inspiring. He found his truths from reading and critical thinking and reasoning. He was his own man. Dan was agnostic—maybe atheist—polyamorous, and fighting stage-4 cancer.

During one of my earlier midlife crises, I invited Dan to join me on a trip to Costa Rica. I wanted to spend time with him not only to foster our friendship but also to learn from him and probe his thinking on a range of things regarding life and happiness. I was struggling to find happiness in my work, although I was outwardly successful. I was also dealing with some of the normal ups and downs of married life and wrestling with some of the fundamental questions about my life, purpose, and happiness.

Dan was contrarian not only in his views on many topics but also in his approach. Doctors had warned that his cancer could be treated in one of two ways. One way would require significant surgery and leave him using an ostomy bag for the rest of his life. This approach would give him the greatest opportunity to beat cancer by carving out as much of the surface area on which the cancer had grown, but it would also mean that the quality of his life, for however long, would be significantly diminished. For a man who looked the picture of health and a person for whom movement and activity was a source of joy, this was too high a price for his happiness. The second option offered by doctors was to pursue a potentially less effective, but also less invasive course of chemotherapy and radiation.

Dan shocked many of his friends when he opted for the latter, but they shouldn't have been surprised. Dan was living a truth that many give lip service to but fall short of actually doing: He was organizing his life around his happiness and desired quality of life, even if he risked potentially living a shorter one.

Although Dan was younger than me and we did not have too much in common in terms of our career journeys and lifestyles at the time, his spirit resonated with something deep and asleep within me. I had not yet constructed the philosophical framework that I now offer you so easily and readily, but when he and I spent that week in Costa Rica, I began to sketch some of the earliest foundational concepts. Although we were, on the surface, two frat brothers hiking, touring the sites, and having fun, below the surface, we were being vulnerable and sharing ideas and perspectives on life. Dan was living his best life, as best I could see, and doing it on his terms. I knew deep down that I was not. Many years earlier, when I had been a college senior and he a freshman, I'd been the big brother, the wiser one, and the one with the answers. Yet in this season, I felt very much like his student.

In the last few days of our trip, almost on a whim, we decided to give scuba diving a try. We were looking for something else to do that was physical, challenging, and engaging to round out our trip. Earlier, we had climbed a volcano, gone river rafting, and soaked in the natural hot springs with the locals. Dan suggested we try scuba diving but insisted that we approach scuba the way he had every other sport and activity in his life: Full on, 100 percent. So for two days, rather than hang out and party, we studied for our certification. I could not have known then that scuba diving would be the beginning of one of my greatest sources of joy and also my quest for truth and meaning in my happiness and life purpose.

I'm happy to share that nearly ten years after his diagnosis, Dan is not only alive but living his best life. He still deals with the ups and downs of occasionally finding something concerning on one of his regular scans and then having to change his treatment options (he had a chemo pump inserted into his liver for years, for example) or endure another surgery.

Still, in between he lives a more active life than me, looks amazing, and centers his life unapologetically around his happiness. While fewer than 15 percent of those diagnosed with stage-4 colon cancer survive, Dan has defied the odds with the path he chose and taught me a powerful lesson about following your authentic truth. Most of all, he has been a living example of when quality can be worth more than quantity. For some, this is an easy thing to say when there are no real or permanent consequences, but for those facing the realities of a terminal illness, it is more than just a bumper-sticker slogan. It could be life or death.

Today, Dan is exploring new frontiers of joy and growth. For example, he recently picked up another hobby: Photography. He enjoys taking some of the most artistic pics of everything from cats to special moments with his friends. He manages to be as technical with his newfound joy as he is artistic and creative. He posts his work on Instagram and enjoys the joy it brings his close friends who are amazed to see him evolving into not only his softer and sillier self but a more creative version of himself. Just a few years prior, Dan took up standup comedy and improv, in part to get more comfortable with public speaking but also to keep exploring new sources of purpose, community, growth, and fulfillment. I have learned so much from Dan and I suspect we could all benefit from taking a page out of his "quality over quantity" playbook.

BEING PRESENT

After a few years of traveling and diving around the world, I learned another powerful lesson about happiness. First, it's important for context that I share how much I love filming, editing, and sharing videos of all my great dives. I never dive without my regulator in one hand and my GoPro camera in the other. I have published nearly seventy shorts on YouTube and Instagram but have hours and hours more of content on my laptop. To be clear, I am an amateur at best and do not boast a big social media following. But the creative process is a source of joy, and I find meaning in sharing bits of the world below with friends and family.

Once I had a chance to dive the Red Sea, one of the world's best dive destinations. Although I entered the sea from Israel, I could also see the shores of Jordan and Egypt from the boat. It was an amazing site to behold—but the real beauty was what was below the water. Yes, the Red Sea is known for its storied parting by Moses as he delivered the Jews out of bondage and fled Egypt, but it's also known to us scuba junkies for its beautiful reefs, comfortable temperatures, and abundant and diverse marine life.

So here I was, on the boat with only a scuba guide and our boat captain. It's rare to have the boat and sea all to yourself in a popular tourist destination like the Red Sea, but that day I did. After doing my equipment check and inflating my BCD (the vest we wear to keep us buoyant), I back rolled off the boat into the Red Sea and felt the cool water engulf my body. It felt amazing as always, but that moment of bliss was immediately followed with utter dread. I realized as I hit the water that I was missing my GoPro camera. Ugh! I had somehow left my camera at the hotel. I was so pissed with myself. I never, ever do that.

For the first few minutes of the dive, I was hardly present. I kept ruminating on how much of an idiot I was to come all this way and leave my camera. Although it was just me and my scuba guide with the entire sea to ourselves, I was far from embracing the magic and potential happiness of the moment. We did not have any other clumsy divers kicking up sand, obstructing a perfect camera shot, or scaring away the magnificent creatures I hoped to see. There was none of that. It was perfect.

Fortunately, I had a gruff and scrappy dive guide, who had spent most of his life serving in the Israeli military. He was hardened and not particularly the warm and fuzzy scuba guide you typically find in most Caribbean tourist destinations. This guy was a hardcore and very serious diver, more like an army drill sergeant than the typical cheerful hippie instructor who opted for a career doing what they loved. So I was awakened from my internal stupor when he grabbed my arm and shook it urgently. He was trying to get my attention and point out something that wasn't obvious to me. Whatever it was, it was small and required me to squint and focus.

Then out of nowhere emerged to my view the most beautiful octopus I had ever seen either in person or on TV. It was bright blue with red spots. Not the poisonous blue-ringed octopus that is infamous in Australia and other parts of the world, but something that looked more like a Spider-Man costume than anything nefarious. It was beautiful, and my spirits were lifted.

At that moment I had an epiphany. In all of my countless dives before then, I had been so focused on filming that I had often failed to be present and experience what was actually before me—but not this time. Not having my camera allowed me to be more present. I hovered over the octopus and stared at it for what seemed like a lifetime. I was noticing every detail and its ever-changing shape and color. It was not spooked by our presence, although we maintained a respectful distance. We studied and perhaps connected with the sentient being for long enough for the image to sear into my brain. I will never forget it. Nor will I forget what happened next. Once again, my scuba guide grabbed my arm so as to not waste time in getting me to refocus my attention elsewhere. This time he pointed up.

In the ocean, humans have no advantage in their environment. Everything that makes us an apex predator on land is almost useless in the ocean. You can't see very far, even if you have 20/20 vision and the water visibility is great. You might hear things from time to time, but most ocean life makes few audible noises and even when you do hear sounds, from a distant dolphin for example, it's hard to tell which direction it's coming from. You can't smell and you can't taste, as both of those senses are not only useless underwater, they are also blocked by your mask and the regulator in your mouth. Lastly, humans are really slow in the ocean. Even a strong swimmer would find that skillset to be rather useless in the open ocean, as you are mostly floating around—more like an astronaut trying to maintain neutral buoyancy. You also can't breathe without the regulator and the compressed air in the tank on your back.

The word scuba is actually an acronym: Self-Contained Underwater Breathing Apparatus. So there you have it. You are more like a simple single-celled organism squiggling around on a petri dish than the fearsome apex creature that rules the rest of the earth. Scuba diving has taught me to be still, to be present, and to be humble. My type-A brain shuts off almost immediately when I splash into the water each time, and the wonderment and imagination of my inner child steps to the front. I am in awe of everything that lives here and grateful that it tolerates my temporary visit.

As my scuba guide's finger pointed frantically above us, I remembered that there are things happening all around at any point in time—above, behind, to either side, and below. There are literally 360 degrees of action that could be happening at any point around you. This time, it was a massive whale shark that was approaching us ever so gently to check out the two foreigners in its universe. Whale sharks are considered the gentle giants of the sea. Although intimidating with an average adult size of eighteen to thirty-two feet long and twenty-one tons (although they can grow to be much larger), they are far from dangerous or aggressive. Even their name is misleading. They are not the type of sharks that your mind might immediately register but rather, more like a whale in how it moves, what it eats, and its grace.

Although this chance encounter happened many years ago, the shelf-life of that experience was enduring for me. In fact, it is still just as fresh and meaningful to me as if it happened yesterday. It was the absence of my camera, which initially annoyed me, that allowed me to experience and absorb the real joy of this chance encounter.

Although I still carry my camera and film, as I always did, I now make an effort to focus on being present. So rather than watch the event unfold through the preview lens of the camera, I simply point and click and then allow my eyes to experience whatever is happening in the moment. It sometimes results in a slightly less impressive shot that is maybe off centered or maybe not even fully capturing the moment in a way that I'm proud of from a production perspective, but the memories last so much longer when I allow them. So does the happiness.

REFLECTION QUESTIONS

1. Are there examples of when you have been willing to make significant trade-offs, take risks, or otherwise bear costs to prioritize your happiness? What assumptions did you make and how did they play out? In reflecting on those decisions, do you have any regrets today?

2. Looking back at a critical juncture in your professional or personal life, can you identify a moment when you instinctively recognized a need to prioritize your happiness but chose a different path due to a perceived obligation, fear of the unknown, or external pressure? What were the long-term emotional or experiential consequences of that choice?

3. If prioritizing your happiness in your current life situation requires you to take a significant "risk" or make an uncomfortable change, what would that look like? What is the smallest, most courageous step you could take toward that shift, even if the outcome is uncertain?

CHAPTER 24

THE TIME VALUE OF HAPPINESS

"It is not how much we have, but how much we enjoy, that makes happiness."

—Charles Spurgeon, "The Candle"

In finance, there are concepts, mathematical formulas, and tools for figuring out what a future thing of perceived value would be worth to you today, if you could in fact have it today. The internal rate of return (IRR) and net present value (NPV) are two such examples.

According to Investopedia, NPV is the "difference between the present value of cash inflows and the present value of cash outflows over a period of time."[1] Similarly, IRR "measures an investment's profitability, taking into account the time value of money...IRR helps investors determine the rate of return they can expect to earn on an investment, considering the timing and size of cash inflows and outflows."[2] Investors will compare a potential investment's IRR with their minimum required return and also compare their potential investment profits by looking at the NPV's.

In plain, common sense terms, IRR and NPV concepts are far simpler if you think about your natural inclinations. The further out you expect to receive money, goods, or services, the less valuable they are to you today. In order for you to be willing to wait for something in the distant future, it needs to be big enough and valuable enough for you to feel incentivized to wait for it. Especially if you have to pay for it. Embedded in your assumption about something's future value is the probability that said future value is real. But regardless, the further out you expect to wait to get that value (i.e., money), the less valuable it might be to you today. The inverse of this is also equally powerful. The sooner and more certain it is that you can have a thing, the more valuable it will be to you.

Do I want to be a millionaire at age ninety or age thirty? I would rather have it at thirty years old so I can enjoy it longer. What would be more attractive to you: a 100 percent chance of receiving $100,000 two years from now, or a 50 percent chance you receive $120,000 five years from now? I'm guessing you would opt for the first option—a bird in hand. And that's even before you calculated the expected value of either scenario or the time value of money. For example, what you would need that number to be to justify waiting for it?

The same concept applies to loaning someone money or making an investment. If I loan my cousins $1,000, and they tell me they'll pay me back in five years, I almost discount the pledge altogether. I would rather assume I won't get it back and treat it as a gift. But if someone tells me they will pay back the $1,000 next week, I don't really consider it a big lift to make the loan at all. If someone tells me they'll pay me back in a year, I might do some calculus around the probability that they'll pay it back and at least begin to get comfortable with the idea that they may or *may not* pay back the loan. But if they say they'll pay me $100 a month for the next twelve months (so a total of $1,200 versus the $1,000 I loaned), I will probably start to feel pretty good about the exchange.

Whether you are familiar with these financial concepts or not, we all instinctively think about the time value of money. You are more likely to buy a house if you think it will double over the next five or seven years that you own it. You are less likely to buy a house that you think will immediately lose value and be underwater by the time you are ready to sell it. This is true in our happiness, and why I have coined the concept "the IRR of happiness."

THE IRR OF HAPPINESS

People often say, "give people their flowers today." Why wait until they are dead?

I would rather experience more of my happiness today or sooner versus potentially, hypothetically experiencing it in some distant future. If I have to wait for some future happiness, it needs to be large enough for it to be worth the wait. If there's a probability that this future happiness might not actually come, it needs to be even bigger for me to accept both time and uncertainty.

The concept of heaven is a great example of a future benefit that billions of people of faith think is worth significant investments today. However, how certain do you need to be that heaven actually exists for you to be a martyr in a holy war, to spend your entire life paying one-tenth of your wages to a religious institution, or to deny yourself the pleasures of the flesh? I am exaggerating a bit to illustrate the point: We sometimes make big investments for future happiness that is not guaranteed. Sometimes it's not even clear how we might begin to calculate the probability that it *could be* real.

Imagine the other sections in this book and how this concept applies to relationships and work. How likely would you be to work for a company until your retirement age if the company-sponsored pension was not guaranteed when you stopped working? How likely would you be to get married if the likelihood of you divorcing and going through a costly separation in two years was 50 percent or greater? What if that probability of you actually being happy in your marriage was less than 25 percent? Would you do it?

Let me state it slightly differently: How likely would you be to marry if there was a 75 percent chance that you'd be miserable? Perhaps you would because you believe the odds are in your favor or the potential upside and perceived future happiness is worth it. Perhaps you would do it for reasons that are far more practical than happiness. That, too, would be okay, but because happiness is not your priority in that decision, your choice might not lead to happiness. You would need to own that reality.

The opposite of these fictitious examples is true as well. If the Ghost of Christmas Future visited and shared with you that you had a 100 percent chance of 1) being happy in your pending marriage, 2) having a large retirement pension from a potential job you're considering, and 3) upon dying, live the rest of your eternal life in a dreamy heaven, chances are you would make that bet on all three—all day, every day!

Regardless of what you believe about your future happiness, I encourage you to consider the probability that your projected future happiness is real, how long you will need to wait for it, and at what cost or opportunity cost. You don't need a calculator to figure out if it's worth it, because there is no right or wrong answer—and it's likely impossible to know anyway, unless you're visited by the Ghost of Christmas Future. The only IRR that matters is the one you've implicitly calculated and considered. But if you don't, you could be walking into a happiness trap.

INSTANT GRATIFICATION

Aiming to experience happiness sooner (as was implied in the IRR of happiness) might be misconstrued as the pursuit of instant gratification or temporary pleasure, which may not necessarily be good in the long run. In fact, some of the greatest rewards and happiness can come from delaying and working hard for your gratification. Similarly, some of our biggest regrets can come from immediate gratification.

As an example, you could eat lots of glazed donuts today and theoretically experience a lot of immediate gratification from the chemical reaction that sweet foods create in your brain. Later you might regret it if this behavior eventually led to weight gain or even just a stomachache. If you remember, at the beginning of our book we talked about sources of happiness that were extrinsic and low in quality and value (represented by the lower left-hand quadrant of the 2x2 chart). There is nothing intrinsically wrong with instant gratification, especially if there aren't major long-term consequences. But you might be more willing to wait awhile for a more certain and high-quality happiness opportunity that had fewer consequences in the future.

There was a study conducted in the late 1960s called the Marshmallow Test that sought to understand the long-term implications for very young children who demonstrated self-control and the ability to delay gratification.[3] In the study, four-year-olds were offered the option of eating a single marshmallow now or eating two later, if they could wait. Some of the kids ate the treat right away, while others found ways to resist the urge for immediate gratification, thereby enjoying two marshmallows instead of one. The research followed the kids for decades and found those that had greater self-control and could defer gratification had better life outcomes in terms of health, economics, and so on.

Many reference this study when pointing to the conventional wisdom that delayed gratification can in fact be a good thing, while immediate gratification is a bad thing. Of course, I am oversimplifying to make the point. But the creator of the study, Dr. Walter Mischel, makes a powerful point that often gets overlooked:

> To me it's a matter of helping kids to have the freedom to make
> choices. Whether or not they choose to eat the marshmallow,
> if they know how to wait for it, is up to them. But they should

have the ability to have a real choice. It doesn't mean that you spend your whole life self-controlling, obviously. A life that's all self-control can be as dismal as a life without any self-control. But it means that you need to have the skills plus the motivation if you want to really optimize your opportunities.[4]

His statement emphasizes that there are choices for *when* and *how* to use self-control. In much of our happiness calculus, we do not (think we) have choice—or we are unaware that the choice has been removed by much of our early and ongoing life programming.

There are many things you enjoy which can actually improve with time. It takes time to build trust and connections in relationships that may blossom in the years to come. It's also true that you might enjoy your job and work more as you master some of the skills that allow you to go from applying a technical use of your talents to a more artistic one.

As for myself, I did not immediately have a profound love for scuba diving. I had to develop not only a command of the technical aspects of diving but also get comfortable with the initial discomfort and eventually do it enough times actually enjoy it. It took many dives before I grew to love it! Now, hundreds of dives later, I can say it's a passion. If I had been overly simplistic and myopic in my time value of happiness application, I might have missed the future payoff that came after investing time and effort into something that had the potential to generate an abundance of joy in the future.

CROWDSOURCING HAPPINESS (THE BIGGEST TRAP)

Crowdsourcing is "the practice of obtaining needed services, ideas, or content by soliciting contributions from a large group of people and especially from the online community rather than from traditional employees or suppliers."[5]

Crowdsourcing is great for quickly tapping the masses for new ideas, money, creativity, and even help. But it is horrible if you are trying to figure out what will bring you happiness. If you believe right now that your happiness is the average of everyone else's happiness, you may be in for a surprise. Worse yet, if you need validation from the crowd that you actually *are* happy in your happy moments, then you have your work cut out for you.

We live in a day and age where we are always on our phones, scrolling Instagram, Facebook, and TikTok. The amount of depression that is now common among teens, and especially young girls, from being inundated with millions of images of what coolness and goodness looks like has destroyed our individual understanding of what "good" actually is. We look to the crowd—our followers, digital and otherwise—to validate not only our self-worth but our own happiness.

As an example, I can't tell you how many times I'm in a nice restaurant and look over to the tables to my left and right and see a group of people photographing their food with their phones and posting to Instagram before they have even taken their first bite. I've actually been at meals myself where everyone was on their phones either scrolling or taking selfies instead of engaging in conversation with the people present at the table.

It is not in itself a bad thing to capture the artistic value and beauty of a plate, nor is there anything wrong with capturing and sharing the moment. However, what I find interesting is that many will post the picture of the perfectly curated maple-drizzled salmon and wait to see what type of feedback they get from their social network. It's almost as if the number of likes and the kind of comments the post generates about the happy moment is where they derive their sense of happiness, rather than enjoying the food itself. The posters might scan for those "Oh my God, that looks amazing" comments before they can taste that the salmon is, in fact, amazing. The poster feels validated and is made happy by their followers' comments, more so than by the joy of the moment they are actually experiencing.

To be clear, the two are not mutually exclusive. However, we have to be aware of what and who is actually the source of our joy. Sadly, I sometimes imagine someone posting a picture of an amazingly plated cheesecake where no one clicks "like" on the post or comments how awesome it is. Does the poster lose some of the happiness that would've otherwise come from the dessert? Is a moment with their friends not as special if it isn't validated by their followers? Are the acceptance and validation that comes from followers what makes them happy, or is it the taste of decadent cheesecake?

You cannot look to the masses to validate that what you are doing is joyful. Otherwise, you have given the power for your happiness to someone who likely cares very little about it. You have to decide what happiness is for you and pursue it for yourself and yourself alone. If something brings you—and no other soul on this planet—happiness, then your happiness is no less for that. In fact, when we seek the validation of others, we've actually delegated our authority to define and enjoy happiness as we see fit.

I have come to grips with the fact that I love posting my videos, even though I have a very small following. I do very little to promote my videos, because crowd validation is not the source of my joy. My happiness does not come from likes and clicks, but rather from creating and sharing. There is a nuanced difference.

Some of the ways I avoid the happiness trap of using social media for validation:

1. Be more present when I am diving (like I did with the Red Sea octopus and whale shark).

2. Enjoy the creative process of editing and production like an artist that paints a painting for themselves, and not a patron.

3. Post my content sometimes weeks or months after creating it. Alternatively, I often post without waiting for immediate reactions.

I do this with the expectation that my joy will mostly come from hopefully exposing someone to something amazing and new.

I am not telling you to get off of social media or stop posting your perfectly plated dinner with friends. That's far too great an ask, and there can be real joy in sharing and receiving experiences. I'm also not suggesting we pretend not to enjoy the "likes" and smiley face emojis our social media posts get. My advice is to simply avoid the extreme of this exchange, when you look to followers to validate your happiness, because I know firsthand that it is a happiness trap.

REFLECTION QUESTIONS

1. When examining your own deeply held beliefs or long-term commitments (e.g., to a specific career path, a traditional family structure, a community ideal), what "future happiness" are you implicitly expecting from them?

2. How certain are you that this projected future happiness will materialize, and how much are you "investing" (time, money, self-denial) today based on that probability? What might be the "opportunity cost" if that future happiness doesn't fully manifest as expected?

3. Can you identify a recent instance where your sense of joy or the perceived "goodness" of a personal experience felt dependent on external validation (e.g., social media reactions, others' comments, public recognition)?

4. How does the pursuit of external validation influence your actions in moments that should be intrinsically joyful (e.g., enjoying a

meal, spending time with friends, pursuing a hobby)? What are you potentially missing out on by delegating the authority to define your happiness to others?

5. How can you apply the lesson of happiness growing with time (like in relationships or mastering a skill) to a current challenge or goal, ensuring you are investing in potential future abundance of joy rather than being "myopic" in your pursuit of immediate pleasure?

CHAPTER 25

THE VALUE OF OPTIONS

"Everybody has plans until they get hit for the first time."

—**Mike Tyson**

The more uncertain the future, the more valuable it is to have options. There are so many areas of life where this is instinctively true. When you are in high school, you apply to multiple colleges, not knowing which will accept you, where you will get the best financial aid package, or what factors you will value the most after your campus visits. Ultimately, the reason you don't apply to just one college is because you want to have options.

In my world of commercial real estate, you would not dream of signing a lease for space that was critical to your business operations without options. You would ensure a lease gave you the option to renew at the end of the initial term at some pre-negotiated rate, or perhaps the ability to expand or terminate if your business took off and needed more space or cratered and needed to close shop. In some of the companies I've worked for, I was granted options as part of my compensation package. Oftentimes, the options gave me the right to buy stock in the company at a discounted price point in the future. Options were great in many respects when I did not know for certain whether the company was going to succeed in the future or not.

The more uncertain you are about the future, the more you must weigh the various probabilities of different outcomes. The more certain you are about the future, the less valuable an option is to you. If you know for certain that a hurricane is going to hit your beach home, you will likely want the most exhaustive insurance coverage for potential flood and wind damage. The same is true for options in every other area of life. Your future desires and sources of happiness are no different.

HAPPINESS EVOLVES

When I was a young child, I loved to read comic books. Reading them brought me joy, as it provided an outlet to escape my reality by imagining myself in distant worlds and situations and sometimes as the comic protagonist. On most Fridays, my mom would drop me off at the comic book store and allow me to buy a handful of comics while she bought groceries. My pleasures were simple and fairly affordable in those days. As a preteen, I could not imagine that I would one day not be interested in collecting comics. (Although I still get super excited when Marvel drops a new movie or series on Disney.)

At each stage of my life—from being a young adult in college to being a young professional to now—I have found happiness in so many different things. In each season, I reflect on the things that brought me pleasure just a few years or decades earlier and think how little they continued to factor into my happiness later. For example, I no longer play with toys, but in elementary school I took immense pride in my collection of nearly one hundred Transformers toys.

The same is true for future happiness. I could not have ever imagined at any point in my life that I would love scuba diving. I've always enjoyed watching nature shows, but I was terrified at the thought of being in the wild and never considered I would be excited to dive with sharks. As I imagine future versions of myself now, I have no idea what will bring me joy in the future.

While there are certain themes that are likely to be more constant and consistent through life, in part because they are tied to our core composition and constitution, there are other aspects of who we are that change meaningfully with time, exposure, and experiences. The more you understand and embrace how you might change, the more likely you are to look for ways to embed options in some of the biggest decisions of your life. You might rent a home rather than purchase until you know for certain that you love the new city that you just moved to. Giving yourself time and options is really a gift to your future self that you likely won't regret.

Just as immediate gratification and pleasure do not necessarily equate to happiness or fulfillment, neither does the knowledge of what you enjoy now ensure that you know what will bring you joy and happiness in the distant future. You must look for ways to create flexibility. And there are some fairly basic ways you can do this in the different aspects of your life.

HEALTH

I work out five to six days a week (and sometimes seven), unless I am sick or traveling. My routine alternates between cardio, legs, upper body, and back. I also stretch daily and occasionally do yoga. Although my diet is not the best, it has improved significantly over the years as I have grown to appreciate the value of eating fewer carbs, consuming fewer sugars, and avoiding the urge to forage late at night. I also sleep and embrace my sleep time. FOMO (fear of missing out), a term coined by my good friend Patrick

James McGinnis,[1] is not nearly as much of a thing for me today as it once was—especially if it gets in the way of my sleep.

However, this was not always the case. It took me seeing early signs in my annual checkups that some of the key indicators for my health were either just "okay" or trending in the wrong direction. Although none of them were existential, the doctor reminded me that if left unchecked, these things could have an impact on my future self. I could imagine how miserable I would be if I wasn't as mobile, couldn't scuba dive or travel to remote places, or do any of the other things that contribute to my current happiness. If my future happiness was netted down to something lower than ideal because I did not do my part now to ensure that I had good health, then I was destroying my future options. By investing a bit more in my health today, I'm creating options for me to enjoy a full range of future activities that are important to my happiness.

ECONOMIC FREEDOM AND MOBILITY

I don't need to tell you how important it is to save and invest to prepare for your future retirement. My financial advisor would ask me to imagine the lifestyle that I thought I might want in the future and insisted that we get really detailed. Together, we built a monthly budget that was necessary to support my future self, for the next thirty, forty, or maybe even fifty years. My future happiness needed to have a budget for traveling, making donations, supporting nieces and nephews with their educational expenses, and the list goes on. I had to take into consideration the role of inflation and also anticipate that not every investment I've made would pay off the way I imagined.

Not long after my first COVID-19 scare, I got really serious about my estate planning and worked with an attorney and my financial advisor to establish not only my will but a living trust that stipulated what I would want done with my estate and surviving wealth in my absence. I initially thought that this would be a morbid exercise, imagining a life for my loved ones who would still be living after I had died. But I knew I had to go through the exercise of anticipating all of the things that I would want done in my death, from the practical to philanthropic.

To my surprise, I actually found the process liberating and quite fun. I imagined the things that I would want to do for my brother, sister, and family members. I imagined the way I would want to support certain philanthropic efforts. These thoughts became super exciting. (Remember, giving gifts can be a source of happiness.) I have no idea if I will be aware of any of this or whether I will continue to experience happiness after I die. Yet knowing that I've played a small or large role in educating the future Robinsons even after I'm gone, for example, brings me happiness and peace today.

One of the things that was not so fun to think about but necessary was the space and time in between my current healthy self and death—the sickly and needy phase of life. I imagined the period of time before I die, but I am not well enough to take care of myself. I imagined sitting up in a nursing home, by myself, or hoping that one of my siblings might take me in if I didn't have a life partner.

That thought exercise drained my happiness, until I realized I could embed some options into my future. I purchased a long-term care policy to help with a potentially expensive final few months or years where I might need in-home nursing and medical beyond what my insurance provides, or when I may need to make certain home improvements so I can more easily navigate a declining state. None of those thoughts were pleasant, but purchasing the insurance policy gave me a bit more peace. Most of all, it gave my future self a bit more economic mobility and certainty, or at least the feeling of such. Setting aside a chunk of enjoyment today, in the form of money from my savings, to purchase this policy is my way of acknowledging that in the future I may very well need or want things that are of no benefit to me today.

RELATIONSHIPS

I have been married and divorced twice. I could write a whole book on what I've learned about myself and love in the process. However, the one thing I am not is discouraged. I want a life partner and imagine my future self will want that too. I think we are social animals who need and depend on meaningful connections and interactions with other people, not only for our emotional health but also our mental and physical health. I don't know if I will ever remarry, but maybe. I don't know if I will integrate my finances with someone again, but maybe. The point is not to make proclamations about what I will or will not do, but rather to leave open the possibility that in the future I might find a person who I can't imagine not being with until the very end. So I date, for the happiness of my current self *and* my future self.

Portfolio Life

I believe strongly that what you do for a living should ladder up to the life you want. Your work should matter. But just as I want options in these non-work areas of my life, I have found it helpful to have options in my work life. The term "portfolio life" was coined by Harvard Business School professor Christina Wallace, but the concept has been around for a while. In fact, before I read her book, I was already moving in that direction. Rather than work for one company, I was creating a portfolio of companies that I advised, consulted, and served on the board of. I actually work more today than I did when I was an executive running national and global businesses. However, today my work comes from a diverse source of places. I have different companies, situations, and people that bring me purpose, belonging, and economics. This may not necessarily be practical for you or even what you desire, but it's yet another way to think about creating options.

The key takeaway in this chapter is to acknowledge that your future self will need flexibility. Your future self will need options because your current self can't possibly envision them all. It's also to acknowledge that your needs and preferences will continue to change in future seasons.

REGULAR CHECK-INS

While you do not know for sure what your future self will desire, you don't have to make big bets that are binary or irreversible. Nor do you have to have a corresponding option (back door) for every decision. You can do regular check-ins with yourself to ask "Am I happy? Are these assumptions about the future still valid? Has anything changed that might impact what my future self will want or need?" At any point in time, you can make changes to redirect your path based on new information—and you should.

I believe that we generally sense these changes in our happiness needs and expectations when they're happening. But sometimes it requires you to steal away and create some quiet space, structure, thinking, meditation, or maybe therapy to really flush out what if anything in your happiness portfolio is evolving. This allows you to be very intentional with the decisions you are making or not making.

Ask yourself: Am I still living in the right city, the right home, with the optimal layout? Am I still finding joy and fulfillment with the partner that I chose to integrate into my life years ago? Does my health make certain activities less enjoyable, and I now need to pick up other things to do? Do I need to revisit my will and estate documents because now there are considerations or people that I want to factor into my estate plan? Your list may vary, but the point is to have some type of regular check-in with yourself.

You might also consider establishing a personal board of advisors, if you don't already have a few trusted people that you can go to, to reflect on and revisit these assumptions with you.

I have a group of buddies from college who are like brothers to me. We talk fairly regularly and occasionally take big trips to get away and really catch up. We are fraternity brothers and have known each other since our freshman year of college. When we get together, we sometimes talk about our highs and lows from the past year, as well as what we now desire for happiness in our next season. My buddies will talk about their kids, their new hobbies, and what they want to do in retirement. We run ideas past each other because sometimes saying it out loud is a way of affirming our intention, while also allowing for some loving interrogation to make sure we've thought it out entirely. Regardless of how you choose to do it, plan for annual self-check-ins to be sure you and your future self are still aligned.

REFLECTION QUESTIONS

1. When you reflect on a significant past decision (e.g., college, a job, a move), how did the presence or absence of options impact the outcome and your subsequent happiness?

2. How has your understanding of what brings you happiness "transformed" over time, similar to the author's shift from comic books to scuba diving? What does this past transformation teach you about the unpredictability of your future desires for joy?

3. In what specific area of your life are you currently making a "big bet" that might be too binary or irreversible, and how might that limit your future self's options for happiness if your desires change?

4. How might embracing the inherent uncertainty of your future needs free you from the pressure of making perfect, irreversible decisions today, allowing for a more adaptable and ultimately happier life journey?

CHAPTER 26

GIVE YOURSELF GRACE

"The best way to predict your future is to invent it."

—Dr. Alan Kay

Therapy has gone from being a topic of taboo to being a topic of relative social acceptance. I've had the benefit of meaningful amounts of individual and relationship therapy and counseling over the years. I've also benefited from retreats, workshops, and individual work that was hard, revealing, and necessary for my journey. This book, as much as it is an opportunity for me to share and raise questions that will hopefully be helpful to you and your journey, has been my own therapy. The issues I have wrestled with for so long are issues I have taken pen to pad to stimulate healing, growth, and grace. Grace is one of the most powerful of all the things I could give myself.

While there is much to be said for doing the hard work of therapy and self-improvement and being accountable for the outcomes of that work, there's something even more powerful to be said for the compassion, love, and grace that we owe ourselves. Life is hard. You are likely doing the best you can with what you have. You were born and immediately instilled with a certain set of values, ideas, and scripts that were not your own. They are still running in the background without you always knowing that they are there, and these baseline scripts can be the most difficult to undo. It is not until you begin to experience pain, suffering, and conflict that you choose to either suffer or do something about changing them. Doing something about it may mean going back and finding the root sources of the program scripts that no longer serve you. It's never too soon or too late to start this purge.

I wrestled with how best to write this book, in part because the call to action will not fit neatly on a bumper sticker. It is tough to reduce this book's big ideas into something clean and actionable for easy consumption and commodification. I wish I had a catchy slogan for how to increase your net happiness or improve its IRR. The fact is that the issue is as varied and nuanced as people are, and a brief, universal summation of that dynamic is not something I could achieve simply or easily.

Even if I could, the hard work of removing all of the obstacles that have been placed—or *you* have placed—between you and your happiness won't be an overnight thing. It's a lifelong undertaking, which does not always translate to memorable taglines. Although in childhood we learned that "an apple a day keeps the doctor away," we later discovered health was far more complicated than that. For starters, you should see the doctor once a year for a checkup—not actually stay away. Second, a nutritious diet, regular exercise, and avoiding unhealthy behaviors such as smoking and tanning could never be replaced by eating apples. Although apples have tons of health benefits, they are also high in sugar. So there. The longer and more factual answer is sometimes harder to make fun and pithy.

You will need to have grace as you keep testing various hypotheses and either find moments of insight and eureka or simply clues. It's also okay to be wrong. This book is an opportunity to go back and revisit some of the old assumptions you may have made about your happiness that no longer serve you. In doing so, you should have compassion for the person—your inner child or younger self or even the you who is reading this right now— because chances are, you've done the best you can with what you have.

You may as of tomorrow begin to change some of the big assumptions regarding your happiness and begin to do the hard work of moving the big rocks around in your terrarium. Moving big rocks is hard and takes time. Have grace for yourself if you don't get it right immediately or find that some decisions you've made are irreversible. However, maybe there are some other big rocks that you can move more quickly or start chipping away at, bit by bit.

Don't let perfection be the enemy of good. Have grace, knowing that even if you've committed to people, jobs, and other aspects of your life that are now structural and impossible to change, such as having kids, you can still find great sources of happiness in the other areas where you still have choice.

In math, we learn that you can't solve an equation that has more variables than constants. If I tell you that $y=A+B$, there is nothing I can do to make sense of that. I need at least two of those letters to be a number in order to solve for the third. If I tell you $y=3+B$, then I can create a table that says what y would be if B were 5. It would be 8. The same is true for our life. Some things are constants and some things we need to hold constant to solve the variables that matter today.

IGNORE THE SUNK COSTS

In economics and finance, there's a term I learned—sunk costs. Sunk costs are investments—monetary, energetic, emotional—that can't be recovered. You spent money on something and there's no way to get that money back. Perhaps you made an investment in a company, started a business, bought a house, or did something that your future self looks back on and says "Wow that was stupid." Or perhaps your future self now sees that the assumptions you made did not pan out. The most important thing I've learned to do in these situations is not to throw good money, energy, or emotion after bad. Cut your losses and move on. If I've lost money, it is now more important what I do with the money I have left to maximize my value going forward, not to double down on an old assumption that I've already proven is wrong because I find it difficult to move on. The same is true with respect to your happiness.

When you show yourself grace, you acknowledge that those assumptions you made in the past were the best you could make at the time. You don't beat yourself up; you learn from them and move on. When you know better, you do better. And sometimes tough experiences are how we learn better and begin reconstructing the future that we now know is possible.

REFLECTION QUESTIONS

1. We contrasted happiness as a working hypothesis (requiring continuous testing and learning) with a fixed theorem. How does embracing this perspective change your approach to pursuing happiness compared to seeking a definitive, unchanging formula for it?

2. Extend grace to yourself, acknowledging that you've done the best you could with what you had. When reflecting on past decisions about your happiness that, in hindsight, didn't serve you, what does having grace for that past self truly mean to you, and how can you practice it moving forward?

3. "When you know better, you do better," and happiness involves "reconstructing the future that we now know is possible." As you conclude this book, what is the single most important insight you've gained about your happiness that you are committed to acting upon?

CHAPTER 27

FIND THE COURAGE

*"It takes courage to grow up and
become who you really are."*

—Attributed to E. E. Cummings

In a flock of birds, the bird at the front of the formation is called the leader. According to researchers, birds take turns being the leader. Any and all birds can fulfill this role. The formation offers significant benefits to the rest of the birds flying above in the classic V formation. In aggregate, they can save as much as 20 to 30 percent of their energy when making their long hauls.[1] Flocks of twenty-five or more can even increase their range by as much as 71 percent.[2] But the lead bird, for however long it leads, will expend more energy than the others as the spear tip, where it not only directs the formation, but cuts the wind drag. Each subsequent row of birds after the lead bird expends less and less energy until you get to the final row. The birds in this row are the biggest beneficiaries of the formation.

Leadership is like that in so many other ways. It not only takes a lot of energy to lead—developing a vision, building support and followership, and ultimately seeing the mission through to completion—it also takes courage. It takes courage to be the first to do something that may initially seem odd or contrarian to the group. Some of the most successful companies at some point had a visionary CEO who was often willing to make huge investments and risk significant losses on the basis of a vision for where they believed the market was going—before the market went there.

Henry Ford was believed to have said about the future demand of cars, "If I had asked people what they wanted [before there were cars], they would have said faster horses." Henry was not following the pack, but rather anticipating it . . . and in some cases, inducing it. Steve Jobs induced demand for iPhones. No one was asking at the time for a phone that was also a mp3 player and a personal computer.

In your own way, you can be a visionary leader for your own happiness. By not being captive to popular culture, institutions, and tradition, you can decide for yourself what will bring you joy and happiness. By not crowdsourcing your happiness, you are willing to go from being in the last row of birds in formation to the front, but it might take courage. When you live an alternative lifestyle, take nontraditional career paths, develop your own faith framework, cultivate independent political thoughts versus partisan ones, and so on, you risk alienation, ostracization, and maybe even persecution. This is when it takes courage.

The opposite of this courage is crowdsourcing a set of beliefs and values from the herd, and not your own conscience. Long before an idea becomes mainstream, or even a policy enforced by rules and laws, it may start off as a radical idea held only by radical people. But later, those radical people will be viewed as wise and visionary if the ideas they promote catch on. Dr. Martin Luther King, Jr., was considered radical by mainstream Americans in the 1960s but later was celebrated as a hero with his own national holiday.

This concept is explained by the Overton Window framework. The Overton Window describes a range of policies that are politically acceptable to the mainstream but were once considered radical.[3] In the case of policy ideas that started out as unthinkable or radical, there is probably a radical or courageous leader who introduced the idea. The idea might start small but over time becomes a social movement that ultimately changes public opinion. At that point, politicians (the last row of birds) feel it's safe to enact policies and laws. But first the radical innovator and thought leader may experience loneliness, judgment, or worse if their ideas undermine the power structures and institutions of the day.

You don't need to necessarily be a martyr to courageously embrace your authentic self and happiness. But chances are that the areas of your life you desire to change that are most entrenched in popular opinion and tradition will be the most challenging to shift. Like the rotating nature of lead birds, it's not necessary for any one of us to carry the burden of changing societal norms. But you have to recognize the power that your individual actions can have on the bigger group.

When I was the leader of large global businesses, I knew that some of my smallest behaviors could be powerful signals to my teams about culture, values, and ultimately the safety of their own behaviors. For example, when I was intentionally seeking better work-life balance and willing to make trade-offs that were out of step with the group norms, I decided I would not check emails after I left work on Friday until Sunday.

In high-performance cultures and environments, the expectation is often that you are *always* on and available. Leaving an important email sitting for a few days could risk sending signals to important stakeholders that you were less committed to the success of the business. The downstream implications could show up in your compensation, opportunities for upward mobility, and so on. To mitigate some of these risks, I would tell people my personal policy and why work-life balance was important to me. I would also share, though I didn't need to, that these boundaries made me a better leader when I was *on*.

While it was likely frustrating at first for those who would test my boundaries, sending an urgent email on a Friday night and expecting an immediate response or asking if I could hop on a call over the weekend, my consistency over time (courage) began to set their expectations of me and create a new norm. Further, by not sending emails to my direct reports over the weekend, I signaled that this behavior was not only acceptable (and they should do the same with their direct reports) but gave them permission to develop their own boundaries. Today, many companies have policies, such as hybrid work schedules or paternity leave, that probably started out as radical ideas in some environments.

Courage does not have to always be tied to some big life-defining decision. It can be the summation of lots of small and seemingly insignificant things. Here are a few examples of both small and big decisions that I have taken that required some courage but brought me in closer alignment with my happiness.

BIG DECISIONS (UNTHINKABLE TO RADICAL)

These choices seemed significant and risky based on the values of the crowd, culture, and institutions:

- Going from Christianity to an agnostic belief system

- Switching from a C-suite role to a portfolio life career track

HYBRID (ACCEPTABLE)

These are choices I made that were significant and took some courage but were not controversial in mainstream thinking:

- Divorce

- Choosing to not have kids

SMALL DECISIONS (POPULAR)

These choices were meaningful to me, but not risky. In fact, they've been applauded.

- Leaving New York City and moving back to Atlanta, where I thought I would be happier even if it meant being farther from my professional network.

- Incorporating scuba diving into every vacation and deprioritizing more popular destinations, activities, and chances to travel with friends.

TRENDY DECISIONS (SENSIBLE)

Complete no-brainers to everyone.

- Prioritizing my happiness as a life philosophy
- Encouraging others to do the same

Regardless of the decisions confronting you, standing between you and your happiness, you may find the need to conjure some measure of courage. This is hard work. However, it is also not a sprint but a marathon. Walk it if you need to, as long as you keep putting one foot in front of the other, you will eventually get there, wherever "there" is for you.

HAVE MORE CURIOSITY THAN CONVICTION

It's not the answer, but ultimately the question behind the question that counts. When I first started serving in executive capacities, I instinctively wanted to show up with the answers. That came from a combination of imposter syndrome and some old habits from my inner "golden child" who is a pleaser and wants to be rewarded for having the right answer. My inner child wants to get stickers, trophies, and validation for being right. My inner child does not want to be wrong. My inner child is afraid of being wrong and forever looks for ways to protect himself from those moments. My inner child is also afraid that others will see that he actually may not have the answer and find him a fraud. This is the imposter syndrome that many suffer from but is particularly at work within people for whom there are great expectations and assumptions about their potential.

I have over the years come to challenge and push back on these instincts. These are not moments of weakness. These are actually moments of strength, if we can suppress the instinct to feel like having the right answer is the only way to be valuable. Having the right answer is not only a very limited way to feel and be viewed as valuable, but it is flawed. As I've discussed in this book, we are more likely to be wrong than right. In important meetings, I no longer need to have a brilliantly laid-out answer that everyone looks around the table in unison and says "That was brilliant." That never happens, by the way. I now find comfort in articulating what I don't know. It is better to have a well-constructed question than a flawed or misinformed answer of conviction. We all learn from the question. Embedded in the question is an understanding about the potential answer. Perhaps the answer is not yet knowable or is unclear and requires us to do follow-up work, run experiments, and test a hypothesis.

There is much wisdom in knowing when to ask the question and be curious. This is true for many areas of our lives. Look for areas where you can replace your conviction with curiosity. Look for areas in your life that are encased blocks of ignorance cement that need to be cracked open with questions and vulnerability. Our conviction can be places where we love the story more than the facts. We may not even want new facts, as they create emotional and psychological discomfort.

Find a safe space and give yourself grace to go back and revisit some of those age-old convictions. Allow the new data to flow in. You don't have to announce on social media that you made some big decision in life that it turns out was wrong. You can find a very quiet way for you to grow and learn from your mistakes. However, it can be very powerful to acknowledge that you made mistakes. It is deeply validating to your inner adult self and your inner child to acknowledge the pain and discomfort that they have felt and say "We're not going to endure that pain anymore" going forward. If you are comfortable and courageous enough to say it out loud, chances are others will benefit from your model of strength and wisdom.

Stepping into Curiosity

The following are steps to help you identify areas where you may need to replace your conviction with your curiosity.

STEP 1

Take out a piece of paper and create four columns with A, B, C, and D at the top of each. Populate each column as depicted in the table. For each belief listed in column A, write its corresponding "why" in B and its role in your happiness in C.

A	B	C	D
Conviction: What do you believe deeply?	**Your Why: What is the source of your belief?**	**Your Happiness: What role does this play in your happiness?**	**Curiosity: What assumptions do you need to revisit?**
List of ideas, creeds, activities, etc., that are core to your belief systems and inform your identity	List of things you know (vs. believe), life data, science, personal experiences, etc., that support your beliefs	High, low, or moderate role	What sources and evidence would increase your conviction (or decrease it)?

STEP 2

For each belief listed in column A, populate column D based on the relationship shares with B and C, as shown in the following table.

A	B	C	D
Conviction: What do you believe deeply?	**Your Why: What is the source of your belief?**	**Your Happiness: What role does this play in your happiness?**	**Curiosity: What assumptions do you need to revisit?**
List of ideas, creeds, activities, etc., that are core to your belief systems and inform your identity	List of things you know (vs. believe), life data, science, personal experiences, etc., that support your beliefs	High, low, or moderate role	What sources and evidence would increase your conviction (or decrease it)?
If A>B and C=High, then populate D			
If A>B and C=Low, consider populating D if C increases or you're naturally curious now that you're aware			
If A<B and C=High, no action required			
If A<B and C=Low, no action required unless you're curious			

A quick reference guide for helping to identify those beliefs that impact your happiness that might benefit from greater curiosity.

STEP 3

Take a moment to reflect. How many beliefs require a bit more curiosity? How many require you to do nothing? If you are like me, you have a few areas that require some revisiting and curiosity. Repeat this exercise from time to time, especially if you find yourself in the middle of a heated debate or navigating a tough decision that impacts your happiness.

There isn't anything inherently wrong with conviction. In fact, it is a great superpower when it's informed and grounded. It was conviction that fueled some of societies' greatest technological innovations, transformational social movements, and scientific breakthroughs. President Kennedy had conviction about space travel and America's leadership in going to the moon. Dr. Martin Luther King, Jr., had conviction in our ability to change hearts, minds, and society through civil disobedience and non-violence. Steve Job and Bill Gates had conviction in the need to democratize the power of computing. President Obama had conviction that every American should have access to healthcare. Both my mother and uncle Dale had conviction that education could transform the lives of me and my brother. And each was right.

I am so grateful for the conviction that each of these people had, because you and I may be better for it. But each began their journey with curiosity, long before they delivered stirring speeches, unveiled game-changing innovation, or dug into their savings for school fees. And during their season of curiosity, I am certain that they were doubted by their friends, family, and society—and I wouldn't even be surprised if they doubted themselves from time to time. That would have made their subsequent conviction season a stronger and more impactful one. They would as a result go on to have the necessary strength and stamina to be the proverbial lead bird in formation.

Whether you are a member of the flock in the last row of the formation or tirelessly leading the V, you have more power than you realize. And chances are, others will benefit when you decide to lean into your truth. But the first step and key to unlocking the power of your conviction starts with cultivating your curiosity.

REFLECTION QUESTIONS

1. Your happiness is like being the lead bird in a formation, enduring wind drag while benefiting the flock. In what specific area of your life (e.g., career, relationships, lifestyle, personal beliefs) do you feel

you are currently acting as a lead bird, bravely defining happiness on your own terms rather than crowdsourcing it?

2. What are the costs (e.g., judgment, loneliness, extra effort) you bear for this courage, and what is the profound energy saving or increased range (in terms of personal joy and fulfillment) you gain by not following the pack?

3. Replace conviction with curiosity, especially in areas that feel like encased blocks of ignorance cement. Identify one deeply held conviction (personal, political, social, or spiritual) that you've been hesitant to question.

4. What is the why behind this conviction, and what emotional or psychological discomfort might arise if you were to genuinely crack it open with new facts or perspectives? How does this conviction influence your happiness or relationships with others?

5. What concrete steps could you take to step into curiosity regarding this conviction, perhaps by seeking out new information, perspectives, or engaging in vulnerable dialogue?

6. As you conclude this book, what is an example of your personal commitment to continuously cultivate curiosity in your life, especially regarding your evolving definition of happiness?

AUTHOR'S NOTE

I have never written a book, and I almost didn't write this one. It's hard enough to think differently; it's even harder to put yourself out there for the universe to critique and pick over. I eventually got over that and found much joy in writing this book. In part because I imagined it might actually help someone else as much as it did me, and maybe, just maybe, it might help a lot of folks. I have some reason to believe it will.

Over the past decades, I have been asked to speak at conferences, on podcasts, and in classrooms around the country. No matter what topic I'm asked to speak on, such as real estate trends, I find a way to weave in the topics I have covered in this book. Rarely does someone rush up to me after a talk and probe my thoughts on real estate markets, but they always want to dig deeper into G.E.L., P.P.P., or the IRR of happiness. I have even met folks who will recall some of these frameworks and share how they helped them, even years later. Those moments gave me the gentle nudge I needed to put pen to paper, figuratively speaking, and here we are.

If now, after reading the book, you find that you have a bit more curiosity about your happiness and the role of work, faith, and relationships in it, my mission is accomplished. As I have said a few times in the book, my goal was and is not to tell you *what* to think, but rather to draw your attention to *how* you think.

At the writing of this book, America is deeply divided politically, socially, and ideologically. While there are some serious policy and moral issues underlying this divide, I believe much of our disconnect stems from an abundance of deep-seated convictions and a dearth of curiosity.

Our convictions make up the tinderbox both blinding and inflaming our country, from social media echo chambers to dining room tables. In a future book, I would like to interrogate the topic of *curiosity over conviction* in greater detail, as I suspect we will need it to bring forth healing and compassion in society. But we have to first be the change we wish to see in others—and for this book, that means having curiosity about those things within us. We have to first free ourselves before we can be agents of freedom in our workspaces, relationships, and communities.

To be clear, my call to action is just that: Be a part of the happiness network effect and encourage others to find their way, just as you will find yours. We're on this journey together.

The journey is lifelong and one that should (and will) move at your own pace. If you are like me, it will be an iterative process of learning and course-correcting at important life milestones. The key is to be intentional. I encourage you to plan for periodic check-ins—either with yourself or with a personal board of advisors—to see how things are going and to adjust your calculus as new variables emerge. The six-month self-assessment tool in the appendix is designed to help with this, and I encourage you to use it on an evergreen basis.

I also welcome your outreach and would love to hear about your progress. My website, www.craigmrobinson.com, is a great way for us to stay connected. You are already better for simply taking your first step toward true and lasting happiness. Your future self thanks you for putting you first. *Congratulations and best of luck!*

STAY IN TOUCH

Book website—https://www.craigmrobinson.com/book
LinkedIn—https://www.linkedin.com/in/craigmrobinson/
Instagram—https://www.instagram.com/keepgoingdeeper/

For questions and to share your progress or for coaching, media, and press inquiries, feel free to email me directly at craig@cmradvisors.us.

APPENDIX

HAPPINESS PROGRESS ASSESSMENT

Hopefully you are reading this because you completed the book (and the end-of-chapter reflection questions) a few months ago, made personal commitments to better organize your life around your authentic happiness, and are now starting to see some results. This six-month check-in is your opportunity to pause and celebrate the hard work of introspection. Your journey toward happiness is a lifelong undertaking—a working hypothesis that requires continuous self-assessment and a great deal of self-compassion.

The questions here are not a test of your progress but a tool for you to honestly reflect on the shifts in your mindset and behaviors, hold yourself accountable to the goals you set, and identify where you may need to apply more intentionality. Approach this self-assessment with the same curiosity and grace you were asked to cultivate throughout the book, and remember that every step of this journey, even the uncomfortable ones, is a courageous act of self-discovery.

Six-Month Happiness Check-In and Self-Assessment

Purpose: To reflect on the shifts in your mindset and behaviors since reading the book. This is not about getting it "right" but about honest self-assessment to guide your path forward.

Take a moment to reflect on some of the beliefs and behaviors that you held six months ago (or when you read the book) and how they impacted your happiness. Use the table below (first column) to jot down some of the more significant ones you committed to addressing. Now, in the second column, write down what changes you've made since then. And finally, in the Results column, reflect on how the changes have impacted your happiness.

	Six Months Ago	Today	Results	
Life Area	**Beliefs and Behaviors**	**Beliefs and Behaviors**	**Happiness Impact**	**Goal for Next Six Months**
Overall				
Work				
Faith				
Relationships				

When you review what you've written, how do you feel about your progress?

1. What are some of your biggest surprises, if any?

2. Are there any additional changes in your beliefs or behaviors that could further enhance your happiness? If yes, use the last column to write down your goals for the next six months.

Revisit this table in six months and repeat the exercise. You might also invite a close friend, spouse, or accountability partner to join you in the discussion and reflection.

Additional Reflection Questions (Optional)

I. FOUNDATIONS OF FULFILLMENT

This section checks in on the core frameworks you've established for understanding and pursuing your happiness.

1. *Happiness Quadrants:* When you think about your sources of happiness and how you now allocate your time and resources, do you feel you are better aligned? What steps might you take to further improve quadrant allocations?

2. *The IRR of Your Happiness:* Reflect on the concept of valuing immediate and certain happiness over distant, uncertain joy. Are you still making "investments" (of time, money, energy) today for a happiness that is far-off and not guaranteed? How are you actively prioritizing a higher "rate of return" on your happiness in the present?

3. *Your "Options" Portfolio:* Recall the chapter on the value of options and creating flexibility. What steps have you taken in the last six months to embed more flexibility into your life (e.g., in your career, health habits, or personal commitments)? What "future self" are you protecting by these choices?

II. CAREER

1. *Revisiting Your G.E.L.:* Have your G, E, or L components (What you're **G**ood at, what **E**xcites you, and the **L**ifestyle you want) become clearer (or changed) in the past six months? Are you making professional choices that intentionally align these three pillars?

2. *Plans to P.P.P.:* What steps have you taken to pivot into better professional alignment? What are your next steps?

3. *Your Season:* You will recall that there are four seasons in our careers—getting in the game, staying in the game, winning the game, and changing the game. What does success look like for your current season? What steps have you taken over the past six months toward this goal?

III. RELATIONSHIP AUDITS AND INTENTIONALITY

This section assesses your progress in navigating the complexities of romantic, familial, and social connections.

1. *Reflecting on Your "Love Apps":* Based on the chapter about inherited love patterns, can you identify a moment in the last six months where an old, unhelpful love app (e.g., from your parents) ran on autopilot? What new, intentional app did you use to override it, or what steps did you take to begin that process?

2. *Setting Boundaries:* Recall the strategies for establishing boundaries with family. Have you successfully set a new boundary or reinforced an existing one with a family member? If so, what was the outcome for your happiness and the health of that relationship? If not, what is holding you back?

3. *The "80/20 Rule" in Practice:* In your romantic relationship(s),
    if applicable, are you still consciously celebrating the 80 percent
    that works? Have you caught yourself starting to fixate on the
    missing 20 percent, and what strategies did you use to refocus on
    the positive? If you're not currently in a romantic relationship but
    desire that type of connection in your life, what does goodness
    look like—type of partner, relationship structure, and so on—and
    what steps have you taken to help improve the odds of having what
    you desire?

IV. MINDSET SHIFTS AND PERSONAL LEADERSHIP

This section examines how you are challenging old beliefs and embracing a
more courageous, authentic way of thinking.

1. *Avoiding the "Happiness Trap":* Think about the chapter on crowd-
    sourcing happiness. Have you been able to find joy in a personal
    experience or creative endeavor *before* it was validated by others
    (e.g., a social media post, a friend's approval)? How does the pur-
    suit of external validation currently influence your definition of a
    "good" experience?

2. *Curiosity Over Conviction:* Recall the "Conviction Curiosity
    Exercise." Is there a deeply held conviction (personal, political, or
    social) that you've begun to approach with more curiosity and less
    certainty? What new insights or perspectives have emerged from
    that shift?

3. *Embracing Grace and Sunk Costs:* Have you identified an old com-
    mitment or a past decision that you were holding on to due to a
    "sunk cost" (emotional, energetic)? What have you done to grant
    yourself grace for that decision, and how are you directing your
    energy toward a new path?

V. ACTION AND ACCOUNTABILITY

This final section is about measuring your courageous steps and the tangible impact on your life.

1. *Small Acts of Courage:* The chapter on leadership highlighted that courage can be found in small decisions. What is one small courageous act you've taken in the last six months (e.g., setting a boundary, starting a new hobby, expressing a contrary opinion) that moved you closer to your authentic happiness?

2. *The Mortality Check-In:* The book began with a powerful call to action stemming from the fragility of life. Have you made any changes in the last six months that align with the urgency of living "your best life" now, rather than deferring happiness for a future that is not guaranteed? What is one thing you are most proud of in this regard?

3. *The Lifelong Journey:* The book's core message is that happiness is an ongoing, evolving process—a "working hypothesis." What is one new goal, insight, or area of focus you want to commit to for the next six months to continue your journey of self-discovery and intentional happiness?

NOTES

PREFACE

1. Gretchen Rubin, *The Happiness Project: Or, Why I Spent a Year Trying to Sing in the Morning, Clean My Closets, Fight Right, Read Aristotle, and Generally Have More Fun* (Harper, 2015).

2. Adam Grant, *Think Again: The Power of Knowing What You Don't Know* (New York: Penguin Books, 2021).

3. Arthur C. Brooks, *From Strength to Strength: Finding Success, Happiness, and Deep Purpose in the Second Half of Life* (New York: Portfolio, 2022).

4. Mark Manson, *The Subtle Art of Not Giving a F*ck: A Counterintuitive Approach to Living a Good Life* (New York: Harper, 2016).

5. Christina Wallace, *The Portfolio Life: How to Future-Proof Your Career, Avoid Burnout, and Build a Life Bigger than Your Business Card* (New York: Balance Publishing, 2023).

6. Scott Galloway, *The Algebra of Happiness: Notes on the Pursuit of Success, Love, and Meaning* (New York: Portfolio, 2019).

INTRODUCTION

1. Megan Brenan, "Americans Largely Satisfied With Their Personal Life," Gallup.com, February 23, 2023, https://news.gallup.com/poll/470888/americans-largely-satisfied-personal-life.aspx/.

2. "United States Unemployment Rate," TradingEconomics.com, accessed August 22, 2025, https://tradingeconomics.com/united-states/unemployment-rate/.

3. Rakesh Kochhar, "The State of the American Middle Class," Pew Research Center, May 31, 2024, https://www.pewresearch.org/race-and-ethnicity/2024/05/31/the-state-of-the-american-middle-class/.

4. "The Share of Americans Without Health Insurance in 2023 Remained Low," Peter G. Peterson Foundation, accessed August 22, 2025, https://www.pgpf.org/article/the-share-of-americans-without-health-insurance-in-2023-remained-low/.

5. Brenan, "Americans Largely Satisfied."

6. Tony Mariotti, "Homeownership Statistics," RubyHome.com, August 23, 2023, https://www.rubyhome.com/blog/homeownership-stats/.

7. "Income, Poverty and Health Insurance Coverage in the United States: 2023," United States Census Bureau, September 10, 2024, https://www.census.gov/newsroom/press-releases/2024/income-poverty-health-insurance-coverage.html/.

8. Gloria Guzman and Melissa Kollar, "Income in the United States: 2023," United States Census Bureau, September 2024, https://www2.census.gov/library/publications/2024/demo/p60-282.pdf/.

9. S. Galan, "Wages and Salaries Worldwide: Statistics and Facts," Statista.com, May 30, 2025, https://www.statista.com/topics/11566/wages-and-salaries-worldwide/.

10. "Adult Literacy in the United States," The National Center for Education Statistics, accessed August 22, 2025, https://nces.ed.gov/pubs2019/2019179/index.asp/.

11. Jasmine Laws, "Map Reveals US Adult Literacy Rates by State," Newsweek.com, updated January 6, 2025, https://www.newsweek.com/map-reveals-us-adult-literacy-rates-state-2010175/.

12. "United States," Freedom House, accessed August 22, 2025, https://freedomhouse.org/country/united-states/.

13. John F. Helliwell et al., "World Happiness Report 2025," WorldHappiness.Report, accessed August 22, 2025, https://www.worldhappiness.report/ed/2025/.

14. Marnie Hunter, "These Are the World's Happiest Countries in 2025," CNN.com, updated March 20, 2025, https://www.cnn.com/travel/worlds-happiest-countries-2025-wellness/.

15. Megan Brenan, "New Low in U.S. 'Very Satisfied' with Personal Life," Gallup.com, January 23, 2025, https://news.gallup.com/poll/655493/new-low-satisfied-personal-life.aspx/.

16. "Major Depression," National Institute of Mental Health, accessed August 22, 2025, https://www.nimh.nih.gov/health/statistics/major-depression/.

17. Kim Parker, Rich Morin, and Juliana Menarche Horowitz, "America in 2050," Pew Research Center, March 21, 2019, https://www.pewresearch.org/social-trends/2019/03/21/america-in-2050/.

18. Hunter, "Happiest Countries."

19. Viktor E. Frankl, *Man's Search for Meaning* (Boston: Beacon Press, 1959).

20. *Psychology Today* staff, "Imposter Syndrome," PsychologyToday.com, accessed August 22, 2025, https://www.psychologytoday.com/us/basics/imposter-syndrome/.

21. "Never Feeling Good Enough," Envision Wellness, accessed August 22, 2025, https://www.envisionwellness.co/high-achievers-not-good-enough/.

22. "Understanding Mental Health in High Performers," BlossomPsychotherapy.ca, July 10, 2024, https://blossompsychotherapy.ca/blog/f/understanding-mental-health-in-high-performers/.

23. Sonja Lyubomirsky, *The How of Happiness: A New Approach to Getting the Life You Want*, (New York: Penguin Books, 2008).

24. Frankl, *Man's Search*.

25. Mihaly Csikszentmihalyi, *Flow: The Psychology of Optimal Experience* (New York: HarperCollins, 2008).

26. Edward L. Deci and Richard M. Ryan, *Perspectives in Social Psychology: Intrinsic Motivation and Self-Determination in Human Behavior* (New York: Springer New York, 2013).

27. Richard G. Tedeschi (ed.), *Posttraumatic Growth: Positive Changes in the Aftermath of Crisis (Personality and Clinical Psychology)* (Mahwah, NJ: Lawrence Erlbaum Associates, Inc., 1998).

28. "Life Expectancy," National Center for Health Statistics, CDC.gov, accessed August 22, 2025, https://www.cdc.gov/nchs/fastats/life-expectancy.htm/.

CHAPTER TWO

1. Mark Manson, *The Subtle Art of Not Giving a F*ck: A Counterintuitive Approach to Living a Good Life* (New York: Harper, 2016).

2. Mark Manson, "The Subtle Art of Not Giving a F*ck—Summarized by the Author," YouTube.com, 37:44, March 4, 2021, https://youtu.be/lz8sUiXAnbs?si=ItAkFBoYByXkcKf1/.

CHAPTER THREE

1. "Having Fewer Choices Can Promote Happiness," Harvard Health, January 16, 2024, https://www.health.harvard.edu/healthbeat/having-fewer-choices-can-promote-happiness/.

2. John F. Helliwell et al., "World Happiness Report 2025," WorldHappiness.Report, accessed August 22, 2025, https://www.worldhappiness.report/ed/2025/.

3. Nicholas Anderson, "The Dominance of East African Distance Running," Science Survey, March 18, 2025, https://thesciencesurvey.com/sports/2025/03/18/the-dominance-of-east-african-distance-running/.

4. Gretchen Rubin, *The Happiness Project, Tenth Anniversary Edition: Or, Why I Spent a Year Trying to Sing in the Morning, Clean My Closets, Fight Right, Read Aristotle, and Generally Have More Fun* (New York: HarperCollins, 2019).

CHAPTER FOUR

1.   TED: The Economics Daily (blog), "Unemployment in November 2009," US Bureau of Labor Statistics, December 9, 2009, https://www.bls.gov/opub/ted/2009/ted_20091208.htm/.

2.   Aaron Hurst and Nicole Resch, "2019 Workforce Purpose Index: Pathways to Fulfillment at Work," Imperative, https://www.imperative.com/wp-content/uploads/2023/04/Imperative-2019-Workforce-Purpose-Index.pdf.

3.   "One Third of Your Life Is Spent at Work," Gettysburg College, https://www.gettysburg.edu/news/stories?id=79db7b34-630c-4f49-ad32-4ab9ea48e72b/.

4.   Richard Fry and Dana Braga, "Older Workers Are Growing in Number and Earning Higher Wages," Pew Research Center, December 14, 2023, https://www.pewresearch.org/social-trends/2023/12/14/older-workers-are-growing-in-number-and-earning-higher-wages/.

CHAPTER FIVE

1.   Héctor García and Francesc Miralles, *Ikigai: The Japanese Secret to a Long and Happy Life* (New York: Penguin Life, 2017).

2.   Christina Wallace, *The Portfolio Life: How to Future-Proof Your Career, Avoid Burnout, and Build a Life Bigger Than Your Business Card* (New York: Balance Publishing, 2023).

CHAPTER SIX

1.   Charles M. Blow, *The Devil You Know: A Black Power Manifesto* (New York: HarperCollins, 2021).

2.   @siliconvalleyfellowship, "Scott Galloway: Two Thirds of Wealth Creation Will Come from These Cities," YouTube.com, January 15, 2025, https://www.youtube.com/shorts/aRkZ2vI_oZ0/.

CHAPTER EIGHT

1.   John Jennings, "Does Money Buy Happiness: Actually, Yes," Forbes.com, updated February 12, 2024, https://www.forbes.com/sites/johnjennings/2024/02/12/money-buys-happiness-after-all/.

2.   Aimee Picchi, "One Study Said Happiness Peaked at $75,000 in Income. Now, Economists Say It's Higher—By a Lot," CBSnews.com, updated March 10, 2023, https://www.cbsnews.com/news/money-happiness-study-daniel-kahneman-500000-versus-75000/.

3. Matthew A. Killingsworth, Daniel Kahneman, and Barbara Mellers, "Income and Emotional Well-Being: A Conflict Resolved," pnas.org, November 29, 2022, https://www.pnas.org/doi/10.1073/pnas.2208661120/.

4. Killingsworth et al., "Income."

5. Issi Romem, PhD, "High-paying Jobs? They're a Dime a Dozen," ADPResearch.com, November 12, 2024, https://www.adpresearch.com/high-paying-jobs-theyre-a-dime-a-dozen/.

6. "Real Median Personal Income in the United States," Federal Reserve Bank of St. Louis, updated September 9, 2025, https://fred.stlouisfed.org/series/MEPAINUSA672N/.

7. "Average Salary in Finland," remotepeople.com, accessed August 22, 2025, https://remotepeople.com/countries/finland/average-salary.

8. *English Standard Version*, Matthew 16:26.

CHAPTER TEN

1. Rachel Chang, "19 Inspirational Maya Angelou Quotes," Biography, January 19, 2021, https://www.biography.com/authors-writers/maya-angelou-quotes/.

2. Michael D. Watkins, *The First 90 Days: Proven Strategies for Getting Up to Speed Faster and Smarter* (Brighton, MA: Harvard Business Review Press, 2013).

3. Youngme Moon, *Different: Escaping the Competitive Herd* (New York: Crown Business Publishing, 2010).

CHAPTER ELEVEN

1. Piers Worth and Matthew D. Smith, "Clearing the Pathways to Self-Transcendence," *Frontiers in Psychology*, vol. 12, April 29, 2021, DOI: 10.3389/fpsyg.2021.648381.

2. "The Leadership and Happiness Laboratory," Harvard Kennedy School Center for Public Leadership, https://www.hks.harvard.edu/centers/cpl/faculty/leadership-and-happiness-laboratory/.

3. *English Standard Version*, Philippians 4:7.

4. Pam Wasserman, "World Population by Religion: A Global Tapestry of Faith," populationeducation.org, January 12, 2024, https://populationeducation.org/world-population-by-religion-a-global-tapestry-of-faith/.

5. Reza Aslan, *Zealot: The Life and Times of Jesus of Nazareth* (New York: Random House, 2013).

6. SDC International Movers, "Cost of Living in the Maldives—the Numbers," sdcinternationalshipping.com, updated May 2025, https://www.sdcinternationalshipping.com/cost-of-living-in-the-maldives/.

7.   Daniel Mazo et al., "Facing Dire Sea Level Rise Threat, Maldives Turns to Climate Change Solutions to Survive," ABCnews.com, November 3, 2021, https://abcnews.go.com/International/facing-dire-sea-level-rise-threat-maldives-turns/story?id=80929487/.

8.   The Association of Religion Data Archives, "National Profiles: Maldives, South-Central Asia, the World," thearda.com, accessed August 22, 2025, https://www.thearda.com/world-religion/national-profiles?u=140c.

9.   Pew Research Center staff, "Mapping the Global Muslim Population," PewResearch.org, October 7, 2009, https://www.pewresearch.org/religion/2009/10/07/mapping-the-global-muslim-population/.

10. "2022 Report on International Religious Freedom: Maldives," US Department of State, accessed August 22, 2025, https://www.state.gov/reports/2022-report-on-international-religious-freedom/maldives/.

11. Gov.uk, "Foreign Travel Advice: Maldives," accessed August 22, 2025, https://www.gov.uk/foreign-travel-advice/maldives/.

12. "An Overview of the Maldives Tourism Industry in 2024," Travel Trade Maldives, January 26, 2025, https://www.traveltrademaldives.com/an-overview-of-the-maldives-tourism-industry-in-2024/.

13. "Country: Maldives," UN Women website, accessed August 22, 2025, https://data.unwomen.org/country/maldives/.

14. "Schneck vs. United States," Landmark Cases, https://landmarkcases.c-span.org/Case/5/Schenck-v.-United-States/.

15. Isabel Wilkerson, *Caste: The Origins of Our Discontents* (New York: Random House, 2020).

16. "History - Brown vs. Board of Education Re-enactment," United States Courts, https://www.uscourts.gov/about-federal-courts/educational-resources/educational-activities/brown-v-board-education-re-enactment/history-brown-v-board-education-re-enactment/.

17. "2022 Report on International Religious Freedom: Burma," US Department of State, accessed August 22, 2025, https://www.state.gov/reports/2022-report-on-international-religious-freedom/burma/.

CHAPTER TWELVE

1.   Ruth Rosen, "Is Heaven a Jewish Idea or Not?," Jews for Jesus, November 13, 2023, https://jewsforjesus.org/answers/is-heaven-a-jewish-idea-or-not/.

2.   Yuval Noah Harari, *Sapiens: A Brief History of Humankind* (New York: HarperCollins, 2014).

3.   Reza Aslan, *Zealot: The Life and Times of Jesus of Nazareth* (New York: Random House, 2013).

CHAPTER THIRTEEN

1. "Social Media and News Fact Sheet," PewResearch.org, accessed August 22, 2025, https://www.pewresearch.org/journalism/fact-sheet/social-media-and-news-fact-sheet/.

2. Max Roser and Esteban Ortiz-Ospina, "Literacy," Our World in Data, updated March 2024, https://ourworldindata.org/literacy/.

3. Christopher John Farley, "Was Jesus Illiterate? Author Reza Aslan Thinks So," *Wall Street Journal*, August 1, 2013, https://www.wsj.com/articles/BL-SEB-76135/.

4. "Data: Literacy Rate 1475 to 2023," Our World in Data, accessed August 22, 2025, https://ourworldindata.org/grapher/cross-country-literacy-rates/.

CHAPTER FIFTEEN

1. Yuval Noah Harari, *Sapiens: A Brief History of Humankind* (New York: HarperCollins, 2014).

2. Jeffrey M. Jones, "U.S. Church Membership Falls Below Majority for First Time," Gallup.com, March 29, 2021, https://news.gallup.com/poll/341963/church-membership-falls-below-majority-first-time.aspx/.

3. Sudina Search, "The Average Length of a Job by Generation: A Look at Workforce Trends," LinkedIn, February 19, 2025, https://www.linkedin.com/pulse/average-length-job-generation-look-workforce-trends-sudina-search-r4wqf/.

4. Rachel Hartman, "Why Do Jobs No Longer Offer Pensions?," US News, Money, December 20, 2023, https://money.usnews.com/money/retirement/articles/why-do-jobs-no-longer-offer-pensions/.

5. Paul D. Romero and Julie M. Whittaker, "A Brief Examination of Union Membership Data," Congress.gov, June 16, 2023, https://www.congress.gov/crs-product/R47596/.

6. "More Than One-Third of American Workers Turn to Freelance Jobs in 2023," Bloomberg.com, accessed August 22, 2025, https://www.bloomberg.com/news/articles/2023-12-12/record-64-million-americans-turn-to-gig-work-in-2023-survey/.

7. E-Solutions, "The Gig Economy: A Workforce Revolution," LinkedIn Pulse, June 5, 2025, https://www.linkedin.com/pulse/gig-economy-workforce-revolution-e-solutions-inc-o799c/.

8. Beth Kempton, "Gig Economy Statistics and Market Trends for 2025," Upwork, November 7, 2024. https://www.upwork.com/resources/gig-economy-statistics.

9. Ray Dalio, *Principles for Dealing with the Changing World Order: Why Nations Succeed and Fail* (New York: Simon & Schuster, 2021).

10. Fareed Zakaria, *Age of Revolutions: Progress and Backlash from 1600 to the Present* (New York: W. W. Norton & Company, 2024).

11. "Creating the United States," Library of Congress, accessed August 22, 2025, https://www.loc.gov/exhibits/creating-the-united-states/.

12. George Washington, "Farewell Address," Arizona State University Center for Political Thought Leadership, September 19, 1796, https://civics.asu.edu/sites/g/files /litvpz456/files/2021-06/Q86 percent20Washington percent2C percent20Farewell percent20Address percent20 percent281796 percent29_CPTL.pdf.

13. Scott Galloway, "Rot," Medium.com, February 2, 2024, https://medium.com /@profgalloway/rot-d59023a2a6f3.

14. Anthony Mann, dir., *The Fall of the Roman Empire*, Paramount Pictures, 1964.

15. Planned Parenthood, "Roe v. Wade Overturned: How the Supreme Court Let Politicians Outlaw Abortion," accessed August 22, 2025, https://www .plannedparenthoodaction.org/issues/abortion/roe-v-wade/.

CHAPTER SIXTEEN

1. University of Pennsylvania, Penn Arts & Sciences faculty, "The Science of Being Social," May 22, 2023, https://omnia.sas.upenn.edu/story/science-being -social/.

2. Julianne Holt-Lunstad, Timothy B. Smith, and J. Bradley Layton, "Social Relationships and Mortality Risk: A Meta-Analytic Review," *PLOS Medicine*, July 27, 2010, DOI: 10.1371/journal.pmed.1000316.

3. UCLA David Geffen School of Medicine, "Health News: Lonely People Have More Inflammation and a Less Responsive Immune System," March 21, 2016, https://medschool.ucla.edu/blog-post/health-effects-of-loneliness/.

4. Aaron Hurst and Nicole Resch, "2019 Workforce Purpose Index: Pathways to Fulfillment at Work," Imperative, https://www.imperative.com/wp-content /uploads/2023/04/Imperative-2019-Workforce-Purpose-Index.pdf.

5. @harvard_business_review, "People Get More Joy From Doing Activities with Others Than from Doing Them Alone," Instagram, July 18, 2025, https://www .instagram.com/p/DMQk2bjNWoa/.

6. Summer Allen, "How Biology Prepares Us for Love and Connection," UC Berkeley's *Greater Good Magazine*, February 24, 2022, https://greatergood .berkeley.edu/article/item/how_biology_prepares_us_for_love_and_ connection/.

7. "Divorce Statistics 2022," Petrelli Previtera LLC, accessed August 22, 2025, https://www.petrellilaw.com/divorce-statistics-for-2022/.

8. "Marriage Rates in 1990 vs. 2020," Our World in Data, accessed August 22, 2025, https://ourworldindata.org/grapher/marriage-rates-in-1990-vs-2020/.

9. "Iran Sentences a Woman to Death for Adultery, State Media Say," AP News, updated November 3, 2023, https://apnews.com/article/iran-death-penalty-adultery-39ac846801400d8d1399ca05f1053ac8/.

10. "Love, Sex, and the Changing Landscape of Infidelity," *The New York Times*, October 28, 2008, https://www.nytimes.com/2008/10/28/health/28well.html/.

11. Daniel A. Cox, "Is America Experiencing an Infidelity Epidemic?," American Survey Center, February 20, 2025, https://www.americansurveycenter.org/newsletter/is-america-experiencing-an-infidelity-epidemic/.

12. Oana Dumitru, "How Many Americans Have Cheated on Their Partners in Monogamous Relationships?," YouGov, October 4, 2022, https://today.yougov.com/society/articles/43605-how-many-americans-have-cheated-their-partner-poll/.

13. Emma Street, "Cheating Statistics 2025: Do Men Really Cheat More Than Women?," Techopedia, September 9, 2024, https://www.techopedia.com/statistics/cheating-statistics/.

14. "Infidelity Rates by Country 2025," World Population Review, accessed August 22, 2025, https://worldpopulationreview.com/country-rankings/infidelity-rates-by-country/.

15. Cox, "Is America Experiencing?"

16. Cox, "Is America Experiencing?"

17. "Infidelity Rates by Country 2025."

18. "The History of Romance," National Women's History Museum, February 13, 2017, https://www.womenshistory.org/articles/history-romance/.

19. Katherine Schaeffer, "For Valentine's Day, Facts about Marriage and Dating in the U.S.," Pew Research Center, February 8, 2024, https://www.pewresearch.org/short-reads/2024/02/08/for-valentines-day-facts-about-marriage-and-dating-in-the-us/.

20. Schaeffer, "For Valentine's Day."

21. Carolina Aragão et al., "The Modern American Family," Pew Research Center, September 14, 2023, https://www.pewresearch.org/social-trends/2023/09/14/the-modern-american-family/.

22. "Are Married People Happier Than Unmarried People?," American Psychological Association, March 2003, https://www.apa.org/news/press/releases/2003/03/married-happy/.

23. Elyakim Kislev, PhD, "5 Good Reasons to Get Married, and 5 Reasons Not To," PsychologyToday.com, December 12, 2022, https://www.psychologytoday.com/us/blog/happy-singlehood/202212/to-marry-or-not-to-marry-5-fair-reasons-for-each-side/.

CHAPTER SEVENTEEN

1. Emily S. Vogels and Colleen McClain, "Key Findings About Online Dating in the U.S.," Pew Research Center, February 2, 2023, https://www.pewresearch.org/short-reads/2023/02/02/key-findings-about-online-dating-in-the-u-s/.

2. "Global Online Dating Market Size, Share, Trends Analysis Report," Market.us, November 1, 2024, https://market.us/report/online-dating-market/.

3. "Report on Customer Statistics for the Calendar Year 2020," Ashley Madison, accessed August 22, 2025, https://www.ashleymadison.com/2020report/.

4. Colleen McClain and Risa Gelles-Watnick, "The Who, Where, and Why of Online Dating in the U.S.," Pew Research Center, February 2, 2023, https://www.pewresearch.org/internet/2023/02/02/the-who-where-and-why-of-online-dating-in-the-u-s/.

5. Vogels and McClain, "Key Findings."

CHAPTER EIGHTEEN

1. Jill Suttie, "How to Manage Expectations to Maximize Happiness," UC Berkeley's *Greater Good Magazine*, July 12, 2022, https://greatergood.berkeley.edu/article/item/how_to_manage_expectations_to_maximize_happiness/.

2. Elisabeth A. Sheff, PhD, CSE, "Updated Estimate of Number of Non-Monogamous People in US," *Psychology Today*, May 27, 2019, https://www.psychologytoday.com/us/blog/the-polyamorists-next-door/201905/updated-estimate-of-number-of-non-monogamous-people-in-us/.

3. Cady Lang, "How American Singles Really Feel About Consensual Non-Monogamy," *Time*, January 24, 2024, https://time.com/6568590/dating-non-monogamy-polyamory-match-singles-in-america/.

CHAPTER NINETEEN

1. Dimitrios Nikolaou, "Happy Mothers, Successful Children: Effects of Maternal Life Satisfaction on Child Outcomes," Ohio State University, October 2012, https://economics.osu.edu/sites/economics.osu.edu/files/Happiness percent26ChildOutcomes_JMP_Nikolaou.pdf/.

CHAPTER TWENTY

1. @Ted-Ed, "The Science of Falling in Love—Shannon Odell," YouTube.com, December 8, 2022, https://youtu.be/f_OPjYQovAE?si=y6_gONFdsYiOgVG_/.

CHAPTER TWENTY-ONE

1.   Gary L. Brase and Sandra L. Brase, "Emotional Regulation of Fertility Decision Making: What Is the Nature and Structure of 'Baby Fever'?," *Emotion* 12(5), August 14, 2011, DOI: 10.1037/a0024954.

2.   Shauna L. Gardino and Linda L. Emanuel, "Choosing Life When Facing Death: Understanding Fertility Preservation Decision-Making for Cancer Patients," *Cancer Treat Res.*, 2010, DOI: 10.1007/978-1-4419-6518-9_34.

3.   Paul Bloom, "What Becoming a Parent Really Does to Your Happiness," TheAtlantic.com, November 2, 2021, https://www.theatlantic.com/family/archive/2021/11/does-having-kids-make-you-happy/620576/.

CHAPTER TWENTY-TWO

1.   "Adult Children Pick Up the Responsibility of 'Aging in Place' Parents," Duke University School of Nursing, November 29, 2023, https://nursing.duke.edu/news/adult-children-pick-responsibility-"aging-place"-parents/.

2.   @harvard_business_review, "People Get More Joy From Doing Activities with Others Than from Doing Them Alone," Instagram, July 18, 2025, https://www.instagram.com/p/C81cA5aP7cC/.

CHAPTER TWENTY-FOUR

1.   Jason Fernando, "Net Present Value (NPV): What It Means and Steps to Calculate It," Investopedia.com, updated August 14, 2024, https://www.investopedia.com/terms/n/npv.asp.

2.   Caroline Banton, "How to Calculate Internal Rate of Return (IRR) in Excel and Google Sheets," Investopedia, updated April 27, 2025, https://www.investopedia.com/articles/investing/102715/calculating-internal-rate-return-using-excel.asp/.

3.   Lea Winderman, "Acing the Marshmallow Test," *APA Monitor* 45(11), December 2014, https://www.apa.org/monitor/2014/12/marshmallow-test/.

4.   Winderman, "Acing."

5.   Merriam-Webster Dictionary, "Crowdsourcing," Merriam-Webster.com, accessed August 22, 2025, https://www.merriam-webster.com/dictionary/crowdsourcing/.

CHAPTER TWENTY-FIVE

1.   Patrick J. McGinnis, *Fear of Missing Out: Practical Decision-Making in a World of Overwhelming Choice* (Naperville, IL: Sourcebooks, 2020).

CHAPTER TWENTY-SEVEN

1. Patricia Waldron, "Why Birds Fly in a V Formation," Science.org, January 15, 2014, https://www.science.org/content/article/why-birds-fly-v-formation/.

2. "Why Do Birds Fly in a V?," Gulo in Nature, accessed August 22, 2025, https://guloinnature.com/why-do-birds-fly-in-a-v/.

3. "The Overton Window," The Mackinac Center for Public Policy, accessed August 22, 2025, https://www.mackinac.org/OvertonWindow/.

ABOUT THE AUTHOR

FOR YEARS, CRAIG ROBINSON HAS EXPLORED the intersection of professional ambition and personal happiness from a unique vantage point: the C-suite. As a seasoned corporate director and former CEO, he has navigated the pressures of the modern workplace while leading global teams toward success. It was while leading a division at WeWork—tasked with designing spaces that fostered happiness and community for clients ranging from Fortune 50 companies to celebrity home offices—that he began to codify the insights that form the foundation of his book, *The Happiness Reboot: The Path to Reclaiming Your Joy*. He has since written a number of articles and been a regular speaker on the topic of fulfillment, leadership, and innovation.

Craig's leadership experience spans roles as Chief Growth Officer for Industrious (now CBRE), CEO of Global Corporate Services at Newmark, and President of the U.S. Region at Colliers International Group Inc., where he oversaw over $1 billion in annual revenue. Today, he channels that expertise into his work as an executive coach, an adjunct professor at Emory Goizueta Business School, and a strategic advisor to growth companies and a private investment firm. He serves as an independent director for

Lessen, Roofstock, and Second Nature and is a member of the Executive Committee of the Harvard Business School Alumni Board.

Craig earned his MBA from Harvard Business School and his BS from MIT. A founding member of the Leadership Now Project, where he advocates for fair democracies, he continues to explore how individuals can build fulfilling lives both in and out of the office.

Outside the boardroom, he finds joy in scuba diving, running, and the simple pleasures of everyday life—believing that happiness is not just a destination, but a practice.

More on Craig at www.craigmrobinson.com